Other Books by Rhoda A. Hendricks

LATIN MADE SIMPLE
CLASSICAL GODS AND HEROES
MYTHOLOGY POCKET CRAMMER
ARCHAEOLOGY POCKET CRAMMER
ARCHAEOLOGY MADE SIMPLE

DISCOVERY OF THE PAST

Rhoda A. Hendricks

DISCOVERY
OF THE PAST

A REVISED EDITION OF
ARCHAEOLOGY MADE SIMPLE

1973

DOUBLEDAY & COMPANY, INC.

Garden City, N.Y.

To my father

ISBN: 0-385-01538-0
Library of Congress Catalog Card Number 74–103754
Copyright © 1964, 1973 by Doubleday & Company, Inc.

Preface

This book was written to present a comprehensive view of the science of archaeology in such a way that the reader may gain a meaningful understanding of the scope of archaeology, an appreciation of its achievements, and a realization of the value and importance of its contributions to our knowledge of the cultures of the past.

The reader is invited to survey the growth and development of archaeology from its early beginnings to its present status as a science and to share in its adventure, excitements, and rewards. The material he will cover has been chosen from the abundant and ever-growing possibilities of selection with the idea of avoiding a detailed or exhaustive treatment that would be too strictly technical or specialized and of interest to scholars only.

The long, hard work of excavation brings to light the archaeological evidence that enables the archaeologist and historian to reconstruct the everyday life of the ancient world as well as the grandeur of antiquity. The topics and sites included within the limits that space allows were selected mainly with the purpose of offering sound information about the more important questions that might arise concerning the subject of archaeology and with the hope of guiding both layman and student along the paths of the pleasures and satisfaction that may be derived from a study of the subject.

I should like to express my gratitude to Miss Martha Sherwood for her faithful companionship and patient support in research and travel from deserts to mountain tops and to Miss Jean Anne Vincent of Doubleday & Company for her helpful co-operation and knowledgeable suggestions in the preparation of this book.

Contents

Contents xiii

CHAPTER FOURTEEN

LIST OF PLATES

DISCOVERY OF THE PAST

CHAPTER ONE

What Is Archaeology?

There has always been a fascination about suddenly finding a strange object lying on the ground—perhaps a coin, or a chunk of brick with odd markings on it. The finder stoops to pick it up. He examines it and speculates. He may even start to guess about it—how old is it, who once owned it, where did it come from, and why was it found at that place? Even more exciting, he may come across a partially hidden object sticking up from its hiding place. His curiosity is aroused and he eagerly digs it up, wondering if the "discovery" is valuable. Most thrilling of all is turning up by chance something completely buried and wholly unexpected. Immediately it captivates his imagination and may start him out on a road of discovery, perhaps leading to an absorbing hobby, or even a career. Taking his find to a local museum, he may learn it is an arrowhead made by American Indians or a piece of ancient Greek pottery, found in the ground he now considers his own.

The lure of discovering things that once belonged to someone else attracts both children and adults. Beyond its wonder and charm, it stimulates thought and brings a spirit of adventure. This has been true throughout the history of mankind. Just imagine a child or a man at the dawn of history coming by chance on a cave painting, gazing at it in amazement and wondering who drew it—when he lived, what he looked like. Or it is not difficult to imagine one of Caesar's legionnaires in south Britain—during the first century B.C.— stumbling without warning on Stonehenge, a circle of gigantic stones erected by primitive Britons almost two thousand years before the birth of Christ. No doubt this ancient place amazed him and made him wonder how its builders, with their bare hands, moved such enormous stones from their quarries and set them one atop another.

At the end of the eighteenth century some of Napoleon's soldiers uncovered the Rosetta Stone in Egypt. It had been buried for hundreds of years in the mud and silt of the Nile Delta. Its decipherment led to unlocking the secret of hieroglyphics, which opened up a whole world of Egyptian history. Within the last ten years both popular and scholarly interests have been aroused by the discovery of the Dead Sea Scrolls. Even more recently—in the fall of 1960—a Greek gold coin from Cyrene in North Africa was found by a gardener, who noticed it shining in some seaweed he was spreading on a garden near the English Channel. It is discoveries such as these that led to the gradual development of the systematic, scientific study of the past known today as archaeology.

Archaeology really began when man first recorded the lives and saved the relics of those who went before him, but it is only within the past two hundred years that it has gradually come to its full maturity as a disciplined science.

Its possibilities in the future are limitless. It may seem that museums—not to mention countless storerooms—are filled with a wealth of material that enables scholars to reconstruct the past, but there is always new subject matter to be studied and interpreted. Each fresh discovery generates new ideas and theories, and it is plain that there is a reservoir of material still untapped. The sites for future exploration lie in all the corners of the earth, and no one can foresee how many are as yet undiscovered.

DEFINITION AND SCOPE

Not only have the finest archaeological remains been left to us by the Greeks, but the word **archaeology** itself is derived from two Greek words: *archaios,* "ancient" or "old," and *logos,* "word" or "study." A simple definition of archaeology would therefore be "the study of things old, or ancient."

A useful definition of archaeology must, however, be more complex. Archaeology first of all includes discovering and excavating all the relics, remains, and signs of ancient times. Many people are not aware of the painstaking preparations necessary to these objectives. Preliminary investigations help archaeologists to decide exactly where to dig. Then a group of experts must be selected to make the expedition and local workers hired to do the manual labor. All data pertinent to a find must be recorded. Items of archaeological importance must be studied in relation to their surroundings and other objects of a similar type. Then the assembled information must be published to make it available to everyone interested.

But the search for tangible evidences of the past is only a part of the archaeologist's work. Beyond that there is the collection, detailed study, and interpretation of everything unearthed. Then his real search begins—for facts and clues that will fill in the gaps and round out our knowledge of past history. It becomes obvious that archaeology's scope is vast and unlimited. It embraces and uses the knowledge of many sciences—history, anthropology, geology, chemistry, and physics, among others. Often it is necessary for the archaeologist to consult with experts in these fields to supplement and substantiate his own findings.

Finally, and most important, the archaeologist fits all the accumulated facts together in their proper relationships to reveal the story of the everyday life, customs, and culture of former civilizations. Some experts place the beginning of written history at about 3500 B.C., when the first records were carved into stone by the Egyptians. It is through the efforts of archaeologists that we have an increasingly clear picture of life in the hundreds of years before written records. In addition, the archaeologist is constantly shedding new light on life during the several thousands of years since that date by uncovering much that has been lost, forgotten, or unrecorded. Thus the scene of the course of civilizations comes alive to a degree impossible without the aid of archaeologists.

THE BEGINNINGS OF ARCHAEOLOGY

As is often the case with beginnings, the first steps in archaeology were uncertain, experimental, and beset with errors. Archaeology's birth was witnessed by isolated individuals. Most of them were curiosity seekers or men whose only thought was material gain for themselves.

Even in quite early times, old buildings that were easily accessible —temples, theaters, arenas—were robbed of their bricks and stones. These were used in new buildings, or to repair damages in existing buildings. It was convenient, cheap, and simple to use bricks that were near at hand or stones that were already cut and could be had for the taking. An outstanding example of this is the Colosseum in

Rome. Bit by bit, stone by stone, it was looted, pilfered, and scattered into other structures of Rome. Hence it was given the irregular shape it has today. This removal of stones from ancient Roman buildings went on periodically until as late as the nineteenth century and did irretrievable damage. Old Roman buildings in the Forum and elsewhere lost their marble facings, which were torn away so the lead pins fastening them to the brick beneath could be taken out, melted down, and made into bullets.

Also in early times, royal tombs, especially those in Egypt's Valley of the Tombs of the Kings, as well as those in Greece and Italy, fell prey to thieves. With no respect for the past or thought of the future, these men broke them open to steal the gold, jewels, and valuables that had been buried with the dead. Thus these things were lost to posterity. But the reckless haste of these men is even more regrettable. Of the things they left behind, many were damaged beyond repair or later destroyed by exposure to the air.

Archaeology began in its full sense when men started to search out antiquities for constructive purposes. Even then progress was slow and often haphazard. In the early days even men with the best of intentions made many mistakes. They were exploring new paths as pioneers, with few footsteps to follow, and their lack of experience in handling archaeological materials caused some losses.

To many archaeologists of that time, it seemed important only to gather objects for museums or private collectors. Although their motives were good, they displayed the same haste and lack of care as the thieves who had preceded them. Pushed by demands of the museums and others who were paying their expenses, they removed many antiquities from their sites without realizing the necessity for recording details.

They never noted the exact location in which the article was found, or other objects that were lying with it, or above or below it. They made no attempt to link a discovered object to its historical locale. That is, perhaps some article was found in Italy—a mirror, a comb, a cooking pot. It may not have been made in Italy. An ancient Italian merchant may have bought it in Greece and brought it home to his wife. In this way it got to the site where archaeologists found it. On the other hand, another object—an Etruscan pot, for instance—could have been found quite close to the place where it was originally made. By knowing the history of one object, archaeologists can tell a good deal about the trade and everyday life of the place where that object was found.

The early archaeologists, however, did not realize these possibilities. They simply dug things up and carried them away. Gradually archaeologists became aware of the historical continuity to which each new-found piece could contribute. Time taught them to work on excavations in an orderly and organized manner. Excavators began to make exact records of each find: the level of digging at which every article was found, and of all things found with it. Careful observation on the spot, note taking, and detailed recording were combined with a scholarly analysis of the objects unearthed. In this way each newly discovered object became part of the vast total picture of history. More important, a scientific approach to archaeology was developed—one which has put it on a solid foundation.

JOHANN JOACHIM WINCKELMANN

The first man among early archaeologists to come to public attention was Johann Joachim Winckelmann. This happened during the transitional period between archaeology's beginning and maturity. The relatively few antiquities known in Winckelmann's time were largely in the collections of wealthy people. During the Renaissance it had become very fashionable to collect Greek and Roman works of art. The owners privately enjoyed them as art—they never considered them as a means of shedding light on the history of the past. Nor did they link themselves to, or unravel the thread of continuity between, their own times and the centuries during which the ancient Greeks and Romans flourished.

In the middle of the eighteenth century Winckelmann was to change all this, changing also the course of archaeology. He brought it from a disconnected collecting of objects into the proper organization of a science. He was one of the first to realize the significance of the things he found in terms of their role in the culture of their period. By explaining his new ideas in his published studies, Winckelmann made archaeology popular for its broader and more exciting possibilities.

Born in Prussia in 1717 of a poor family, Winckelmann began to develop an interest in ancient art and culture when he was a young boy. Fortunately for us, this pursuit continued to be a driving force throughout his life. Winckelmann received a fairly comprehensive formal education, in the course of which he maintained and enlarged his love for classical writings, art, and culture.

His studies continued informally when he became librarian to Cardinal Passionei, and later to Cardinal Albani. Constantly eager for knowledge, Winckelmann learned all he could about the antiquities in and about Rome. Then he traveled south of Naples to see the temples at Paestum, and the newly unearthed ruins of Pompeii and Herculaneum. These showed the strong influence of the Greeks who had settled in, and transferred their culture to, southern Italy when Rome was only a crude settlement of huts along the Tiber River. Winckelmann visited these sites when they were under the control of the King of the Two Sicilies. The King carefully guarded all information about the discoveries made there—a common practice in the eighteenth century. He did, however, give Winckelmann permission to visit his collection and see the objects in it which had come from Pompeii and Herculaneum.

In 1764 Winckelmann produced his monumental work, *Geschichte der Kunst des Altertums* [History of Ancient Art]. This was based on the objects and buildings he had seen at Pompeii and Herculaneum. It not only gave an account of Greek art, but correlated the descriptions of the various artifacts with the culture and lives of the people who had inhabited those sites in the first century A.D. before the eruption of Mt. Vesuvius destroyed them.

During his later life Winckelmann gained wide recognition for his accomplishments. He was received and honored by important European figures, among them Maria Theresa, Empress of Austria. Obviously this also helped the cause of archaeology, for as Winckelmann became known, so too did his subject.

In 1768 Johann Joachim Winckelmann met a violent death in Italy. He was stabbed in his hotel room in Trieste by a man to whom he had shown some gold coins given to him by Maria Theresa. Although the murderer was apprehended, Winckelmann's loss to the world of archaeology was a tragedy.

During the fifty-one years of his life he had introduced a new method to archaeology. No longer would archaeological observations spring from subjective thinking; in the future they would arise from carefully weighed judgment based on pertinent material.

By the end of the eighteenth century and the beginning of the nineteenth century, the point of view toward archaeology had begun to shift. Due to the efforts of Winckelmann and men like him, archaeology had started on a new course. Various nations had become interested. One of the first was France under the leadership of Napoleon, who took a group of trained men to Egypt with him to study the antiquities there. In addition, the information gathered through the use of archaeology's newborn scientific approach was becoming available to everyone interested, whether professional archaeologist or enthusiastic amateur.

This trend was to lead archaeology steadily away from the control of a few private individuals and put it into the trust of scholars and students, who would nourish this budding science until it accumulated dividends and reached its full development in the present century.

CHAPTER TWO

The Significance of Archaeology

THE CONTRIBUTION OF ARCHAEOLOGY

As a systematic field of study guided by scholars, archaeology has great value. It brings to everyone—layman and scholar—the unprecedented opportunity to see reconstructed ancient sites, and thus to understand history better. The material connected with these sites is kept as it was found, or put into a form as close to the original as modern scientific methods permit. Whenever it is possible, related objects remain together and furnish a basis for comparative and thorough study. As a result, archaeology has taken on a new meaning not only for the archaeologist, but for everyone—artist, sculptor, architect, historian, linguist, tourist.

National Museums The changing political picture in nineteenth-century Europe indirectly influenced the growth of archaeology. As nations became unified and the nobility lost their power and wealth, large archaeological collections fell into the hands of public museums. Gradually more and more ancient archaeological material appeared in the museums of cities such as Paris, Berlin, and London. As a result, these articles became available to students and scholars, who could examine them and contribute to the mounting sum of archaeological knowledge. As more and more people became interested and created a new demand for antiquities, the museums of various countries began to compete with each other to add to their store of prizes. Thus the museums began actively to search far afield to acquire objects for display.

Expeditions Fortunately the energies of the national museums were well directed, and the museums worked hand in hand with the early leaders of this budding science. When men were sent out to gather new material for museum collections, they were generally sent under the supervision of archaeologists trained in field work. These expeditions carried on their work as scientifically as possible, considering the extent to which archaeology had then progressed. As a result, the hunter of items for museum showcases—the archaeologist who watched over the methods of excavation, (which were still in the experimental stage)—and the scholar, who was now learning to make full use of everything unearthed and to appraise its significance carefully, worked together to increase mankind's knowledge of the past.

Use of Archaeology One can go into almost any museum and look at the tangible remains of the past. These may vary from an Indian arrowhead to the Venus de Milo statue, from a delicately wrought coin to an Egyptian sarcophagus. In addition, one can go to a library, in the museum or elsewhere, and avail oneself of all the descriptive and interpretive writings produced in connection with the objects seen.

The same applies to the great wealth of archaeological material that cannot be put into any museum, but remains standing in its original location, just as it has stood through the centuries—Hadrian's Wall in Britain, for example, or the pyramids of Egypt, or the Indian cliff dwellings of the southwestern United States. At many such sites the visitor can often see not only what has been left in place, but also the smaller objects—statuettes, pottery, coins—that must be protected in a museum nearby. Usually this museum is a closely related part of the excavation site itself.

Classification of Antiquities The remains of ancient civilizations can be classified in various ways. For example, they can be grouped according to location. Under this system one group would include all objects that are aboveground and needed no unearthing—as, for example, the Roman aqueducts. In contrast are the greater number of articles that have been partially or totally buried and were uncovered either by chance or by planned excavation. A third group would be the unknown number of antiquities yet to be found by one means or another.

Archaeologists sometimes classify ancient relics into two groups, without regard for how or where they were found, but based on their origin. The first and smaller group includes whatever man used in former times, but did not make himself. This would encompass everything used in its natural form, such as the grains of corn left in an ancient storage jar. By far the larger group, and the one more valuable to the archaeologist not only because of its size but because of the abundant information it yields, would include everything man made for himself, either practical or aesthetic. These are called **artifacts** (from the Latin words *ars,* "art" or "skill," and *facere,* "to make").

Whatever grouping or classification is given to ancient remains, they are invaluable to us as the sum total of all that has been left by former civilizations and as keys to the past.

BRANCHES OF ARCHAEOLOGY

Archaeology has come into its full stature during the twentieth century. It no longer covers a narrow field jealously guarded by a few participants. Today, museums, universities, and nations send expeditions into the far-flung parts of the globe, and the numerous countries where antiquities are found maintain active archaeological services.

Modern archaeology is not only well organized and equipped, it is divided into numerous branches—for example, **numismatics** (the study of coins), **palaeography** (the study of ancient manuscripts), **epigraphy** (the study of ancient inscriptions), **ceramics** (the art of making pottery). As each field contributes its share of detailed information to the whole picture, this knowledge becomes accessible to other archaeologists and specialists through publications of all kinds.

No longer is knowledge of the findings at one site restricted almost exclusively to those involved with that location. On the contrary, this knowledge is passed on throughout the realm of archaeology. Each piece in the jigsaw puzzle receives its proper recognition. One bit of information, as it goes along the line, is checked and rechecked, examined and criticized by one scholar after another, and it may be corroborated, reversed, or modified, but the end result is to the benefit of all. In this way the individual who first studies a piece of pottery or a coin found in any part of the world can—with the aid of photography, of the printed and spoken word, of all the scientific means known to archaeology—receive untold help in identifying, dating, classifying, and interpreting his new material.

Anthropology Anthropology is, in general, the study of man—more specifically, the study of man's physical and mental development from the earliest times to the present. It is concerned with man's interaction in particular groups, races, or environments within definite global and historical limits. Anthropology and archaeology are interrelated in that the artifacts of a people must be known, studied, and interpreted if we are to understand their total culture. The time and culture type, as well as the origin, of different peoples are of the utmost importance to the anthropologist. If the culture is an ancient one, the archaeologist furnishes the artifacts for the anthropologist to study, and together they add to the total knowledge of that culture. This is especially important for the period of pre-history, whose peoples have left us no written records of their social and cultural life. The material unearthed by archaeologists can fill wide gaps in the story of mankind by giving anthropologists the artifacts and their dates, either exact or comparative, from which to rebuild the scene of past cultures.

Ethnology Ethnology is the branch of anthropology concerned with the physical and mental differences between peoples as seen in their social and cultural life. When the field archaeologist's findings on a particular people have been gathered and interpreted, a comparison with similar finds and analyses on another group can shed light on many questions. Major among them are the causes for migrations of peoples and the problems involved in establishing and maintaining colonies.

It is sometimes possible to trace an entire population from its apparent point of origin through long difficult wanderings to the place where it finally settled. Because each local or national group of people has certain culture characteristics and customs that distinguish it from others, it can be followed with relative accuracy as it moves from one area to another. The method of building houses, burying the dead, fashioning weapons, tools, personal ornaments, household necessities—all reveal something distinctive about the people involved.

Not only the migrations of the mainland Greeks to the Aegean Islands and thence to Asia Minor, but the establishment of Greek colonies in all of the Mediterranean area can be followed in this way. So also can the rise and fall of one culture after another in any one locality—with the Minoan civilization of Mycenae and Tiryns, and the settlement of Cnossus on Crete. However, unless all of the resources of archaeology—a study of pottery, coins, ancient literary sources, and other artifacts—are brought together, a thread of culture cannot be traced in this way. A co-operative effort is necessary to draw exact and accurate conclusions within the full potential of existing information and the power of human skill to deal with it.

Commerce Closely associated with reconstructing the migration and establishment of colonies by various tribes is the contribution that archaeologists can make to the study of commerce and trade. When the many different artifacts turned up by excavators have been arranged and sorted, they fall into two large groups: those made by native artisans and those imported from a distance. As populations increased, the trend toward specialization grew, and in its highly developed stage this meant that one city, district, or even nation concentrated on perfecting those articles that its natural resources permitted its skilled workers to produce with some mastery. These goods were then exported and the things needed were imported. Gradually a brisk commerce grew up throughout the entire Mediterranean region in this manner.

Each country established colonies where necessary natural resources could be found. Spain and Britain were important to the Romans as sources of tin. Colonies on the Black Sea and the northern coast of Africa supplied grain to the homeland. Mines on the island of Cyprus furnished copper.

Our word "copper," incidentally, comes from the Greek form of Cyprus, *Kypris*. Our word "parchment," also, comes in a slightly changed form from the name of a city in Asia Minor, Pergamum, which was foremost in preparing animal skins to be used as writing material.

Marble from quarries of the Aegean Islands went into the buildings of Greek colonists in southern Italy and Sicily. In Egypt the abundance of sand made glassmaking both practical and profitable. The quality of the clay in Attica, ancient Greece, made it extremely suitable for pottery making. As a result, the Athenians and others in that district reached a point of perfection in the making and painting of vases that has never been surpassed.

When colonies increased in number and trade flourished widely, the currency of each city traveled with its products. Thus coinage has left us one definite and serviceable clue to the paths of commerce. The geologist, chemist, metallurgist, among other experts, can supply the answers about the place where the raw material in an object had its origin and the place where it was made. By following the course of an article from its origin to its final ancient resting place, where it reappeared in an excavation, the archaeologist can develop a rather accurate map of old commercial routes.

Architecture Archaeology can contribute its share to architecture by amassing, assimilating, and interpreting many facts related to it. The architect is able to examine the square arch, as developed by the Egyptians, and the round arch of Etruscan buildings and Roman aqueducts. He compares the simple, squat columns at the Palace of Minos with the ornate grace of a Corinthian column. He looks above the Lion Gate at Mycenae to see how the Greeks relieved architectural stress. In the Roman baths he finds that under-the-floor and between-the-walls heating is not new.

The architect can study ancient architectural techniques in detailed drawings and photographs and by reading accounts supplementing them. He may not be able to see the Parthenon at first hand, but with the extensive information about it available to him he cannot help but appreciate and learn from its beautiful perfection of structure. In the same way he can study the functional design of the Colosseum, with its underground network of elevators, or the perfect and unequaled acoustics of the Theater at Epidaurus.

Art Painting and sculpture are uncommonly indebted to archaeology. During their race to acquire pieces of sculpture for their gardens and palaces, the Renaissance nobles paid large sums for ancient Greek and Roman works. As private collections grew larger and the number of easily removable antiquities standing aboveground diminished, the greedy sought farther and deeper afield. By the second half of the eighteenth century they were tapping underground sources, and these early archaeologists, excavating in their search for sculpture to fill collectors' museums, unearthed treasures that might otherwise have remained lost to the modern world.

Painting Painting is both fragile and perishable. The colors that once adorned marble buildings to help cut the glare from the sun, have, affected by time and the weather, almost completely disappeared. So, too, have the colors which made ancient statues even more lifelike than could the sculptor's skill. Ancient painting—especially portraiture—was often done on wood. As a result, only a few examples of this type have come down to us. Although a relatively small percentage of the art of antiquity has survived, what it reveals of the past as interpreted by the archaeologist has definite value for the art student.

Until the middle of the Stone Age, about ten to fifteen thousand years ago, man was wholly taken up with the essentials of living and staying alive—hunting for food, fashioning weapons and implements, protecting himself and his family from animal or human enemies. At that point his development permitted him some free time for the entertainment and satisfaction of decorating his cave home. In northern Africa, Stone Age man drew pictures of the animals he knew or hunted—elephants and tigers. In southern France and in Spain he painted the animals of that region—horses, deer, and bison. Other paintings show the appearance and everyday activities of Stone Age men and women, as seen through their own eyes. Protected from the elements, these paintings have retained their fine colors and tell us that, as far back as the Stone Age, man was able to create pictures that reveal a high degree of skill both in making paint colors and in their application. Adding to this his ability to draw, he had the tools to produce an artistically pleasing result.

The temple walls of ancient Egypt were decorated with a variety of pictures showing animals, men and women, battles, and scenes of everyday life. These paintings were generally colored carvings done on the building stones. They served several purposes: to decorate the temples, to tell passers-by of the pharaohs' accomplishments, and to preserve that information. It was indeed preserved throughout the centuries, for these carved records have been invaluable to today's archaeologist and to the student of Egyptian history.

As we do today, people of ancient times liked paintings in their palaces and homes. Perhaps the best-known wall paintings are those from Pompeii, but there are many others. Entire scenes were painted on walls to add depth or charm to a room. A wide decorative band in a geometric pattern often surrounded the painting. Archaeologists have been able to remove the dirt and deposit of the years from such paintings and to restore them intact for everyone to see. More than this, archaeologists have transferred wall paintings from their original locations and set them up in museums, where they are safer and available to a larger number of people.

Archaeologists make their greatest contribution, however, to the large field of vase painting. A major reason for this is that earthenware was made by all peoples of antiquity and was used widely for many purposes. Wherever clay could be found, it was molded into containers of all sizes and shapes. It was not long before the painter's art combined with that of the potter. Painting on pottery began with simple patterns and, especially in Greece and Italy, went on to more detailed designs and pictures.

Almost any excavation site yields pottery. In some instances, a painted piece of pottery may be found intact or almost unharmed, perhaps in a tomb or grave, but such an occurrence is as rare as it is desirable. Usually a painted vase is found in fragments. In that case the painting, be it geometric design or descriptive scene, would be of little value to the world of art if the archaeologist could not restore it. With his background knowledge of the many types of vases—their origin, development, dates—the archaeologist is able to rebuild a broken vase. It may be that a few pieces are missing, or that only a few are found. It may be that fragments of many painted vases are found together in one spot, making a hodgepodge of bits of pottery. Combining his knowledge and skill with modern methods of reconstruction, the archaeologist can restore the vase painting in the approximate or even exact form it had when it disappeared in ancient times.

Archaeology adds breadth and order to the history of art by laying man's achievements open to study.

Literature The great bulk of ancient literary writing that is extant comes to us almost entirely by way of the monasteries of the Middle Ages. There the monks painstakingly copied and recopied manuscripts by hand, preserving them for their own study and ultimately for ours. There is also a sizable quantity of writing that has been preserved by one means or another and has survived untouched for hundreds of years. Archaeologists have turned up much of this literature.

In Egypt, where the papyrus reed grew plentifully in the Nile

River, pens were made from the sharpened reed, and a kind of paper was produced by splitting the reed and pressing it into long, thin sheets. This papyrus was sturdy and made an excellent writing surface.

When a scribe had finished writing on the papyrus, it was rolled up and stored in a pottery jar. These jars were placed in the library of the pharaoh, priest, or noble, within his easy reach when he wished to read the book. Often these "books" consisted of one or more papyrus rolls.

It was almost essential when an Egyptian died that he be equipped with a copy of the so-called *Book of the Dead*. This was a papyrus roll—or often more than one, because it was a book of some length —on which were written words of magical charms that could assist the deceased when he appeared for judgment or in other situations of his life in the future world. Many times the *Book of the Dead* was beautifully illustrated in color.

The relative secrecy of the tombs and the dry air of Egypt have kept many of the books and fragments from disintegrating. As a result, archaeologists' excavations have brought numerous papyrus rolls out of the darkness of their storage places and reopened them to people concerned with literature and history. These papyrus rolls contain many types of writing and include songs and poems, plays, stories, as well as more serious works on the sciences—especially mathematics.

In recent years similar scrolls, made not of papyrus but of leather and even of copper, have been discovered in caves not far from the edge of the Dead Sea. These Dead Sea Scrolls, approximately two thousand years old, contain biblical and religious writings of tremendous importance. Archaeologists and other scholars are still engaged in the exacting task of piecing together and translating the hundreds of fragments.

Linguistics The study of a language and its relationship to other languages is called linguistics. Archaeology has also added to the horizons of this science by interpreting many of the lost languages which were developed when language was in its infancy. The data-processing computer is an invaluable aid in deciphering ancient languages and scripts. Whether the archaeologist discovers the picture writing of the American Indians, the cuneiform of the Babylonians, or the hieroglyphics of the Egyptians, that find is important to the linguist.

The writing may be on papyrus, stone, or clay; it may be the inscription on a vase or a coin—the linguistics student is not concerned with the medium, but with what it can tell him. He wants to know how each language began and developed, what changes took place and when, how it sounded, what its structure was, what its dialects were—all the possible meanings which made that language a form of communication. Then, by comparison and contrast, he can establish basic principles about each group of languages and the entire family of languages.

Mythology Classical mythology deals with ancient gods and goddesses, heroes, legends, and folk tales. It is a fertile spring which has enriched all Western poetry and prose. By revealing the origins of these myths and showing how they changed with each retelling, archaeology plays its part in reconstructing our cultural heritage.

Insight into mythological characters and stories has come from many sources, particularly from sculpture and vase paintings. All sizes of statues of deities have been found, from the large temple gods and smaller ones used in private homes to very small ones (generally of the lesser deities) made for purely decorative purposes —a pendant or similar piece of jewelry. Myths were favorite subjects for Greek and Roman artists, who used them extensively in ornamenting vases. Each new archaeological find dealing with mythology—a piece of sculpture or pottery—adds invaluable information to the total picture.

History As we have said, archaeology's greatest contribution is to the broad and fascinating story of history. Archaeologists have illuminated the whole dark period of prehistory by supplying solid, factual information about it. They have not only uncovered prehistoric events but have given them a proper relationship in time and place.

Even when history began to be recorded, only a few outstanding events received recognition. In the four or five thousand years of "recorded" history, the greater number of events have passed by unnoticed. Only in recent times, with increased communication and information storage facilities, has history been written down, step by step, detail by detail.

Prehistory In the long stretch of time before historical records, mankind reached varying heights of culture in widely scattered parts of the globe. Early man started as an isolated creature, occupied solely with survival. Then men gradually learned they could accomplish more with less energy expended by working together and helping each other. So men began to live in groups. Sometimes these took the form of separate tribes, villages, or communities, but the result was always the same—each unit developed a characteristic way of life, or culture. Each of these cultures had basic activities in common with the others—making implements and tools, growing or killing their food, protecting themselves from enemies and the elements, burying their dead.

But when Stone Age man built his sacred monument at Stonehenge, his stone tomb in France, or decorated his everyday pottery with paint, he was leaving behind a record also marked by the development that made his group different from others. The kinds of stones, building materials, metals used and shaped by early men, their earthenware and grains, even bones and ashes—all tell a tale. The archaeologist reads the record of prehistory not in writing, but by discovering and knowing the distinctive characteristics of each group as revealed in everything they used and built.

Chronological order is essential to history. Because man first used the stones he found around him for making things, the first period in the prehistory of mankind is known as the Stone Age. Because man learned and improved his use of stone as much by accident as by experience, the Stone Age is the longest period of mankind's history. In writing the saga of prehistory, archaeologists have found enough distinguishing differences to break the total broad Stone Age into three major divisions: the **palaeolithic, mesolithic,** and **neolithic** periods.

Palaeolithic Age Archaeologists call the first time for which we know anything of man's activities the Palaeolithic Age. The word palaeolithic comes from the Greek words *palaios,* "old," and *lithos,* "stone." Thus this period is also often called the Old Stone Age. It began at the earliest time in prehistory that man took stones and shaped them, however crudely, for his own use. Stones—especially flint—and bones were used as tools by palaeolithic man, who lived in caves and hunted to supply himself with food.

Just how long ago the Stone Age began has been determined by the British archaeologist Dr. Louis S. B. Leakey and his wife, Mary, who, after close to thirty years of purposeful work in the Olduvai Gorge in Tanganyika, found the remains of the earliest man known. In 1959, at the edge of a prehistoric lake, they discovered the skull of a young man, complete except for the lower jaw, first thought to be about 600,000 years old. Dated by the potassium-argon process, it is now estimated to be at least 1,750,000 years old. From the numerous artifacts excavated at the site it is known that this man, called Zinjanthropus, meaning East African Man, was a toolmaker. Also found at Olduvai Gorge were the remains of a child of about eleven or twelve years of age of an even earlier date.

Palaeolithic man's struggle against his difficult environment was ended, at least in much of the world's northern half, by the end of the glacial epoch. Fortunately man had not been wiped out by the Ice Age—four long periods when the ice advanced and receded—but had learned how to survive. During this time he discovered fire, which kept him warm. He learned to make better tools and to travel farther from his cave in search of game. The end of the glacial period, when the ice retreated as slowly as it had come, is also taken as the end of the Palaeolithic Age. This was approximately 40,000 years ago.

Mesolithic Age   When man emerged from the glacial epoch, he entered a new period in his development. This Mesolithic Age—from the Greek *mesos,* "middle"—was one in which man's tools and implements show a marked advance in number and quality. Man began to fashion axes and to use ivory. He began to clothe himself. He carved drawings on stone and horn, and painted astonishingly good pictures on the walls of his caves.

The Mesolithic Age, or Middle Stone Age, did not come to an end relatively suddenly, as did the preceding era, but merged into the period that followed it. This occurred at different times in different places. If we were to give a cause for the gradual shift from the Mesolithic Age to a more advanced age, it would be that whenever environment permitted, Middle Stone Age man settled in one district and began farming, domesticating animals, weaving, making pottery. In addition he vastly improved the necessary objects of everyday life. He broadened their range and refined their decoration.

Gradually he learned to carry on many of the other activities in community living that make a civilization. In the favorable and warm climate of Egypt this change took place much earlier than it did in northern Europe. On the other hand, there are still some places in the world where man has not yet, or has only quite recently, left the Mesolithic Age. Generally, however, the Middle Stone Age is considered to have ended about 8000 B.C.

Neolithic Age When civilization dawned on the banks of the Nile River, the third and last Stone Age came to that region. Archaeologists have given it the name neolithic, from the Greek word *neos,* meaning "new." It is also called the New or Late Stone Age.

By this time man's stone implements had reached a high point of development and were generally made of flint, which could be ground on his whetstone into weapons, chisels, and even saws. Pottery made cooking easier and lent itself to the artist's brush. The more neolithic man did with his perfected tools and the more he saw their usefulness in making what he needed and wanted for himself—houses, pottery, ships—the closer he came to the end of the New Stone Age.

At approximately 5000 to 4000 B.C., man discovered copper and found that it made even better tools than did stone. As is true of all changes in history, the transition from stone to metal was a slow, gradual one and cannot be fixed at any one point in prehistory. But the use of copper led to bronze and other metals, and man was on his way toward the limitless possibilities of civilization.

Recorded History The beginning of recorded history can be set to coincide with the first document in writing that has survived and come down to us. The credit for the first fixed and recorded date in history, as opposed to prehistory, goes to the ancient Egyptians, who introduced a calendar in 4241 B.C. This date is established according to our reckoning and is still only approximate. It is known for certain that the Egyptians began to trace the course of time by a calendar, calculated according to astronomical observations, at about that date.

If we accept the year 4241 B.C. as the initial date, we can develop a chronological table of all the events that followed, provided they are known to have taken place in a given year, or at some time with a known relationship to another event with an established date. In this manner archaeology brings into focus the panorama of history in a continuous narrative of what man has done during the approximately six thousand years since the calendar was invented and written records began to appear.

HISTORY OF PEOPLES AND CIVILIZATION

There are many possible subdivisions in the field of history. If we look at history as the story of man and his development, it falls into two broad divisions: the history of peoples and the history of civilizations.

History of Peoples When the archaeologist speaks of culture and civilization he does not use the two words precisely as synonyms. To him, culture is a term that applies to a group of people having certain traits and characteristics in common and sharing the same stage of progress. Hence a culture may be, and usually is, given an adjective that limits and defines it—for example, a *primitive* culture, or *advanced* culture, or *Mayan* culture, or *Hellenic* culture. Thus we see that the adjective tells something about time and space, which are essentials of history, and that when archaeologists describe a culture, they do so as fully as their observations permit.

When we consider the history of peoples from an archaeologist's approach, it is important to keep in mind that he is concerned primarily with ancient peoples. He makes every effort to reconstruct especially that history which has come through the ages in unwritten form, or history which has been recorded but must be appraised, reinforced, and interpreted in the new light shed by its relics and remains.

History of Civilization Civilization is a state of society characterized by relative progress in the development of the arts, science, and statecraft. The civilizing process began with the first cave man and continues today. The more advanced and refined a culture of the past became, the more it contributed to the development of civilization. Some cultures, however, were quite primitive compared to their contemporaries and reached only a low level of civilization.

By finding, classifying, and comparing and contrasting the artifacts of one culture with those of another, archaeologists are able to determine where the people who developed it belong on the scale of human progress. A chronology can show which culture followed which, but not which was more civilized. Often, as at the fall of the Roman Empire, the later culture was the less civilized.

It is not the case that a culture or a number of cultures began by being primitive and then proceeded to climb the ladder of civilization steadily and without interruption. It is one of archaeology's truths that all cultures of the past—even if they rose to great heights of civilization—declined and fell, caught by the fact that humans are never without motion and flux, and are therefore faced with only two possibilities: progress or decay. The best known example of this is the Roman Empire, but all ancient cultures disappeared from the scene, or they would not be subject matter for archaeology.

It may happen, too, that a civilized culture makes every effort to raise a contemporary but more primitive culture to its own level of civilization. Because time and capacity are essential to the advancement of a culture, forced progress is usually limited and precarious. The Romans proved this by their attempt to "Romanize" the many peoples and cultures they held under domination. They were moderately successful with those cultures that already had reached a high point of civilization, such as the Egyptian. But they were unable to Romanize less advanced and complex peoples, as, for example, the Britons and Germans, who reverted to their former lower level of civilization soon after the Roman occupation ended.

In this age when the words "new" and "modern" are so overworked, it is well to consider the light that archaeology sheds on the history of civilization. As we examine each basic ingredient of civilization, it is hard to find one that is really new or modern. Language and literature, art and architecture, philosophy and mathematics, are obviously old disciplines. In many of these areas "modern" civilization has made "new" changes, but has sometimes found it difficult to improve on old methods or ideas.

With the aid of archaeology twentieth-century man can see his relationship to the men of ancient times, from whom all civilization has evolved. Archaeology reveals when and how each bearer handed on the torch of civilization. It teaches the successes and failures of the past, which may carry lessons for the present and future.

RECONSTRUCTING THE PAST

Until a century or two ago, that part of the past that fell before and outside the memory of men living at the time, or within a few generations of it, was an almost unopened book. A few pages from the past had been handed down by word of mouth, or even in writing. Their accuracy depended on human judgment, with only the shallowest of evidence, if any, to verify statements that varied according to the individual.

Within the last hundred years, archaeology has helped to change our whole approach to the past. As archaeologists' spades removed the accumulation of hundreds of years from sites which had long been buried—and many of which had been partially or totally forgotten, as artifacts were brought to light—and as the remains of the past were recovered in steadily mounting numbers, the history of mankind began to be a living document. Archaeologists not only removed the covering of darkness from the past, but also gave to the past a new birth.

CHAPTER THREE

Methods of Dating

Since the archaeologist's primary purpose is to help clarify past history through his excavations and conclusions, the matter of dating is of the utmost importance.

There are a number of methods of dating available to the archaeologist and historian. By knowing the dates of pottery, coins, brick marks on building material, or inscriptions found at the site, the archaeologist knows roughly the corresponding dates of the relics found with them. Literary evidence—dates given in the writings of classical authors, especially the Greek historians—is an additional way of placing events in ancient times. At the other end of the scale is the newly developed use of carbon 14 to set archaeological material in its proper chronological perspective.

To have a clear idea of how the various methods of dating produce the results they do, it is necessary to have some general understanding of each of them separately.

POTTERY

Most of the major inventions in the history of mankind were born of necessity. Inventions which proved satisfactory endured, and were improved upon or embellished in the course of time. When man needed containers, bowls, and cups for cooking or storing his food and drink, he took what was at hand and shaped it for his use. In the earliest times man made his vessels out of leather, tied or sewn into the desired shape, or of straw, woven into baskets.

In localities where clay was plentiful, as it was in most regions, it was readily moistened with water, molded, and then set in the sun to dry, forming the first pottery. The transition to pottery took place during the Stone Age, at least five or six thousand years ago, although baskets and leather containers remained in use also.

With the appearance of metal came the making of jars and vases out of copper, which could be bent with little difficulty into the required shapes. Soon silver and even gold were used in this fashion. Metal vessels, however, had the disadvantage of not standing up against fire. They were, therefore, impractical for use in cooking.

It was not long before man improved his techniques by inventing tools to shape and mold the moist clay. As time went on, he learned to bake pottery by fire, giving it added sturdiness. Then he devised methods for making his pottery in greater variety and more exactly to a set model. Methods of firing were also refined when ovens were used to bake the clay evenly, which gave it more durability. Archaeologists have found pottery dating from the Neolithic Age that was molded by hand, but baked in an open fire, and even decorated with lines and designs scratched into the clay before it hardened.

Definition Pottery includes all vessels made from moistened clay and shaped, usually in rounded form, either by the hands alone or with the aid of a tool, or on a wheel, and then baked by a fire or in an oven until it is hardened.

A coarse kind of pottery fashioned from clay is called **earthenware.** Earthenware is made fairly simply and quickly and can easily be shaped into a countless variety of vessels serving everyday needs. For these reasons it has been made in most areas of the world in greater quantity than perhaps any other article.

The word **ceramic** applies to the art of making articles from clay and comes from the Greek word *keramos,* meaning "potter's clay" or "pottery."

Pottery Making As is true of all things in common use, the art of pottery making, or ceramics, developed with comparative rapidity. Pottery making involves several steps, which run almost parallel to the stages of its development from earliest times.

First, and obviously, the potter must have clay within easy reach. The quality of the finished product will depend to a large extent on the type of clay that goes into it. The best clay, whether found in the ground or in a river bed, was free from impurities, offered the proper degree of plasticity, and hardened without cracking in the drying or firing process. When the painter began to add his skill to the potter's technique, the color of the clay and the way its surface reacted to the paintbrush became extremely important.

If clay was not of the right consistency in its natural state, the finished product would not be satisfactory. Early potters learned to make clay smoother by removing pebbles and other foreign matter. If it was too damp, they made it drier by adding bits of dried grasses or sand. They made it more moist by kneading in the right amount of water.

For centuries pottery received its shape from the potter, who formed the raw clay with his fingers and possibly some tools. He pressed it into shape or built it up gradually by adding bits of clay or by twisting long strips of clay into a crude pot which could then be smoothed off.

But it was inevitable that a means of shaping pottery by something other than the potter's own fingers and hands was sought. The next development was to press the clay against a mold of the shape desired. The mold could then be destroyed or reused, depending on the material of which it was made. By this method the potter formed the main body of the piece of pottery, but had to add the finishing touches—rim, lip, or handle—by hand.

The final stage in making pottery was reached with the invention of the potter's wheel. This took place at different times among people of various cultures, but can be put during the Bronze Age, or sometime after 3000 B.C., in the eastern Mediterranean regions. The invention of the potter's wheel meant that the body of the piece could be made rounder, more even in shape, and thinner in texture, with a fool-proof regularity. It also freed the potter's hands somewhat so that he could work toward precision. Pots made on a wheel, however, were not necessarily better than those of a highly skilled manual worker who had achieved an advanced technique by long experience and practice. But by using a wheel, more potters could turn out a better product.

When the moist clay had been molded into its final form, the excess water had to be removed. In the early history of ceramics this was achieved by leaving the vessel to dry in the air, preferably in the sun, or next to a fire. If the vessel was to hold a liquid, however, this type of drying was not enough, since it would be too porous and would soften again as the liquid was absorbed into its pores. Again necessity supplied the answer. This time the need for drying the clay more quickly and with a higher degree of heat was filled by the use of a closed fire or oven invented for the purpose. It is quite possible that the first ovens were simple pits dug into the ground. Later, the ovens were built aboveground, where it was easier to maintain a steady and constant heat.

It was natural that, since earthenware was used in such quantity, decoration was added to it early in the development of ceramics. We know from finds in Egyptian graves that ornamentation was applied to pottery there by the fifth millennium B.C. Designs and even paintings have been found on many vases of that time. Egyptian potters had perfected their skill to a marked extent and were already using the potter's wheel and baking their clay vessels in a closed oven. In addition, Egyptian potters revealed their imaginativeness in a rich variety of forms and shapes.

Vase Painting The technique of vase painting also went through several phases and followed a natural pattern of development before it reached its height. The first and simplest designs man attempted were applied to the clay with a sharp implement or whatever would achieve the desired effect. Since straight lines are easier to draw than rounded ones, most of the more primitive pottery had incised geometric decorations. Later, as skills developed, the designs became more advanced, with difficult circular or scroll-like lines.

It is quite likely that the use of paint appeared when man attempted the graphic representation of non-geometric subjects—the paintbrush could give a freer and less rigid effect. At first flowers, animals, humans, and plants were painted in a geometric rather than lifelike manner, but as the artists's ability grew, they became more natural and realistic.

As soon as the art of painting was combined with the art of pottery making, it became apparent that there was a definite relationship between the clay's ingredients and the paint. Because clay was taken directly from the ground or a stream bed, its color varied greatly, according to the composition of the earth and the absence or presence of different materials—especially iron. When the clay was fired, the iron was oxidized. As the amount of iron in the clay varied, different colors resulted, opening up to painters the possibilities of a whole range of color. They could then produce pottery of almost any shade from gray-white to gray-black, with yellows and reds in between. In addition some of the ancient Egyptian pottery shows the application of glazes produced by using a variety of other minerals contained in the earth, clay, or glass. In this way they achieved some vivid tones and brilliant effects.

Attic Pottery Although pottery making as an art began in Egypt and Mesopotamia and gained impetus from the several inventions made there, Athens was leading in pottery production by the end of the seventh century B.C. One reason for this was that the clay of Attica—the district in which Athens was located—was of excellent quality. Even more important, as painted pottery became more popular and painters' skills developed, there came a division of labor. No longer was it usual that a highly skilled potter was also a superior painter. In the final development, the artisan who made the vase and the artist who painted it were two separate individuals, each a master in his own field.

Black-figure Vases The painted pottery of Athens falls into two large groups. The first and earlier is called the **black-figure.** The easiest background to use in vase painting is the natural color of the clay. In this case, the Attic clay was a fine shade of red. The simplest method by which the paint could be applied was by adding it directly to the red-clay background. Since the major part of the drawing of the figures—human, animal, and the like—was done in black paint, with a few other colors and lines added to bring out the details, this type of painting in black upon a red background was given the name black-figure.

Red-figure Vases By the fifth century B.C. Athenian artists had attained such delicacy and perfection in painting black-figure vases that they began to need a new medium of expression. This brought about the second and more intricate style, the **red-figure** vase. This was a reversal of the black-figure technique. Instead of painting black figures, they now painted the background completely in black, leaving the figures to stand forth in the natural red color of the clay.

The great intricacy of design and creativity in subject matter of the Attic red-figure vases made Athenian artists the undisputed leaders in the art of pottery making. Indeed, it became an Athenian industry. There was a large section in Athens where the potters lived and worked, and Athens lured all of the best potters, painters, and apprentices by enticing offers of privileges. By perfecting the manufacture of pottery, Athens developed a sought-after product it could ship to all parts of the civilized world in exchange for goods the rugged and rocky country lacked. Athenian vase painters paralleled the potters in the perfection of their skill—to the extent that both have yet to be surpassed in the art of pottery making.

Vase Shapes The Greek vases were shaped like the earlier metal types and display a variety of styles within the several groupings of cups, bowls, jars, and pots.

Etruscan Pottery As we have said, Grecian potters and painters were unequaled in their arts. The potters of northern and central Italy, where the Greek influence had not penetrated deeply, evolved

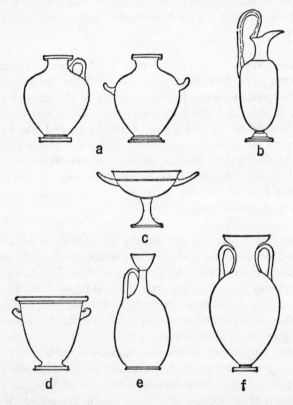

*Forms of Greek Pottery: a–*Hydria, *water jugs. b–*Oenochoe, *a wine jug. c–*Cylix, *a drinking cup. d–*Krater, *a bowl for mixing water and wine. e–*Lekythos, *an oil bottle. f–*Amphora, *a storage jar*

a technique that was quite different. The Etruscans, who lived north of the Tiber River in Etruria, made their pottery by hand, almost entirely without the aid of a wheel. The result was a coarser and heavier style. Etruscan pottery was also characterized by its color, ornamentation, and variation in form.

Typical Etruscan pottery was black. The clay was darkened either by the application of coloring or by the way in which it was fired. Archaeologists believe the Etruscans may have added something to their fires which made the smoke turn it black. For this reason, the name *bucchero,* an Italian word from the Greek word *boukaros,* meaning "dark-red clay," or *bucchero nero* meaning in Italian "black pottery," has been given to typical Etruscan pottery. Some of the Etruscan pottery was yellow, brown, or the more conventional red, but the *bucchero* was the predominant type.

Etruscan decoration was more plastic or sculpturelike than graphic. Instead of using the paintbrush, the Etruscans seemed to follow the pattern of their excellent bronze work and drew or incised designs on their pottery, or executed them in relief with molds and stamps carrying the engraved pattern. Due in part to the methods of ornamentation, geometric and stylized designs were used most often.

In shape and form, the typical Etruscan drinking cup showed the widest divergence from the graceful Greek cylix. Its proportions were different and sometimes it had three or four legs.

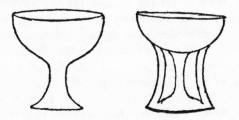

Etruscan drinking cups

Roman Pottery The Roman pottery of central Italy, like the Etruscan, was usually modeled or incised to give it decoration. In its early stages it was not as fine or beautiful as it became later on, when the Romans adapted the superior eastern Mediterranean pottery to their own uses.

The Romans made extensive use of **terra cotta,** from the words "earth" and "cooked" or "baked," for many purposes, especially for figurines, lamps, and household articles. This was earthenware with the clay's natural brownish or reddish tint. It was often painted and glazed. The term *impasto,* from the Italian *pasta,* "paste," is applied to Roman pottery because its decorative color was generally applied thickly, in the manner of paste.

Ostrakon In Greece, where pottery was plentiful and fragments of pottery even more so, it became the custom to use broken pieces of pottery—much as we might use torn or small pieces of paper—for the purpose of voting. The Greek word *ostrakon* means "shell" or "tile" and was the name applied to a fragment of broken pottery on which a vote could be cast. The Greeks, especially the Athenians, used to banish political dissenters for a temporary period—usually ten years. They cast their votes by marking an *ostrakon* or pottery fragment, and this custom was given the name "ostracism." Thus the Athenians put their pottery to every possible use, whether it was whole or in fragments.

Potsherds Archaeologists, too, can make use of pieces of broken pottery found at excavation sites. These are called **potsherds** and are of great value in establishing chronology. With the methods of dating currently available, even small fragments can be useful.

A chemical examination of the clay can usually disclose the region from which it came. Since the demand for pottery was widespread and constant, each locale developed its own industry, and the pottery factories of each area developed certain individual characteristics. The color and type of clay, the shape of the vessel, the method of decoration or design, the process of manufacturing—all tell their story about the origins of a vase or fragment.

For example, if the clay is not native to the area in which the potsherd was found, then the article was an import and provides clues about trade and commerce, relations with the city or state where the pottery was made, and the cultural level of both exporter and importer. Thus each tiny piece adds to the story of history.

Of even greater value are vases found whole or only partially broken. They were often placed in graves to serve the deceased in life after death and are therefore usually the best examples of the potter's art. Occasionally undamaged vases are found elsewhere, but tombs are the best source.

Signatures Although Attic potters and vase painters inherited their crafts from the Egyptians and peoples of western Asia, they went on to even greater achievement. By the time an artist had attained some degree of skill, he felt both pride in his work and a spirit of competition. At first potters and then painters, too, wanted recognition and began to claim credit for their own work. A Greek vase made early in the seventh century B.C. bears the signature of the potter. And it was not long before Attic vases appeared with two signatures—of the artist as well as the potter.

Many of the artisans were slaves or foreigners, especially in Athens, where the pottery industry grew to a great size and highly skilled workers were in great demand. As a result, a foreign name usually meant that the artist or craftsman, and not the piece of pottery, came from another country. In some potteries, the owner's stamp or signature was also put on each piece.

The signature or name often appeared on the base of a pot and when such was the case, only the pot base could tell the archaeologist what he needed to know about the vase's origins and dates. The conventional way in which a vessel was signed was "[name] made me" and "[name] painted me." A vase might be signed by the potter and the painter, or by one alone, or by one name followed by "made and painted me." Thus EUPHRONIOS MEPOIESEN [Euphronios made me] indicated that the vase was made by the potter Euphronios, one of the most skilled of the red-figure potters. KLITIAS EGRAPHSEN [Clitias painted (me or it)] was the signature of a famous vase painter, who specialized in subjects having to do with the story of Achilles.

Roman pottery was signed in a similar fashion—as, FIRMINUS FECIT [Firminus made (me or it)], and MARCUS PINXIT [Marcus painted (me or it)]. With Roman vases, too, the name of the factory owner or of the person for whom it was made would be placed on the vessel.

Dating Pottery By grouping, classifying, and studying in detail all the types of pottery found, archaeologists can fix the date of any one piece of pottery within the narrow bounds of about a quarter of a century. When there are additional sources for cross reference, such as the mention and dating of a celebrated potter or painter by an ancient writer, the chronology can be quite accurate and can also aid in fixing other dates in relation to the whole picture.

Pottery can also supply archaeologists and historians with many facts about the culture of the people living at the time it was produced and painted. As soon as vase painters began to depict human and animal figures, they turned to nature and life for their inspiration. Therefore they drew their material from what they could see around them every day.

As a result, archaeologists are furnished with a wealth of graphic, authentic information—directly from the artists who saw at first hand the sights they reproduced on clay. There are even vases that give us a detailed picture of the various stages in the technique of the potter's art. They show the potter at his wheel, molding a vase, and drying or firing it. Mythology was also a fertile and popular source of illustrations. Gods, heroes, and religious rituals all appear frequently in vase painting, revealing facts about the religious customs, fables, superstitions, and folklore of the ancients. Domestic scenes, athletics and sports, weapons, dress and hair styles of both men and women, domestic animals, hunting scenes, musical instruments, farming implements and methods, flowers, arts and crafts, and many other subjects make their appearance on painted vessels and serve as vivid photographs of the life and times of centuries long past.

COINAGE

Currency The custom of barter is well known to children, who "swap" or exhange articles which to them have equal value. Many cultures in the past used barter as the sole means of exchange. Eventually certain products or services took on a standard value in barter—for example, it was not long ago that a cow or a sack of grain could be taken to college by a student to pay his tuition. But the barter system must necessarily prove unsatisfactory as the level of trade becomes more complex. There are various reasons for this. One is that values are not always exactly equal, and smaller units or divisions become necessary. For example, if a canoe were valued at one and one-half cows, how could it be purchased? Another reason is that the unit of exchange may not always be convenient to carry around. Also it may not be one which the recipient wants or has any use for. A cow has value only if a man needs one. It has no value as currency to the man who must pay his creditor in grain. It may also be true that as one group of people begins to trade with another, the second group has an entirely different medium of exchange.

Gradually animals and grain were replaced by metals—gold, silver, copper, or bronze—in the form of an ingot, ring, or bar. The kind of metal used and its weight determined its value. Even when metal came to replace cattle, the value of each metal unit was in proportion to the value of an ox or cow and the weight showed the ratio between them. Thus the Greek *talanton,* meaning "something weighed" or "balance," was a unit of gold weighing a little more than eight grams and having the same value as an ox. If the talanton was made of silver, copper, or bronze, its weight was increased to make up for the difference in value in relation to gold.

Coinage In the process of development, **talents** appeared in the shape of an outstretched oxhide or cowhide to indicate that the metal talent was of a value equal to the animal. When definite, established weight measurements were applied to metal currency, mankind was close to the invention of coinage as such. As soon as designs were stamped on the money, currency became coinage.

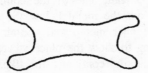

*Metal talent representing
an outstretched cowhide*

Ingots and Coins It is not definitely known where the first coins were made, or who should receive the credit for inventing them. We do know that currency—gold or silver shaped into ingots for convenience and weight regularity, but without any design—was used for some time before the appearance of coinage. The use of coins came from a need to indicate the weight or value of each piece, which was done by the designs stamped on them. This also made counterfeiting—coating ingots of cheaper metal with the precious metals of currency—more difficult. This step in the development of coinage may have taken place first in China or Greece or Asia Minor, or some other area where trade flourished.

Punch Marks The first step in the transition from plain, shaped ingots to actual coinage was the use of a punch mark stamped into the side of the ingot deeply enough to reveal the metal inside. A punch mark was a simple geometric device in a shape such as a triangle, square, or circle, that cut down into the center of the metal and lay bare the base metal of counterfeits, or proved that the silver, gold, or electrum (an alloy of silver and gold) in the pure ingots was genuine.

Designs From using a punch mark on one side of an ingot it was a short and natural step to introducing a design on the other side to indicate the city, kingdom, or state represented by that coin. It is fairly certain that this step took place by about 700 B.C. in Lydia, a kingdom in Asia Minor strategically located as a trading center, which had a real use for coinage in its commerce. The Greeks, however, were using coins by the seventh century B.C. Their coins were becoming standard in size, weight, value, and in other aspects that we now take for granted but which actually were developed slowly over many years in ancient times.

In time, punch marks gave way to more decorative designs and became the **reverse,** or tail, side of the coin. Generally this side continued to be cut into the metal below the surface more or less deeply to expose the inner metal, and contained the necessary information and lettering to show the place where the coin originated, the artist who designed the coin, and the like. On the **obverse,** or head side of the coin, the artist began to display his talents to the full.

It was the Greeks who brought coinage to the peak of artistic refinement and beauty. The Greeks became traders because their mainland was too small and unproductive to support their population, and its many miles of coastline gave them opportunity and zest for sailing. The Greeks established colonies on the shores of Asia Minor, the Black Sea, Sicily, southern Italy, and as far away as Spain and the African coast. In time, each colony and each important city developed its own distinctive coins and took a competitive pride in doing so. These individual, characteristic designs not only showed the value and weight of the coin but made it possible for those who could not read, or who spoke a foreign tongue, to identify the coin quickly and accurately.

It is quite likely that the first coins and the earliest series of coins of several denominations based on the same standard of value were struck for merchants and bankers. This probably took place first in Asia Minor. No matter how plain the device, it nevertheless was distinctive and identified the individual whose guarantee was clearly marked on his coins for all to see. By the middle of the sixth century B.C. the use of currency minted and guaranteed by the state was widespread. Coinage of this type—of standard weight and known value—circulated widely.

Soon electrum, abundant only in Asia Minor, was replaced by pure silver and gold in sections where they were plentiful. Since gold was scarcer than silver, it became more valuable. Currency issued on the gold standard could, therefore, be set at a lighter weight than the silver, but with equal value. Obviously gold and silver mines became most important to each state.

Gold coinage first replaced electrum in Lydia under King Croesus, who issued a series bearing the distinctive Lydian lion design in the sixth century B.C. The island of Aegina, in the Aegean Sea near Athens, had a turtle or tortoise on its silver currency. The winged horse of Corinth; the head of Athena, patron goddess of Athens, with her owl on the reverse; the nymph Arethusa, sacred to Syracuse, circled with dolphins—all these designs bore witness to the origins of the coins they decorated.

Method of Striking Coins Greek coins were not only excellently made, but they were all made by hand. These coins were struck by the anvil-and-hammer method. A piece of bronze, or die, with the design for the head side of the coin, was set into the top of the anvil. The hammer held the punch die into which had been cut the pattern for the tail of the coin.

A blank piece of metal—silver, gold, bronze or occasionally electrum—was heated at the nearby hearth until it would best receive the designs from the punch and anvil dies. This blank, which was to become the finished coin when struck, was at first quite varied and irregular in shape. Later it evolved a more oval shape, somewhat resembling a bean. As minting processes were perfected, it became rounder and more regular and standardized. The heated blank was placed directly over the lower die on the anvil and the upper or punch die was set as squarely above it as possible. The punch was struck with a sharp hammer blow, and the coin was ready for the marketplace.

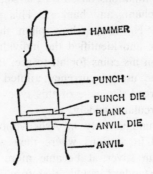

Striking a coin

Overstriking and Countermarking One of the labor- and time-saving methods that soon developed was overstriking. By taking old, used coins from another mint and heating them, a second, poorer city or state could strike its own designs over them. The result was a simply and quickly made coin.

This practice was not always honest, for even in those days counterfeiting was a problem. Sometimes perfectly good coins of one place were countermarked by others and then put into circulation as their own. This was more commonly done by individuals—usually bankers or merchants—than by states. The overstruck punch mark was very small, but definite enough to represent the man for whom it was countermarked.

Dating by Coins The scientific study of coinage is known as **numismatics.** Numismatists have studied and classified ancient coins so closely that they can give archaeologists a detailed description of coin types in the sequence in which they were issued during the seven hundred best years of ancient history. So it is through the joint efforts of numismatists and archaeologists that old currency and coinage are used in dating and can furnish historians with invaluable chronological evidence.

The name **hoard** is given to a group of coins found together. When a hoard or even one coin is unearthed at an excavation site, it, like pottery, can supply evidence of its own time. With expert information on the various mints in operation, archaeologists can re-create the history of one coin. A coin that can be given a fairly exact date can, in turn, give a date to the level of excavation at which it was found.

It has been established that the anvil, or obverse, die did not wear out as quickly as the punch, or reverse, die, which was struck with a hammer. Thus the coinage of a certain state and mint can be classified and arranged in a definite series, showing which coins were struck earlier, and which later.

Overstruck and countermarked coins shed light on a longer time span—from the date they were first used through the time they were re-used. And they provide clues to interaction—who had to re-use old coins, or who was counterfeiting coins.

When the name of the artist who created the design and engraved the die appears on the coin, that is an additional aid in dating. Also variations in devices, marks, techniques, and types go a long way toward explaining something about the dates of coins. For example, when one design was used over a long period of time, it underwent certain changes in the process of development. This can be seen clearly in the coinage of the island of Aegina, where the precision with which the turtle was drawn progressed from the seventh-century archaic type—with the suggestion of a shell by means of beading down the turtle's back or around the neck—to a clear-cut and unmistakable tortoise shell in the later period of the fourth century B.C.

Value of Coinage When portraits came to be used on coins, as they did by the fifth century B.C., they established not only a coin's date, but the physical appearance of the individual portrayed. A mintage honoring Mithridates, King of Pontus, or Julius Caesar, or Hadrian, occasionally provides realistic graphic information. And such coins also reveal much about the art of the states that minted them. As we have also seen, coins minted in one state and found in another tell a great deal about trade and commerce.

BRICK MARKS

Egyptian Brick Marks Fifteen centuries before Christ, artists in Thebes illustrated in a tomb the method of brickmaking then common in Egypt. It is startling to realize that in the tremendous stretch of time since then, very little has changed in the trade and skill of making or laying bricks.

At about the same time—1400 B.C.—the Egyptians began to stamp their bricks. The stamp block was usually made with the required device or name in hieroglyphics. This was used to mark the surface of each brick.

Brick-stamp designs varied according to function and purpose. The pride of a brickmaker in his work, or of a ruler in the building he was erecting, led to his name on the stamp. For convenience, a brick stamp might bear the mark of the ultimate destination of the bricks upon which it was impressed—as, for instance, the name of the person for whom a tomb was being built. A ruling monarch might be honored—and flattered—by the imprint of his name on bricks.

No matter what the motive or purpose, the result is the same: more chronological data for archaeologists and historians. The names of the pharaohs and their dates, as well as many other dates in the history of ancient Egypt, can be ascertained through brick marks, which add to the sum total of dating evidence.

Greek Brick Marks The Greeks used stamps in a similar fashion to mark tiles of terra cotta and other clay objects with a design often including the name of a contemporary official.

Roman Brick Marks Under the Republic, Rome was ruled by two officials, called **consuls,** who were elected annually for a twelve-month term of office. From Roman records, inscriptions, and literary evidence, the chronological sequence of these consuls has been established. The dates of the Roman emperors are known also. The Romans built mainly with brick, the building material at hand. When marble was used, it was generally applied as facing to the brick. To increase their personal and political prestige, the Roman consuls and emperors used stamps extensively on their building bricks and have thus handed down a permanent and accurate record of dates for archaeologists.

The Roman brick stamps were characteristically circular, and were engraved into a wooden, terra-cotta, or bronze die. The inscription was generally written in a circle or semicircle around the central device, which was the potter's sign or mark. Additional information often named the owner of the pottery where the bricks were made, and the place from which the clay came. The name on a brick mark of one or both consuls in office at the time, or of the emperor, indirectly gives the date when the tile was made. Sometimes the name of a legion by or for whom a building—such as those in a permanent camp—was erected, appears on brick stamps and furnishes dating evidence in far-flung parts of the Roman Empire, as in Roman Britain.

Each brick bearing an informative stamp served a useful purpose not only in the construction of a building but in the reconstruction of antiquity and the history of the past. Thus the name of the Egyptian Pharaoh Rameses II in hieroglyphics; or of Nebuchadnezzar, ruler of Babylon, in cuneiform characters; or of the Roman Emperor Hadrian in Latin lettering on a brick stamp, is significant. When the marked bricks of an area are arranged in sequence, they provide a long series of dates, establishing a chronology. Then, almost as in a jigsaw puzzle, gaps in such a series can usually be filled in by cross references with other dating material, such as vases and coinage.

EPIGRAPHY

Definition The word **epigraphy** comes from the Greek preposition *epi,* meaning "on" or "upon," and the verb *graphein,* meaning "to write." The science of epigraphy deals with ancient writings or inscriptions of all kinds on durable material, such as pottery, metal, stone, and the like. It also includes their decipherment, translation, explanation, and evaluation. The ancients have left much tangible written evidence, giving a wealth of factual information that can be used by the epigraphist as he, in turn, helps to reconstruct the story of the past for archaeologists and historians.

Inscriptions The word **inscription** comes from the Latin preposition *in,* meaning "in" or "upon," and the verb *scribere,* meaning "to write," and therefore parallels the meaning of the word epigraphy, which refers to the actual study of inscriptions. An inscription is writing of any type that is cut into, or raised upon, a hard surface and therefore endures. The material may have been clay, stone, wood, metal, or any other durable medium that receives and preserves thought. The system may range from symbolic picture writing to phonetic alphabets or even abbreviated script.

The instrument used for writing depended in part on the message's purpose and on where it was written. For writing on stone, marble, or wood, a paintbrush, or a chisel or other sharp carving tool may have been used, or, more effectively, a combination of the two, as was common in Egypt. Writing on soft clay was done with a tool that could make imprints; on harder surfaces, such as pottery, it was painted, or sometimes incised. On a hard metal or stone, the writing might be carved or incised, raised in relief, or struck with a punch and hammer, as on coins.

It is usually true that once people begin to record their words and ideas for posterity, they will find a method to make them endure and, once they have perfected this method, they will retain it. The hieroglyphic picture writing of the Aztec Calendar Stone and the shortened numeral forms and common words of a Roman tombstone both exist today, still expressing ideas of fifteenth-century Central American Indians or of the ancient Romans.

The method, the tools and surfaces, the style of writing, the stage of language development, the signatures and other names found in inscriptions everywhere—on tombs, public buildings, household articles, coins, tablets, temples, pottery—all supply archaeologists with information that bridges countless gaps in our knowledge.

LITERARY EVIDENCE

The writings of any man must be subjective to a certain extent. The degree of subjectivity varies according to the writer's character and the subject matter. If the writer has a good reputation and the material allows for objectivity, we expect a reliable and informative result.

This holds true of classical Greek and Roman writers, just as it does today. Classical writings which we now accept as valid have passed the tests of historical reliability established by scholars over a long period of time. By weighing and using the information handed down by the writers of antiquity, archaeologists can co-ordinate it with the knowledge yielded by their spades. As we have seen, classical authors furnish valuable evidence for fixing dates. When we know the date of a writer, or when he recounts events connected to a time sequence known by other means—pottery, coins, and the like— or when he supplies the dates, or talks about contemporary matters, we have further helpful clues that are constantly clarifying the mysteries of the past.

Classical Greek Writers Homer's description of Troy in the *Iliad*—its walls and its surroundings—was alive and vivid enough to convince a young German boy, Heinrich Schliemann, that Troy had indeed been a real place. This conviction led him, many centuries after the *Iliad* was written, to the place where Troy had been—and to years of excavation at that site, as well as at other places described by Homer, Mycenae and Tiryns in particular.

When Pindar, a Greek poet of the fifth century B.C., glorified the victors at the national games held at Olympia, Nemea, Corinth, and Delphi, we may assume that his descriptions are authentic and can be relied on by historians and archaeologists.

The Greek historian Herodotus traveled extensively in the entire eastern Mediterranean area and then set down what he saw and heard. He lived in the time of Greece's greatness, but it was also a period when the Persians brought invasion and war as their empire increased in power. Herodotus' description of Babylon re-creates for us a picture of that great city, most of whose bricks have long since disappeared into dust. We do not know exactly how the Egyptians accomplished the feat of preserving their dead by mummification, but Herodotus gives an account of this process. It is he, too, who tells us that it took one hundred thousand men twenty years to build the Great Pyramid, the tomb of the Pharaoh Khufu.

In the second century A.D., Pausanias, a Greek traveler and geographer, made a leisurely tour of Greece and wrote a detailed account of all he saw. This has been a mine of information ever since and has served as a guidepost to archaeologists and students of Greek antiquities, both in respect to monuments that survive and those that do not. He tells of the great gold and ivory statue of Athena which, during his own time, stood inside the Parthenon on the Acropolis at Athens, but which is known to archaeologists only by literary references such as this.

Classical Roman Writers The Roman writer Pliny the Elder recorded for posterity the four colors—shades of white, yellow, red, and black—which the most famous Greek painters used. He described the details of their paintings, their artistic innovations, and the superior quality of their painting. Archaeologists, therefore, are provided with a foundation upon which to reconstruct Greek painting, even though much of it has disappeared, due to its fragility. Pliny lost his life when Mt. Vesuvius erupted in A.D. 79, destroying life at Pompeii and Herculaneum. We learn of this from a letter written by his nephew, Pliny the Younger, which gives an account of that disaster and even of the day on which it began, August 24.

When an exact date for a monument or other object cannot be determined, a relative date can sometimes be fixed through a writer's mention of it. If we can accept such descriptions as accurate, that is all to the good. Detailed observations, measurements, and descriptions are, in this way, invaluable mines from which archaeologists can gather not only dates but clear pictures of the past.

CARBON 14

To Dr. Willard Frank Libby, an American nuclear scientist, goes the credit for devising a way to put chemistry and the physical sciences to work for archaeology and using this combination as a means of dating relics of the past. His new method is accurate to within about two hundred years in dating archaeological material up to sixty thousand years old, and the margin of error is continually being narrowed.

In the late 1940s, Dr. Libby, working with carbon-14 atoms and many organic materials of known and unknown ages, developed the method of dating called carbon 14. Since then Dr. Libby and scores of other scientists have refined this testing process until it has become ever more accurate and simplified. To understand carbon-14 dating and its value to archaeology, some explanation of the scientific principles behind it is necessary.

Carbon 14 and the Carbon Cycle Carbon 14 is a radioactive isotope (variant) of carbon, has an atomic weight of fourteen, or two more than regular carbon. It is relatively scarce, found in a ratio of one carbon-14 atom to a trillion carbon-12 atoms.

Nitrogen, which makes up 80 per cent of the atmosphere, is broken by the force of cosmic radiation into several substances, one of which is carbon 14. When carbon combines with oxygen, carbon dioxide is formed. Carbon dioxide is an essential element in giving life to all plants and thus becomes part of all animals. In a constant cycle, carbon dioxide is taken in from the air by plants and turned into chlorophyll and carbohydrates. Animals breathe in oxygen and consume plants and breathe out carbon dioxide, to start the cycle again. During their lifetimes all plants and animals absorb a certain amount of carbon 14.

When death comes to living organisms, the process is reversed and radioactive carbon-14 atoms are given off by the dead organic matter, but at a very slow rate. The decrease in the number of atoms of radioactive carbon in plants and animals when life stops is at a fixed rate of progression. After 5568 years half of the radiocarbon atoms have left the dead organism; during the next period of 5568 years, half of the remaining atoms disappear, leaving one quarter of the original number. In the following 5568 years the remaining atoms are again reduced to half their number; and this numerical decrease goes on continuously.

Dating by Carbon 14 All living matter contains a constant ratio of carbon 14 to regular carbon. When the plant or animal dies, it begins to lose carbon 14, but the regular carbon remains. By measuring the amount of regular carbon in a specimen, therefore, a scientist can figure out mathematically how much carbon 14 there was *while the specimen was alive.* Then, with electronic counting devices, he can discover how much carbon 14 remains and therefore how old the specimen is. For example, if there is half the carbon 14 there was when the specimen was alive, the plant or animal died 5568 years ago; one quarter of the original amount, 11,136 years ago. Dr. Libby tested matter of a known date as well as that of unknown age and balanced them one against the other, to prove the validity of his carbon-14 method of dating. Great strides have been made in his technique since it was first put to use. As the field of electronics grows and the number of experiments with carbon 14 increases, the percentage of error becomes less and the accuracy of the count becomes greater. Carbon-14 dating is considered accurate up to about 50,000 years in the past.

It has been proved that, although charcoal is the easiest material with which to work, all things that were once living reveal their dates to the electronic counter. Care must be taken, however, that the samples tested are pure and do not contain any modern foreign matter.

Potassium-Argon Dating Another scientific method of dating is the potassium-argon process, which can date matter that was living millions of years ago. Potassium 40 is converted at a constant but very slow rate into calcium 40 and argon 40. Because calcium 40 cannot be distinguished from other types of calcium atoms, the argon 40 atoms are used instead. By measuring the amount of change with extremely precise instruments, scientists can determine when the process started. Volcanic ash is ideal for this kind of dating. The potassium-argon method was used by Dr. Garniss H. Curtis and Dr. Jack F. Evernden, geologists at the University of California, to date the fossils found by Dr. and Mrs. Leakey at Olduvai Gorge.

As the sciences continue to work side by side in dating material from the past, the entire time chart of history is exposed to changes and variations of all kinds, but is constantly becoming more exact.

It must be remembered, however, that an answer is not always arrived at as mechanically as the availability of new scientific techniques might suggest. After a date comes out of the laboratory, it must be interpreted by men who, with all their training and knowledge, must assemble all the available facts and fit the pieces into the total picture of history. On the other hand, the objectivity of science holds the subjectivity of man's judgment in restraint.

CHAPTER FOUR

Discovery of Ancient Sites

HOW ANCIENT SITES WERE DESTROYED

Forces of Destruction Natural forces causing destruction were as effective in ancient days as they are in modern times. If one has ever seen the ravages upon everything in its path of a dust or wind storm, of fire, earthquake, or volcano, one knows that even marble cannot stand undamaged. Sometimes the causes of destruction at ancient sites are quite obvious, but often only the excavator's work and the archaeologist's research can explain the happenings. In certain instances the explanation still remains tentative, due to insufficient evidence.

Flooding If a city was built on a river, lake, or sea, the natural rise and fall of the water level, floods, and high tides often caused cave-ins or earthslides which undermined buildings on the banks. In time this could bring about their partial or total collapse. This was especially true of western Asia and similar areas where unbaked brick was the chief building material. In such cases destruction was usually quite complete, and rebuilding did not take place because it was impractical. On the other hand some buildings are so well constructed they seem impervious to the batterings of storm and flood. A temple in Naples has stood for centuries with its floor covered by water.

The changing course of a river sometimes led to the abandonment or decline of a town that depended on the river for its livelihood and could not exist without it. It is quite likely this was why Ur gradually lost its importance, for the Euphrates River slowly piled up silt and moved away from the city.

Earthquakes and Volcanoes An earthquake, quite plainly, can overthrow everything in its path. Throughout history, heavy earthquakes or series of quakes have caused widespread destruction. Many sites in Central America were damaged this way, and in Greece little remains of the once famous site of the Nemean games but a few temple foundations and toppled-over marble columns. If losses were not extensive, rebuilding generally took place, but otherwise it did not.

Another of nature's great destroyers is the volcano. It cannot be estimated how many ancient ruins might be deeply buried under volcanic lava, because there have always been settlements close to mountains that are active or potential volcanoes. The famous eruption of Mt. Vesuvius, in the first century A.D., destroyed the cities of Pompeii and Herculaneum without the least warning. Tragic though this was when it occurred two thousand years ago, it has provided an unparalleled visual record of life in these two sites, almost as though the inhabitants actually lived only a few years ago.

War Sieges and defeats in battles of ancient times were usually accompanied by fire. If a town was overwhelmingly defeated and the conquered population led away into captivity, the town was often given over to the elements, with no one left to combat them. When the Greeks besieged Troy for ten years, they did a great deal of damage that was repaired either hastily or not at all. In the end the Greeks set fire to the entire city, forcing the remaining Trojans to flee and seek new homes.

Drought and Famine Just as flooding can destroy, so too can a long, intense dry period. In both cases crops are affected adversely, and famine may occur. When famine is prolonged and cannot be overcome, inhabitants who are able to go elsewhere to find food, abandoning their former homes and town. In such instances there is generally no evidence that can be unearthed by excavation to indicate that famine once drove the people from the site. By eliminating the causes that would have left traces, however, and by other means, famine can often be inferred with some degree of certainty. Quite probably in Crete the Palace of King Minos at Cnossus was left empty after famine or plague, and so fell prey to the power of winds and dust.

HOW ANCIENT SITES WERE BURIED

Once an ancient site or structure was destroyed or abandoned, nature took over. The speed and extent to which remains became buried depended on the building materials used, and on the weather conditions of the locale.

Heedless of human affairs, the winds continued to blow, piling up dust and dirt over abandoned ruins and carrying with them the seeds of grasses, weeds, and trees. These took root and raised the level of earth even higher. The rains kept on falling, causing erosion and washing silt over the land. In some places the snows fell and ice formed, leading to thaws that brought floods which deposited a layer of mud over ruins that once stood erect—but now lay covered even more deeply.

Compare this to an old barn that falls away and crumbles slowly: the superstructure slides into and around the foundations, starting the process by which the ground level steadily rises to bury whatever remains, year after year, decade after decade, century after century.

Rebuilding When a town grew up in a given location, or when a building—a temple, for example—was erected at a certain spot, this was usually because the place had definite advantages. When a site was ruined or left vacant for any reason, it was quite often reoccupied or rebuilt simply because the location was a good one. This might take place after some time had elapsed, but when it did happen, the new was generally built upon the remains of the old.

In this manner a number of cities rose upon the ruins of Troy, and the Parthenon stands today upon the foundations of an earlier temple. It happens, also, that desirable spots such as Rome or Athens have been inhabited almost continuously, undergoing many periods of rebuilding. Hence one site may hide another just beneath it, and the archaeologist must always consider this possibility.

HOW A BURIED SITE IS DISCOVERED

The discovery of ancient remains depends on a variety of circumstances. A site may be entirely visible aboveground, as are the pyramids of Mexico, or parts of walls or columns may be standing in sight. On the other hand, sites may be completely buried and found only after careful thought—or a hunch, as was the case with the Troy of the Trojan War. Or a bomb, missing its target, may lay bare part of a large potential archaeological site, as happened during World War II, when a hole was torn open in the hillside above Palestrina, Italy, revealing part of an extensive Temple of Fortune. Built in Roman times, it had lain buried for an untold number of years.

Other sites, such as Pompeii, may be known through literary evidence, but lie covered for centuries until rediscovered by the chance unearthing of an artifact, or by a planned excavation. Ancient sites in desirable locations were often rebuilt many times, as was ancient Troy, where eight cities were built atop the ruins of the original settlement. It was indeed a good location—close enough to the sea to carry on a flourishing trade, but far enough inland for protection against surprise attacks. Sometimes an inhabited spot was destroyed, abandoned, or simply became a small village, and remained so for centuries until resettled on a larger scale. This happened especially to settlements that almost disappeared during the Dark Ages in Europe and then began to grow again during the Middle Ages. As trade and commerce flourished once more, they sometimes grew far beyond their original size. Such was the old Roman camp and walled city on the Thames River called Londinium—it emerged later as London.

Along the southern coast of England there are mounds which have been given the name **kitchen middens,** because they were formed where the early inhabitants of that area dumped in a pile the things they did not want. Over the centuries these piles have been buried by earth and growing things, but still retain their shape. Elsewhere, particularly in regions where sundried brick was the building material, mounds have grown up over the sites of ancient habitation and stand forth on the landscape. A trace of a building or settlement of antiquity in the form of a mound of this type is called a **tell.**

When remains of a structure—a temple, wall, or tower—stand aboveground or can be traced in outline, it is fairly certain that they are only a small part of an entire site which now lies buried below the surface. In such cases the promise of further archaeological finds, as excavation radiates out from the original point, is well founded. When it is known that a large area was once thickly settled and highly civilized, as were Peru and the Yucatán Peninsula, a search of nearby jungle sections is likely to uncover more statues or buildings which have been swallowed up, but also protected, by the thick growth since Incan and Mayan times.

In short, any faint suggestion of an ancient site, provided it is based on logical evidence—circumstantial or otherwise—is apt to reward the excavator who knows how to read and interpret the clues before him.

Aerial Photography A new method of locating ancient sites came with the development of the camera and the airplane. In the beginning, attempts to take aerial photographs were experimental and scattered, but as advances were made in both photography and flying, it became apparent that photography would open up new vistas to archaeologists. Great impetus was given to aerial photography during World War I. The years that followed brought an increasing realization of its value for archaeologists, as photographs of various sites were followed by excavations which clearly indicated the truth of what the camera's eye saw. During World War II extensive, detailed photographs were taken from the air. When they are enlarged and examined, many archaeological sites, such as the ancient wall at Canterbury or the Etruscan tombs in Italy, stood out clearly.

Aerial photographs not only reveal archaeological sites that might otherwise go unnoticed, but they are timesaving short cuts which often eliminate lengthy and unnecessary digging. The film provides a record that can be used to check and support what is already suspected. Because aerial photographs can reproduce a far larger ground area than someone looking at a site from ground level can see, they vividly show the connections and interrelationships of ground patterns.

The archaeologist wants to know what is below the soil's surface. A road, a wall, building foundations, or other remnants of the past may lie below the hills and fields. Even though remains have been covered over for centuries, what is below the surface must affect the topsoil as it exists today.

When the earth above an ancient site is cultivated, the ruins below will stand out on the photograph in a darker shade than other areas. Growing crops will often show influences of the presence or absence of remains over which they are growing. Thus one patch of grain may be more sparse or abundant than the rest of the field. Or it may show a variation in color, according to the depth at which the soil beneath was disturbed in ancient times, changing its quality, drainage, or fertility.

In uncultivated fields certain varieties of wild flowers may indicate they are flourishing above something that changed the soil in the past, and may etch out the details of an ancient structure. Soil thus altered shows up in a photograph as though the cause that produced its distinctive characteristics were drawn in outline, furnishing archaeologists with exact locations of sections to be excavated. Aerial photography has been so perfected that it is now a major tool in unraveling the entanglements still lying below the soil and disclosing the work of the ancients.

Ground Photography Ground photography has also proved its worth. Its main advantage is in saving time and effort, which in turn leads to saving money in the excavation process. Ground photography has been developed and used extensively in Italy to follow up the findings of aerial photography—especially where numerous Etruscan tombs were located from the air by the presence of round shadows on the film. It is also helpful in verifying hunches based on other evidence, such as a rise in the ground level.

Extensive, thorough excavation of each and every mound or tomb would be costly and time-consuming. Instead, a hole is bored deep into the center of a tomb, and a minute camera is lowered into it. The camera takes flash photos that tell which tombs still contain the artifacts that were buried with the dead and have their wall frescoes well preserved. In this way the excavator knows ahead of time what things of archaeological value he can expect to find when the earth and debris above the tomb entrance have been cleared away. He can also excavate the tombs in the most fruitful order, putting first those which contain the best archaeological remains.

Skin Diving With the appearance of skin diving, archaeologists have been provided with a new instrument for discovering ancient artifacts. It has long been known that many remains lie below water as well as land, but until skin diving developed only a fraction of this area could be explored.

When ships sailed from one country to another they often carried valuable cargoes, representative of many nations. A cargo of glass from Egypt or of vases from Greece did not always reach its destination. An ancient ship which foundered and sank near a port can be reached today by divers equipped with Aqua Lungs, masks, and underwater cameras—if the spot is not too deep. In this way, a ship laden with **amphorae** (Greek storage jugs) was located on the floor of the Mediterranean Sea close to Marseilles.

When a body of water was located near an ancient sanctuary, people tended to throw articles into it as offerings to a deity, or just for good luck. Skin divers have brought to the surface many artifacts of this nature. These finds are generally most helpful to archaeologists, because worshipers usually offered beautifully wrought things —made of gold, silver, precious and semiprecious stones—to their deities.

AN ARCHAEOLOGICAL EXPEDITION

Financing an Expedition An archaeological expedition may be privately organized and financed, but this is the exception rather than the rule, because the cost is high and financial returns are nonexistent or negligible. Heinrich Schliemann and Sir Arthur Evans, for example, financed their own expeditions, the former at Troy, Mycenae, and Tiryns, and the latter at Cnossus. Several others have done the same.

But more often sponsors of excavation work are private and public organizations or institutions, especially since archaeology has grown into a science in the twentieth century. Such sponsors are large museums, universities, or national governments. The British Museum, or the University of Pennsylvania, or the Italian Government, or the American School of Classical Studies in Athens might lead an archaeological expedition to a particular site. When a site is extensive enough to require digging over a long time by a series of expeditions, more than one institution may be involved, in a cooperative venture. Sometimes the government of the country where the site is located offers additional aid.

Selecting a Site Certain factors enter into the choice of an excavation. Foremost, of course, is that the site selected should give promise of a productive yield. This is usually determined by the physical signs and evidences of buried remains. As we have seen, standing remains, mounds rising on the landscape, darkened areas on photographic plates, literary evidence, even a single artifact—all indicate potential sites for excavation. On the whole it is a matter of logic, depending on the potential archaeological and historical value of the ruin, artifact, or site under consideration, that leads to the decision to dig in a certain location.

The Director and Staff   When sufficient funds have been allocated to send an expedition into the field, a director must be chosen. It is no simple matter to head an archaeological expedition, because the demands upon the leader are numerous and exacting, and he must be extremely versatile. First of all, the director should be a scholar well versed both in the specific area of study before him and in archaeology's many branches. He should be able to select a small but able staff to accompany him, preferably including experts in the major fields of archaeological research—pottery, numismatics, architecture, and inscriptions. Their final success depends upon the breadth of their combined knowledge, and on their ability to work together and separately.

In addition, the director is responsible for the expedition from beginning to end. He must supervise the preparations, and when the site has been reached he must hire and supervise the native workmen. He is also responsible for the accuracy and detail of the excavation's records, and ultimately for publishing its findings and related material.

The Gang   It is the gang of natives that does the actual digging, and its size is variable, according to the size of the project. The director and his staff closely supervise the gang, no matter what its size. The foreman of the diggers watches carefully as each member of the gang works with the soil. Some break away the earth with picks, some shovel it into baskets, others carry it to a dump pile or, in extensive excavations, to the dump car of the small railroad that hauls it to a distant dump pile. If the excavation is spread out over a large area, the gang of workmen may be divided up into a convenient number of small gangs, each under its own foreman.

The natives are usually surprisingly quick and adept at spotting an artifact or anything important, and the foreman must be the most alert of all. Each man is not only encouraged to use his eyes, but is equally discouraged from stealing by the money reward he is given, based on the importance of each find he makes. In this way each bit of soil receives a close inspection as it passes from hand to hand in its journey from the place where it has lain for years to the dump. Any find or possible clue turned up by the gang of workers is brought to the attention of a staff member, who handles it as he sees fit.

Since excavation work is expensive, the expedition's director must see that funds and time are not wasted, but are put to the best possible use. He must not neglect areas that might yield finds, but, on the other hand, must avoid unnecessary digging. In localities where the weather—excessive heat or cold or rainy seasons—makes living and digging conditions seasonal, it is even more necessary to make the most of each dig or campaign. The more thorough the preparation before a campaign is launched and the more direct the approach at the site, the more successful will be the entire expedition.

The Digging   The actual spot where digging begins at a site depends on decisions made before the expedition starts out and on the surface signs that corroborate or change these decisions. When the expedition is ready to go to work in the field, one or more trial trenches, or shafts, are dug at what seem to be strategic places. If a trench yields nothing of archaeological value below the surface, it is abandoned in favor of one that discloses something—stonework, walls, or objects.

It is of the utmost importance that whatever is brought to light should remain undisturbed in the exact place where it is found until a complete record, including maps, measurements, drawings and photographs, is made of all the details involved in the find. If this is not done, much information will be lost and cannot be retrieved, once the digging goes on and disturbs the spot. If it is done with care and thought, the entire scene can later be brought back, layer by layer, by words and pictures that describe every detail. Even things that appear to be unimportant during the digging may prove valuable clues upon evaluation of the whole.

It is essential to chronology that all finds—artifacts, walls, buildings—be noted without exception, each in its own stratum, as the excavation progresses down into the ground. Digging is destructive to a large extent, as it lays bare further antiquities below, but careful note taking can preserve all the knowledge gained at each level. When destruction and rebuilding have taken place in the past, the layer of earth in which remains and relics are found will contribute to the final dating. A lower stratum must be of earlier date than the upper, and articles found together in any stratum must have been left there at the same point of time in antiquity.

This can be seen clearly at some excavation sites where the earth has been left for just this purpose. The name **martyra,** from the Greek word *martys,* meaning "a witness," is a towerlike piece of earth that is left standing as the excavation takes place around it. In other words, everything else in the area is dug away except for the martyra, which then becomes a witness to the various strata through which the excavators have dug. The depth of the dig and the stratification are illustrated in this way. There is actually a cross section, not only of earth but of time, showing both the differences in the soil and the relative sequence of dates at which changes took place.

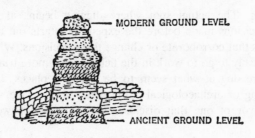

MODERN GROUND LEVEL

ANCIENT GROUND LEVEL

Martyra

RECONSTRUCTION

Artifacts Artifacts found during the course of excavation contribute their share to dating the level of excavation at which they were found. They also aid in reconstructing the picture of early life as it was at each layer. After an artifact has been studied thoroughly it will be put in storage or, if it is a fine example of its type in good condition, into a museum. When funds permit, it is preferable to build and maintain a museum in connection with each site, so that all the material is at hand to be seen or easily studied.

Just as every artifact does its part toward the reconstruction of the past, so does the site as a whole. It is the aim of all archaeologists to present a final picture that will resemble the original as closely as scientific methods allow. The scattered stones of a wall will be replaced, the fallen drums of a column will be erected again, the broken statue will be rebuilt, the shattered vase will be restored. All this is done on the basis of all the evidence at hand, so that the result is the truest possible. For this reason, it has become the practice of modern archaeologists to leave everything *in situ,* meaning "in place" or "in position," as it existed in ancient times.

CHAPTER FIVE

Archaeology in Egypt

IMPORTANT DATES IN EGYPTIAN HISTORY*

4241 B.C.	First Calendar
c. 3400–3200 B.C.	King Menes; Old Kingdom begins; First Dynasty; Capital at Memphis
c. 3000 B.C.	Great Pyramids at Gizeh; Fourth Dynasty
c. 2600–2400 B.C.	Old Kingdom ends; Seventh Dynasty
c. 2375 B.C.	Middle Kingdom begins; Eleventh Dynasty; Capital at Thebes
c. 1800–1600 B.C.	Conquest and rule by Hyksos
1580 B.C.	Middle Kingdom ends; New Kingdom begins Eighteenth Dynasty
1550 B.C.	Amenhotep I ruling; Capital at Tell-el Amarna
1450 B.C.	Thutmose III ruling
c. 1380 B.C.	Ikhnaton ruling
c. 1358 B.C.	Tutankhamen ruling
c. 1200 B.C.	Twentieth Dynasty
c. 930 B.C.	Twenty-second Dynasty
672 B.C.	Conquered by Assyrians
525 B.C.	Conquered by Persians; made part of Persian Empire
c. 330 B.C.	Conquered by Alexander the Great
168 B.C.	Submitted to Roman domination
c. A.D. 635	Conquered by Arabs

* There is considerable disagreement among classical scholars regarding the dates of Egyptian and Babylonian dynasties, Assyrian reigns, and so on. The dates used in this book are those used by several reputable sources, but they may be several hundred years earlier or later than other sources. The question of chronology and the various theories of dating are very specialized branches of archaeology and ancient history and are, we believe, beyond the scope of this book. Interested readers are referred to scholarly journals and books on chronology, many of which are on the shelves of university and other large libraries.

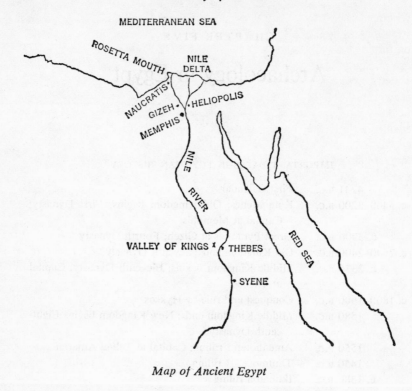

Map of Ancient Egypt

SIR W. M. FLINDERS PETRIE

The name of Sir William Matthew Flinders Petrie is almost synonymous with Egyptian chronology and nineteenth-century Egyptology. He carried on extensive excavation work and, with his orderly mind and systematic methods, applied all his skill and knowledge toward making exact measurements and working out methods of chronology.

Born in London in 1853, W. M. Flinders Petrie set out for Egypt when he was still in his twenties. He soon earned a reputation as a sound scholar and authoritative archaeologist. He studied the pyramids in detail, finding and excavating a number of the more important sites. He not only unearthed a number of tombs but located Naucratis, the ancient Greek colony at the mouth of the Nile. After carrying out concentrated excavations in Egypt and Palestine, he received a professorship in Egyptology at London's University College. As a venerated authority, Petrie was later knighted for his extensive contributions to archaeology. Toward the end of his long life, he carried on further excavation work in Palestine and died in Jerusalem at the age of eighty-nine.

Petrie was among the first to recognize the importance of a time sequence based on and correlated with archaeological finds, particularly artifacts such as vases and pieces of sculpture. When the smaller objects that appear in almost any excavation are examined, certain common characteristics become apparent. If, for example, large quantities of pottery are studied, subdivisions can be made according to styles, types of shape, decoration, painting, glazing, and the like. A further division is also possible on the basis of the pieces that show signs of having been made during the best period of any one grouping, or at its beginnings or decline. When time relationships have been arrived at in this manner, it becomes possible to establish the time sequence of an entire category of objects.

Since the Egyptian calendar was based on astronomical observations, notably on the rising in definite cycles of the Dog Star, Sirius or Sothis, it can be computed that the Egyptians invented their calendar about 4241 B.C. The Egyptians themselves kept king lists or records of their pharaohs and when they ruled. Classical authors, chiefly the Greek historians, furnish additional data for building a chronological history of Egypt during the Dynastic period—that is, from the time when King Menes united Upper and Lower Egypt to form one kingdom about 3400–3200 B.C. The dates of each dynasty are not fixed beyond dispute, but they do act as labels to which contemporary events can be pinned and to which classifications of archaeological materials can be assigned. In other words, it is almost as satisfactory to speak of monuments and artifacts as belonging to a certain dynasty as it would be to give them dates reckoned by our calendar.

SEQUENCE DATING

Dates for the period between the invention of the calendar and the reign of Menes, as well as for the time preceding the Egyptian calendar, however, remained confused until Sir W. M. Flinders Petrie overcame the problem. He grouped the archaeological material that antedated the fixed chronology of Egyptian history into categories which were subdivided on the basis of all available evidence. He then set up sequence dates running from 1 to 100 to act as divisions of time, quite apart from any attempt at dating according to a calendar. Thus a grouping of pottery might belong to sequence date 45 or, abbreviated, s.D. 45. Another grouping of pottery of later manufacture might belong to s.D. 60; of earlier, to s.D. 25, and so on. With this system of sequence dating, Petrie brought method and regularity to Egyptian chronology and put it on a sound, comprehensible footing.

HIEROGLYPHICS

Definition The Greeks conferred the name hieroglyphics on ancient Egyptian writing. It comes from the two Greek words, *hieros,* "sacred," and *glyphein,* "to carve." Hence hieroglyphics meant sacred carvings or writings, because they were used by Egyptian scribes—who were generally priests—for recording religious matters. Although hieroglyphic writing had been produced in great abundance since it appeared at about 3000 B.C., the time of the first pharaohs, and could be seen everywhere on ancient Egyptian monuments, temples, and statues, it could not be read by the Greeks of the time. Nor could it be read by anyone since the ancient Egyptians until Jean François Champollion, in 1822, provided the key to decipherment. Before that time Egyptian hieroglyphics had remained an insoluble mystery. The ability to read hieroglyphics brought with it a wealth of detailed knowledge and a storehouse of information communicated directly from the ancient Egyptians themselves.

The type of writing employed in hieroglyphics and the way it was done were largely determined, as is true of most writing, by the writing materials. Hieroglyphics were commonly used on stone, carved or cut into temple walls, columns, monuments, and the like. Occasionally they were applied as relief sculpture, standing out from a flat surface, or painted over in bright color so they would stand out. At other times they were painted directly on the stone, or were written on papyrus with ink and a reed pen.

Hieratic and Demotic Scripts The formal, carefully executed hieroglyphics carved in stone were preferred for important documents and monuments, but the more practical system of writing on papyrus became popular for less important works. This method was much faster than carving the formal hieroglyphics, and as a result abbreviated characters and greater simplicity developed. The rapidly written cursive script became a new branch of hieroglyphics called **hieratic.** When the abbreviated form of the hieratic is compared with the hieroglyphic sign of the same meaning, the resemblance between the two can be readily seen. The comparative simplicity of the hieratic form is also apparent.

The hieratic script was used chiefly for literature, secular writings in general, letters, and accounts. By about the seventh century B.C. an even shorter and more cursive form of handwriting grew out of the hieratic. This was used mainly, although by no means exclusively, for secular documents of all kinds and was given the name **demotic.** Both the hieratic and demotic types of hieroglyphics were used also for inscriptions and religious writings, a fact evidenced by their presence on temples, tombs, and monuments, and by the use of the demotic script on one section of the Rosetta stone.

Development of Hieroglyphic Writing The stages through which hieroglyphic writing passed can be traced with relative ease. In its early form, a picture or sign was used to stand for a noun. Thus a drawing or outline of a house or a man would be the word "house" or "man." Next came the use of that picture or sign, perhaps in a simpler form, to depict both the word it portrayed and one or more ideas closely associated with it. An example might be "house" and "home"; or "man," "father," and "boy." A symbol of this sort, which represents an idea or an object, is called an **ideograph.**

From that point it was a short step to the use of the same symbol to represent a group of words derived from a common root word, even though there might be differences in their meanings. Not long after, another transition took place and a symbol came to indicate the *sounds* (rather than the *meanings*) of words. A symbol that designates a sound is known as a **phonetic sign.** Only consonants were represented in hieroglyphics, with the result that a word sign might be identical for more than one word, despite the fact that their phonetic pronunciations, as well as their meanings, were quite dissimilar and had no relationship to each other. A parallel illustration of the same process would be using one sign to represent a group of

English words containing consonants in like order, but different vowels—for example: *cat, cut, cot.* Most of the Egyptian words were short and had only a few letters.

The next and most highly developed phase was the use of a sign to represent not a word or the stem of a word but an alphabetic sound. Signs standing for the sound of a single consonant were probably arrived at through a process of simplification, by taking all or part of a symbol that represented the dominant—possibly the first—sound in a common word whose hieroglyphic symbol had already become shortened and phonetic. For example, some form of the sign meaning *cat, cut, cot,* might have come to indicate simply the sound *k.*

It is not to be thought, however, that one step disappeared from use when another appeared. Hieroglyphic writing was a composite system of writing in which all varieties of signs and characters—more or less complex pictures, phonetic signs, alphabetic symbols, in many possible combinations—might appear side by side to clarify or determine word values.

JEAN FRANÇOIS CHAMPOLLION

In 1790 Jean François Champollion was born in southwestern France. He showed the fine quality of his intellectual powers at such an early age that his brother Jacques Joseph, twelve years his senior, soon began to watch over and guide his younger brother's talents. Champollion *le jeune* (the younger) displayed such extraordinary linguistic facility that by the time he was sixteen he was master of Greek, Latin, and enough Oriental languages to give him the foundation necessary for his future as a brilliant scholar.

At nineteen he became a professor of history at the University of Grenoble. With the facilities at hand, Champollion continued to increase his store of knowledge, especially that pertaining to Egypt, and added other ancient languages to those he already knew. In his study of comparative linguistics, Champollion soon realized that there are basic principles common to all languages. This recognition increased the ease with which he could handle any and all languages.

Champollion founded the Egyptian section of the Louvre in Paris, and several years later, in 1828, went to Egypt on a scientific expedition. In 1831 he was given the newly created chair of Egyptology at the Collège de France and was preparing for publication his research on Egypt when he died the following year, while only in his early forties.

THE ROSETTA STONE

The Nile River empties into the Mediterranean Sea through a group of mouths. They are shaped like the Greek capital letter Δ (delta) upside down, and hence this section is called the Delta. Year after year the flooding of the Nile brought muddy silt to the Delta region. The town of Rosetta, located on the western branch of the Delta, did not escape this annual deposit of mud. In 1799 some soldiers in Napoleon's army were digging at a spot about four miles north of the town to rebuild a fort, when they uncovered a basalt **stele in** its bed of mud. A stele is a stone slab bearing an inscription or used as a gravestone. This was the most important of many discoveries studied by trained men in Napoleon's army.

Champollion was only nine years old when the Rosetta Stone was brought to light, but he was to be the one who—almost a quarter of a century later—would first read what was written on it. This black, irregularly shaped slab was almost a foot thick, about three and three-quarters feet high, and two and a third feet wide. On its polished side was written a decree issued approximately two thousand years earlier, in 196 B.C., by an assembly of Egyptian priests at Memphis, giving thanks to Ptolemy V and recording the events of his reign. The same decree was repeated three times: in a band across the top, written in the ancient Egyptian hieroglyphic writing, in a middle section written in the simplified hieroglyphic script called demotic, and in the bottom band in Greek. Twenty centuries of exposure to the river mud and water had worn away the outer edges of the heavy volcanic stone, but the damage was not great enough to prevent reading the Greek lower section. One of Napoleon's officers translated the Greek and soon realized the possibilities offered by this trilingual inscription—by learning the meaning of the entire passage from the Greek version a linguist could eventually match specific words to specific hieroglyphics.

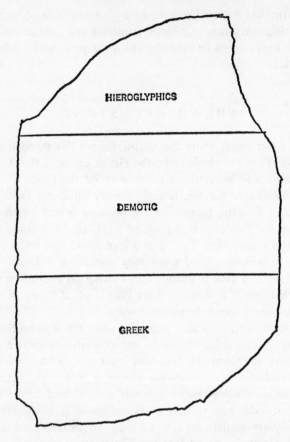

HIEROGLYPHICS

DEMOTIC

GREEK

The Rosetta Stone

Ancient Greek writers, such as the historian Herodotus, had recorded the impossibility of understanding hieroglyphic symbols. Many people tried to decipher them, but unsuccessfully. Champollion, working on the theory that the Rosetta Stone hieroglyphics were not mere pictures but phonetic signs, was to solve the puzzle.

Obelisk of Philae A clue to deciphering the upper hieroglyphic and demotic inscriptions was presented when an obelisk inscribed in both Greek and hieroglyphics was discovered in 1822, on the island of Philae in the Nile River. Until then one of the chief difficulties had been deciding where one word ended and another began. But on the obelisk, as on the Rosetta Stone, there was a **cartouche** around the group of characters representing the name Ptolemy. A cartouche is an oval ring around the written name of a royal personage or deity, to set it apart for emphasis in an inscription or on a papyrus. This made it possible to convert each separate character into its phonetic counterpart. In addition there was on the obelisk a cartouche containing the name Cleopatra. By comparing the two cartouches, the characters common to both could readily be identified and the others could be supplied from the Greek names of Ptolemaios and Cleopatra. In this way a basic phonetic alphabet of these hieroglyphic characters could be constructed.

Cartouches of Ptolemaios (top) *and Cleopatra* (bottom) *on the oblelisk of Philae*

Decipherment The gap between knowing the phonetic pronunciation of hieroglyphic characters and understanding their meanings and grammatical construction was, however, a wide one. Using his extensive knowledge of linguistics, Champollion solved the hieroglyphics mystery by translating the phonetic symbols into meaningful language. He also realized that, as is true of all languages, Egyptian had undergone many changes and refinements in the course of its development through the centuries, and he approached it accordingly. Champollion well earned his distinction as the founder of Egyptology when his key unlocked the countless secrets hidden in hieroglyphic papyri and inscriptions. The Rosetta Stone is now on display at the British Museum.

THE PYRAMIDS OF EGYPT

Pyramids The pyramid shape was not indigenous to Egypt alone, but was used in varying sizes, shapes, and purposes in widespread parts of the world, from Mexico to Greece. A pyramid is characteristically built with four sides rising gradually from a square base to an actual or theoretical point above the center of the ground square.

Gizeh Perhaps the best known pyramids are those built by the pharaohs of Egypt, especially during the Fourth Dynasty, from about 3000 to 2400 B.C. Of these, the largest and most famous are the three at Gizeh constructed to be the burial places of Khufu, Khafre, and Menkaure. Gizeh was a spot on the desert not far from the Nile River and Memphis. It was the capital of Egypt during the Old Kingdom period.

The Great Pyramid It was at Gizeh that the Pharaoh Khufu, or Cheops, had a massive structure constructed as a sepulcher for himself and his queen about the twenty-ninth century B.C., or almost five thousand years ago. As Egyptian kings of the Pyramid Age commonly did, he planned and started his pyramid tomb when he succeeded to the throne. In this way he could supervise and direct the work, so that his burial place would be as he wanted it. Thus he could be sure it was properly equipped to furnish him with all he would need after death.

The saga of the Great Pyramid of Khufu began at the stone quarries up the Nile, where the huge limestone blocks were cut. The smallest blocks weighed over two tons, and between two and three million were cut altogether. Each block was marked with the exact location it would have when it was placed in Khufu's pyramid at Gizeh. So precisely were they measured and cut that they fitted together with almost imperceptible joints. By sheer manpower, assisted only by ropes and pulleys, the huge blocks were pulled on rollers to the river, where they were loaded on barges to be floated downstream to their destination.

There are various theories about the method used to raise the limestone blocks into position at the pyramid site. It is possible that, after the first layers of stone had been put into place and it became too difficult to lift the remaining ones into position above them, a means was devised to pull them up by pulleys and ropes. This might have been accomplished by piling up an embankment of earth against the sides of the completed lower section of the pyramid. A ramp of this type would have enabled the men standing on the flat surface above to drag the blocks up from the level of the desert floor. As the pyramid increased in height, the ramp could be built up farther, to the point necessary to correspond to the next layer of blocks, and the process repeated, and so on to the top. When the pyramid was completed, the dirt could be removed. The entire outside was encased in a layer of limestone, but these facing stones were taken off at some time in the past to be used for building material elsewhere.

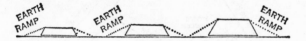

One of the theories put forward as to how pyramids were built. The earth ramp was removed after the pyramid had been completed

Pyramid Temple   When the last limestone block had been raised— almost five hundred feet—and set into its position atop the Great Pyramid, about one hundred thousand slaves had labored for twenty years. The purpose of this colossal undertaking had been to provide one man, the Pharaoh Khufu, with a tomb that would be a safe and unmolested home for his life after death. Deep within it lay his body, sealed into a gigantic stone structure that covers over twelve acres of ground and measures close to seven hundred and fifty feet on each of the four sides at the base. This, however, was only the tomb.

The body had to be sustained in the next life. To that end, those who remained on earth would bring drink and food to the pyramid temple, a chapel placed near the pyramid, usually to the east. In the pyramid temple was a fine portrait statue of the pharaoh, sculptured in stone. Colonnades, wall sculptures and paintings, and window lighting made the temple a place of beauty and dignity.

The customary entrance to a pyramid's burial chamber was by a passageway from the north side, which was sealed tightly after the coffin of the dead pharaoh had been set inside. In the case of the

Pyramid of Khufu, one passage led from the north side to an unfinished chamber below. Branching from this, another climbed to the side passage of the Queen's Chamber and on through a wider and higher section, known as the Grand Gallery, to the King's Chamber. It is apparent that the architects of the pyramids understood the principles of relieving architectural stress and weight, for there is a series of five small chambers above the King's Chamber, evidently built to serve this purpose.

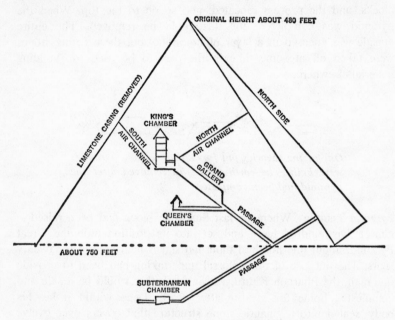

ORIGINAL HEIGHT ABOUT 480 FEET

LIMESTONE CASING (REMOVED)

KING'S CHAMBER

SOUTH AIR CHANNEL

NORTH AIR CHANNEL

NORTH SIDE

GRAND GALLERY

PASSAGE

QUEEN'S CHAMBER

ABOUT 750 FEET

PASSAGE

SUBTERRANEAN CHAMBER

The Pyramid of Khufu

Mummies The Egyptians practiced a method of embalming their dead to arrest decomposition so that the body would be able to enjoy the life after death and make use of the objects with which it was surrounded in the tomb.

Over the course of many centuries the process of mummification underwent continuous change. Basically, however, it was thought to have involved removal of all internal organs, except the heart, through an incision on the left side of the body. The corpse was next immersed in a salt solution for several weeks, during which most of the fat was dissolved. The body was then packed with preservatives, plastered with a substance similar to what we now call plaster of Paris, and wrapped in bandages.

Mastabas The several royal residents of the pyramids were not alone on the desert at Gizeh. They were surrounded by many tombs of the nobles and other contemporary great families. Here, too, were the tombs of the pharaoh's relatives, his court, and household. These tombs were eclipsed by the mighty pyramids that stretched for many miles along the desert, because they were smaller and were differently constructed. A tomb of this type in the royal cemetery at Gizeh was known as a **mastaba.** The mastabas, also built of stone, were rectangular or oblong, with walls that slanted inward to a flat top.

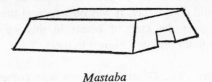

Mastaba

Mastaba burial chambers were in the ground below, as they were in the pyramids, and the place where the coffin actually rested was disguised to prevent robbery and desecration. The chapel in the mastaba served the same purpose as did the temple beside the pyramid, and was generally beautifully decorated with painted bas-reliefs on the walls. These scenes re-create the everyday activities and interests of the Egyptians of about 3000 B.C. Here are depicted their homes, furniture, jewelry, their arts and crafts—the making of pottery, papyrus, glass, linen—their agriculture, and their religious practices, all recorded for posterity by the sculptors and painters of ages past.

SPHINXES

Definition A sphinx was a mythical creature of the ancient world, with a lion's body and the head of a human. The sphinx appeared in most parts of the eastern Mediterranean, especially in Greece, Egypt, and western Aisa. The Greek sphinx—usually combining the head of a woman with the lion's body—was rarely depicted, although it was often mentioned in mythology. It did occasionally appear elsewhere, notably in vase painting and for other decorative purposes. In western Asia, particularly in the region of the Tigris and Euphrates rivers, the lion's body was generally given wings.

The word sphinx should send one's thoughts to Egypt in general and to the Great Sphinx in particular—and rightly so. As far as we know, this type of figure, with its animal and human characteristics, originated in Egypt and was imitated by other peoples, who made it their own by changing its appearance instead of copying it exactly. The Egyptian sphinx had a human head on the lion's body, but it was always the head of a man.

Sphinxes were symbols of great power and strength, and signified indestructibility based on divine protection, just as the lion emblem of royal power still does today. It was only natural that the Egyptians should make use of the king of beasts in this way, since it was native to their country and well known to them.

The Great Sphinx   The Great Sphinx not only comes to mind first, but it seems to have been the first to appear in history. We do not know exactly when this huge sphinx was sculptured, but it was probably during the time of King Khafre, or Chephren, who ruled in the Fourth Dynasty, about 3000 B.C., and built one of the Great Pyramids at Gizeh. Since that time the majestic sphinx, also at Gizeh, has withstood the ravages of desert winds and blowing sands, and of mutilation in times past. It remains a royal figure looking out upon the surrounding scene, attesting to the might and power of the pharaohs. The Great Sphinx (or The Sphinx), created mostly from rock, is in a couchant position, which gives it a calm and imperturbable dignity. Some parts that could not be carved from the rock were added by building them up with masonry work. It is evident from the headdress that a pharaoh is represented.

The constantly shifting desert sands eventually accumulated around the base of this huge image, and early in the nineteenth century excavations were undertaken and periodically continued to learn more about it. During these excavations the purpose for which the Great Sphinx had been built became apparent when a small temple was discovered between the two forepaws. There was also evidence that there had been a sacred road along which processions approached The Sphinx and temple. This road crossed the desert on a level considerably above that of the temple and then ended in a flight of steps, which led down to a platform and then to a second flight descending to the temple itself.

Because the level of the desert shifts constantly, it is not easy to set definite measurements for the height of The Sphinx, but it averages between 65 and 70 feet over-all, from the temple to the highest point—the top of the headdress. It is about 140 to 150 feet in length. The Great Sphinx is not the largest to be found in Egypt, but is by far the most famous monument of its kind. An alabaster sphinx at Memphis is the largest, and there were many others in a variety of sizes. Many of the temples in Egypt were approached by avenues lined on both sides with sphinxes.

OBELISKS

In Paris, New York, London, and Rome there are obelisks which in the nineteenth century were carried from their original locations in Egypt and set up for all to see. It was not an easy task to move these obelisks, which weighed many tons each, and transport them across the water. It was, however, far more difficult for the ancient Egyptians to hew them out of the rock, to carry them long distances from the quarries, and to raise them to standing positions at their destinations—all mainly by the force of manpower and whatever equipment they could invent or devise.

Obelisks were generally cut in one piece from granite, were almost square, and rose gradually to a pyramid-shaped top. They were of various heights, but many ranged between 50 and 75 feet, and some even reached one hundred feet. The tallest obelisk in existence today was found at Heliopolis in Egypt. It is a little over one hundred feet tall and now stands in Rome, where it was taken in the fourth century A.D. by the Emperor Constantine.

Obelisks probably first came into use during the period of the Old Kingdom (c. 3400–2400 B.C.), but were not numerous until the period of the Middle Kingdom. They were often erected before temple entrances, and obelisks used in this way still stand at Karnak and Luxor. Others were set up inside temples, or, in the case of smaller ones, in tombs. More often than not, they were erected on low platforms or pedestals.

In Egyptian religion the ruler and the sun were merged into one idea, so that the sun, which was worshiped, was embodied in the king, who thus became sacred. The pyramidal peaks of obelisks were once covered with metal—gold, if possible, or copper—to catch the sun's light and at the same time the pointed top reached toward the sun. Many obelisks were set up by the ancient Egyptians at Heliopolis, the City of the Sun.

Far up the Nile River, at a place called Syene—the site of the modern Aswan—were the quarries from which the obelisks came, because there the granite was fine in quality and color. We know from one still in position at the quarry that an obelisk was usually a **monolith**—that is, cut from one piece of stone—and the obelisk was hewn from the granite in a horizontal position by cracking away the stone from the outer surface with heat and water—a practice still used by some primitive peoples today—and then dropping balls of rock on the outlined shaft to shape it and separate it from the surrounding stone. This quarrying method was crude but effective.

When the obelisk had been cut free except for the supporting rock on its lower surface, it was held by ropes until it was finally raised from its bed and rolled onto the flat ground beside the now empty trench. The shaping was done entirely at the quarry and the hieroglyphic writing that covered most of the obelisks could have been done there, but was more likely done after the obelisk had been taken to the place where it was to be erected.

From the quarry the obelisk was pulled by rollers manned by hundreds of men to a barge that transported it to the spot for which it was destined. This was no simple matter, as an obelisk, unless it was quite small, might weigh anywhere from seventy-five to four hundred tons. It was all the more difficult when we consider that, with little more than ropes, levers, pulleys, earth embankments, wooden rollers, and muscle, this massive stone not only had to be taken from the quarry to the river and from the river to its ultimate location, but had to be erected when it reached the site, sometimes on a pedestal and sometimes inside a building.

VALLEY OF THE TOMBS OF THE KINGS

Egyptian Future Life The ancient Egyptians' strong belief in a life after death that closely resembled their everyday life on earth led them to great lengths in preparing for it. Much of this preparation was based on the need for a safe burial place, with room for all the material possessions that made earthly life comfortable. The more noted and wealthy the individual, the finer and bigger was his tomb.

Royal Necropolis During the Egyptian Empire (about 1580 to 1150 B.C.) the important personages of the time—pharaohs, nobles, builders, and generals—were buried more than four hundred miles up the Nile River from Memphis, near Thebes. Thebes lay mainly on the Nile's east side, and beyond the river's western bank was a plain backed by cliffs. Into these cliffs natural rock tombs were cut, giving a measure of security to those buried within.

An ancient cemetery is called a **necropolis,** or city of the dead, from the Greek words *nekros,* "the dead," and *polis,* "city." Like the pyramids, the tombs were often near or combined with chapels which are sometimes known as tomb chapels. In spite of their isolation and the attempt to keep their locations secret by sealing and covering the entrances, these tombs fell prey to robbers, who searched for them by night at the risk of both legal punishment and priestly retaliation.

Removal of the Sarcophagi When the Theban line of pharaohs came to an end about 1150 B.C., almost every tomb in the Valley of the Tombs of the Kings had been plundered. But when Thebes was no longer the capital, the royal necropolis in the valley became even more vulnerable to robbers, who took whatever valuables—jewelry, precious stones, and the like—they could find.

In this situation the Egyptian priests, out of respect for the dead kings, moved as many of the bodies as they could and arranged them within a single tomb in a secluded part of the valley. Considering that a royal personage was generally buried in a stone coffin called a **sarcophagus,** and that most of the royal sarcophagi were made of granite, it was no mean task for the priests to get them from their original burial places to this common tomb, located well below the ground and at the end of a long corridor. When this had been accomplished, the entrance to the tomb was filled in, and there these ancient pharaohs' mummies lay in their sarcophagi until late in the nineteenth century—when excavation brought them back to the light of the world.

The Valley of the Tombs of the Kings has now been quite thoroughly excavated. The tomb entrances and the sepulchers themselves, with their temples, illumine the burial methods of the period when the city of Thebes was at its height. Flights of steps, passages and corridors, anterooms, and burial chambers deep within the cliffs all give witness to the precautions taken to equip the dead person for his future life, to sustain him in it by replenishing the offerings of food and drink periodically, and to protect him and all the valuable possessions with which he was surrounded from the sacrilegious acts of pilferers. Of perhaps greater worth to archaeologists, however, are the sculptures and decorations on the walls of the rooms and the sides of the coffins. Many are still bright with color, and all tell of the beliefs, lives, and interests of these rulers of almost four thousand years ago.

LORD CARNARVON AND HOWARD CARTER

Lord Carnarvon George Edward Stanhope Molyneux Herbert, Earl of Carnarvon in North Wales, was born in 1866 and received his education at Eton and Cambridge. With Howard Carter he explored the cliffs of the Valley of the Tombs of the Kings in Egypt, where they found and excavated a number of tombs.

Howard Carter Howard Carter, born in 1873, was educated by private tutors and later was fortunate enough to work under Sir W. M. Flinders Petrie, the noted Egyptologist. Carter had had fifteen years of archaeological work in Egypt and had discovered several tombs of importance, among them those of Queen Hatshepsut and of Pharaoh Thutmose IV, by the time Lord Carnarvon joined him in his excavations in 1906.

After World War I, Carter made one of the most famous of all archaeological discoveries—one that was to shed light on Egypt's past beyond even his most hopeful dreams: he found the almost untouched tomb of Pharaoh Tutankhamen, who ruled in the fourteenth century B.C.

This was in November 1922. Lord Carnarvon was in England when this great event occurred, but, summoned by Carter, he returned to Egypt and the two men shared together the thrill and wonder of the archaeological treasures brought back into the light of the Valley of the Tombs of the Kings after they had lain in the darkness of the tomb for almost thirty-four centuries. Howard Carter lived until 1939 and made a detailed study of the wealth of material left by King Tutankhamen, but Lord Carnarvon died only five months after Carter had come upon the tomb's entrance.

KING TUTANKHAMEN

King Tutankhamen About 1350 B.C. Egypt was ruled by a boy king who was destined to contribute little to Egypt during his short reign, but a great deal to the world of archaeology thirty-three hundred years later. When King Tutankhamen died at the age of seventeen or eighteen, he was buried in a splendid tomb equipped with all he would need for his life among the dead. Unlike other burial places, however, his was not broken into and despoiled of its precious contents, but remained largely intact until Howard Carter found it in 1922. It has furnished archaeologists and historians with a perfect example of a royal tomb and unparalleled material for study.

King Tut's Tomb Tutankhamen's tomb was extremely well hidden in its cliffside location in the valley and by the debris cast down upon it from the tomb of Rameses VI, which was later built above it. Although it had been entered in the past—probably soon after the young king died and while there was still living memory of its whereabouts and contents—the ancient robbers stole very little, for one reason or another, and its discovery was indeed a momentous one. This tomb is a unique example of the riches and luxury that surrounded members of the ancient Egyptian royalty and nobility in this world and permitted them to go well provided for and proudly to the next life.

A flight of steps led to a sealed door and a corridor that sloped downward through the limestone hillside to the entrance of the royal antechamber, a room about twelve feet wide and twice as long. Off this antechamber, and sunk below its floor level, opened another room or annex about twelve feet square. At the antechamber's far end lay the sealed entrance to a room approximately the same size—the actual burial hall or sepulchral chamber. Guarded by two fine gold-decorated wooden statues of the young pharaoh, the doors opened onto the dazzling sight of a golden coffin. This beautiful casing protected the granite sarcophagus in which the royal resident of the tomb rested, preserved by the secrets of ancient Egyptian embalming methods and the preservative qualities of the dry Egyptian atmosphere.

When the numerous and fabulously wrought objects that had been put into the tomb with this fourteenth-century B.C. Pharaoh Tutankhamen are totaled up, it becomes evident that the twentieth century A.D. has inherited a storehouse of gold, alabaster, inlaid wood, gilt,

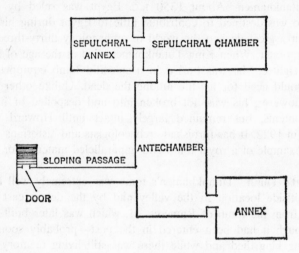

Tomb of King Tutankhamen

precious stones, and statuary, all testifying to the superior workmanship and the wealth of that period. Statues of the young ruler, carved from wood and ornamented with gold, his death mask of gold, shrines, chests, couches heavily decorated with gold, perfume vases of alabaster, many articles of jewelry on his mummified body, give witness to royal splendor and luxury. When we realize how young Tutankhamen was at the time of his death and that due to his short reign his tomb was both small and modest in comparison to those of the greater pharaohs who preceded and followed him in Egyptian history, we get some idea of the tremendous riches those other tombs must have contained before their contents were stolen and scattered.

The items found within the tomb of King Tutankhamen closely parallel those in the palace of the living king and are of the utmost importance in re-creating his way of life, and that of his nobles, for historians and archaeologists. Painting and embossing on furnishings, doors, and walls narrate scenes and events in the young pharaoh's life and reproduce the atmosphere of ancient Egypt during the Eighteenth Dynasty with a precision and definitiveness that no other archaeological find or composite study even had prior to 1922.

THEBES

During the Empire period, from about 1550 to 1200 B.C., the Egyptian capital was about four hundred miles up the Nile River at Thebes. At the height of its development this huge city spread out and covered several miles on both sides of the river. As we have seen, the limestone cliffs which rose not far from the west bank held the tombs of the pharaohs and nobles in the Valley of the Tombs of the Kings, and the walls of their great tomb temples illustrated in relief sculpture the might of the Egyptian Empire.

The larger part of Thebes once lay on the east bank, but most of it, built of sun-dried brick, has long since disappeared into the sands of the desert. Today there is little trace of this bustling port of antiquity, except for the ruins of the Temple of Luxor and the Temple of Karnak, the latter an enormous and magnificent sanctuary.

Luxor The Temple of Luxor was built to Amen, the god of Thebes, under Amenhotep III, who ruled at about 1400 B.C., and the pharaohs who followed him. Erected close to the river south of the town, it had a great court and colonnade with a huge **pylon** entrance, as was then customary in the larger Egyptian temples. (A pylon is actually an entrance or gateway, but in the form of a good-sized building. Its walls taper up and in, somewhat like those of a pyramid.) Before the temple were two obelisks, pointing toward the sun, with which Amen became associated in the form of Amen-Ra, the sun god and chief deity. From the Temple of Luxor a road leads northeast toward the Temple of Karnak.

Karnak By far the greater temple at Thebes is the Temple of Karnak, also built to the patron god Amen. It was constructed over a long period of time and is a great sanctuary, consisting of one large temple and several smaller ones enclosed by an entrance pylon and walls. The approach is along an avenue lined with sphinxes, which leads through the main pylon gate, facing the river, to a large colonnaded courtyard.

The central core of the temple is the Great Hall beyond, with another pylon giving access to it. Here were once many columns—134 in all—arranged in sixteen rows and supporting the roof of the Great Hall. The two rows in the center were considerably higher than the others, forming a clerestory that allowed light to enter the Great Hall through its windows.

Beyond, and also entered through pylons, lie other courts, in one of which an obelisk still stands—the lone survivor of the pair placed there by Queen Hatshepsut, who reigned at the beginning of the fifteenth century B.C. in the Eighteenth Dynasty.

Everywhere within the temple there were splendor, color, and carving, glorifying the pharaohs and their deeds of battle and conquest. The carvings remain on the columns and the walls, with their

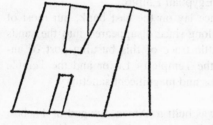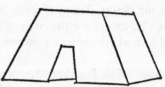

Two types of Pylons: Double (left) *and single* (right)

colors only slightly faded. Thanks to circumstance and the efforts of archaeologists, much of the glory of ancient Thebes remains—its color only slightly faded.

Abu Simbel   Two temples were carved out of the living rock cliffs along the west bank of the Nile at Abu Simbel, south of Aswan in the thirteenth century B.C. The Great Temple honored the sun god Re-Harakhte of Heliopolis, whose representation was carved in a niche over the entrance, and the pharaoh Rameses II. Four colossal, sixty-seven-foot seated statues of the pharoah were carved into the façade. The Small Temple farther north, dedicated to the local cow-goddess Hathor, had six niches with two representations of

Rameses' chief wife Nefertari in the guise of the goddess, flanked by gigantic statues of the pharaoh.

When the construction of the Aswan High Dam was first projected in the 1950s, incidentally precipitating the Suez Crisis in 1956, these ancient temples were threatened by the waters of Lake Nasser, the reservoir that would be formed behind the dam. Thanks to a great feat of engineering and over four years of work that entailed careful recording by photography and architectural drawings, these ancient monuments were dismantled, removed to ground 200 feet higher and 700 feet farther back, and reassembled. When this extraordinary undertaking was successful, plans were made to preserve a number of other monuments including temples and pavilions at Philae that had also been doomed to total inundation.

CHAPTER SIX

Archaeology in the Middle and Near East

IMPORTANT DATES IN ASSYRIAN HISTORY

c. 3000 B.C.	Semites in Assyria
c. 1200 B.C.	Extended territory to north; conquered Babylonia; Mitanni from northwest took Nineveh
c. 1150 B.C.	Rise of Assyrian power
c. 750–612 B.C.	Assyrian Empire
732 B.C.	Assyrians took Damascus
722 B.C.	Rule of Sargon II; Nineveh made the capital
705–681 B.C.	Sennacherib; destroyed Babylon
670–651 B.C.	Assyrians captured Egypt
c. 612 B.C.	Nineveh destroyed by Babylonians, Medes, and Persians; end of Assyrian Empire

IMPORTANT DATES IN PERSIAN HISTORY

558–529 B.C.	King Cyrus
549 B.C.	Captured the Medes; Persian Empire
546–540 B.C.	Persia took Lydia and western Asia Minor
539 B.C.	Persia took Babylon
525 B.C.	King Cambyses took Egypt
521–485 B.C.	King Darius
490 B.C.	Invasion of Greece; defeated at Battle of Marathon
485–465 B.C.	King Xerxes
480 B.C.	Battle of Thermopylae won by Persians; Battle of Salamis; Persian fleet defeated
479 B.C.	Greeks defeated Persians in Battle of Plataea
331–330 B.C.	Alexander of Macedon captured Babylon, Susa, and Persepolis, end of Persian power

IMPORTANT DATES IN BABYLONIAN HISTORY

2050 B.C.	Babylon captured by Amorites from the west
2050–1750 B.C.	Growth of Babylon and Babylonia under Amorites
1948–1905 B.C.	Rule of Hammurabi; Babylon made the capital; laws codified
c. 1900 B.C.	Kassites from the northeast
c. 1750 B.C.	Kassites seize power in Babylonia
689 B.C.	Babylon destroyed by Assyrians under Sennacherib
586 B.C.	King Nebuchadnezzar of Chaldea captured Jerusalem and led Jews into captivity in Babylonia
538 B.C.	Persians under King Cyrus took Babylon

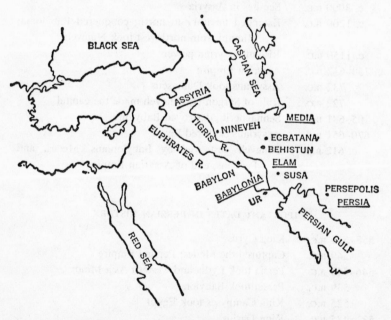

Map of Assyria, Persia, and Babylonia

IMPORTANT DATES IN ASIA MINOR

c. 2500 B.C.	Hittites into Asia Minor from north
c. 2000 B.C.	King Anitta; kingdom of Hatti in control; capital at Hattusas

c. 1900 B.C.	Beginning of First Hittite Empire
c. 1750 B.C.	King Mursil I seized Babylon
c. 1600 B.C.	End of First Hittite Empire
c. 1400 B.C.	Beginning of Second Hittite Empire; King Suppilulyuma captured Syrians and Mitanni and Assyrians
c. 1350 B.C.	Hittite Empire in control of western Asia
c. 1240 B.C.	Trojan War
c. 1200 B.C.	Greeks, Phrygians, and Armenians from Europe into Asia Minor; end of Hittite power
c. 800 B.C.	Lydia rose to control Asia Minor; capital at Sardes
c. 700 B.C.	Lydia turned back invasion of Medes
546 B.C.	Persians under King Cyrus took Sardes

Map of Asia Minor

CUNEIFORM WRITING

Definition   The name **cuneiform** was given to the writing of the
ancient Babylonians, Chaldeans, Assyrians, and Persians, because it
described its chief characteristic. In Latin, *cuneus* means "wedge."
In cuneiform a wedge or triangular shape resulted from the application of a sharp writing instrument, or stylus, to wet clay. When the
clay tablet dried, it presented a permanent record written in wedge-
shaped characters.

Development of Cuneiform   The development of the wedge-shaped
writing of the ancient Babylonians somewhat parallels that of the
Egyptian hieroglyphics. At first the writing was in the form of drawings on stone, and the pictures portrayed objects. Picture writing of
this sort seems to have made its appearance in Egypt and Babylonia
at about the same time. From Babylonia it spread to adjacent peoples.

It is natural to use whatever writing material is at hand and can
be had cheaply and in quantity. In western Asia this was not the
papyrus reed, but clay, which was abundant in the valley of the
Tigris and Euphrates rivers.

As in Egypt, the type of writing was adapted to the medium. It is
not easy to draw small picture symbols on wet clay, nor does this
method lend itself to speed, but it is fairly simple and quick to im-
press a mark upon the moist surface with a pointed instrument. As a
result, the Babylonians began to use a reed stylus, with which they
could readily inscribe their clay tablets. When the point of the writing

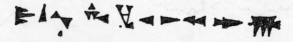

Examples of cuneiform writing

implement touched the wet clay surface, it made a wider depression than it did when it was lifted from it. This formed the wedge-shaped or triangular type of writing.

These small wedge-shaped marks could be used, in the earliest cuneiform writing, to form pictures of the objects later symbolized in the picture-writing **(pictograph)** stage. Then, as in the case of hieroglyphics, the cuneiform characters began to designate the ideas suggested by the objects—for example, the pictograph for "house" could also be applied as an ideograph to refer to "family"; or an eye could mean "see" or "look." The next advance was to characters having a phonetic value to represent the sounds derived from the character, or a certain part of it, as it was read aloud. This process of change came about partly because a simpler and more set kind of character was preferable to the time-consuming and less expressive picture drawing. Phonetic writing based on various combinations and styles of wedges offered more diversity and ease.

SIR HENRY RAWLINSON

Only a few years after the decipherment of Egyptian hieroglyphics by Champollion, Henry Creswicke Rawlinson, aged seventeen, began his army career by going to India. Born in England in 1810, he lived to be eighty-five and devoted his entire life to matters concerned with western Asia. As an officer in the British Army and a political representative of the British Government, and also as a student of western Asia, he received wide acclaim. During his career —especially as an agent, and later director, of the East India Company—his chief contributions were to Persian and Indian studies. He studied and wrote on the history of Babylonia and Assyria and on the written languages of the ancient peoples in the Tigris and Euphrates valleys. He was given recognition for his many accomplishments when he was knighted.

As with hieroglyphics, cuneiform writing had gone through various phases from picture writing through ideographs to syllabic and alphabetic representations. There were many cuneiform inscriptions found, as there had been hieroglyphics, but until the early nineteenth century these too remained a mystery. As a young British officer in Persia, Henry Rawlinson was fired with an interest in an-

cient cuneiform writing and with a determination to decipher it.
While he was stationed in the vicinity of Baghdad he pursued his
avocation and carried it through to a successful completion.

THE BEHISTUN ROCK

In western Asia at the time of Darius I, King of the Persians from
521–485 B.C., travel was largely on foot, or, for longer distances, on
horseback. If goods had to be transported, they were carried by caravan. The land was covered by a network of major roads or caravan
routes, with minor roads branching off at all points, and by a series
of watering and stopping places. One of the more important routes
was the one running between the great commercial cities of Babylon
and Ecbatana. It had been built two hundred years earlier by the
Medes as their capital. Travelers on this caravan route often stopped
at the excellent resting place near where the village of Behistun in
Iran is now located. Here, at the base of a lofty mountain rising almost four thousand feet into the sky, they could refresh themselves
and their animals with spring waters.

When Cambyses II was absent from Persia in 522 B.C., a period
of rebellion began under the leadership of Gaumata, who set himself
up as heir to the throne on Cambyses' death. After hard fighting the
revolt was suppressed by Darius I, who then attained the throne. To
record this event and to fortify his position, Darius I selected a spot
on the mountain beside the caravan stop. Here, at a point high
enough out of reach to prevent defacing but clearly visible to all, he
caused a great relief to be sculptured in the rock face. The carvings
in life-sized figures showed Darius with two attendants behind him
and the defeated rebel Gaumata lying beneath his feet. Nine other
rebel leaders stand roped together in front of Darius, and the Persian
god of good and light, Ahura Mazda, is symbolized above.

This great sculptured panel—400 feet above the caravans—proclaimed the rightful sovereignty of King Darius and attracted the
attention of all who stopped at the springs below. For those who
could read, the story was also told in writing. Below the relief sculptures there was a text in Old Persian cuneiform writing, giving a history of the revolt and the power of Persia. Since everyone who
stopped to rest and look was not a native Persian, but might speak or

read other languages, Darius had his scribes repeat the inscription in Babylonian—the language of the ancient Sumerians, Assyrians, and Babylonians—and in Susian—the language of the Elamites and those who lived to the south and east in the area of Susa which was made the capital of Persia by Cyrus, the father of Cambyses. All three messages were written in cuneiform characters and stood in columns almost four yards high. The columns, however, varied somewhat in size because the languages ranged from the alphabetic cuneiform of the Persians to the Babylonian cuneiform, composed of several hundred phonetic or syllabic characters. The area on the rocky cliff covered by the three inscriptions and the relief panel was about twenty-five feet high, and twice as wide over-all.

The Behistun Rock and Henry Rawlinson did for cuneiform what the Rosetta Stone and Jean François Champollion did for hieroglyphics. In both cases, reading knowledge of the languages—the

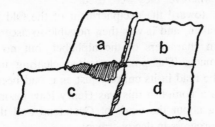

The Behistun Rock: a–Babylonian inscription. b–Sculpture. c–Susian inscription. d–Old Persian inscription

ancient Persian, Assyrian, and Babylonian cuneiform writing, and the old Egyptian hieroglyphic writing—had long since passed into oblivion and there was very little to go on when it came to deciphering them. It was helpful that the inscriptions—those on the Behistun Rock and the Rosetta Stone—that were to make decipherment possible were both in more than one language and were quite lengthy. In addition, each of the stones had been worked on by other scholars, who had laid some of the groundwork that made the ultimate solution somewhat less difficult. Both men, however, deserve full credit for their achievements. They were able to finish their work in a thorough manner because of their unique skills with languages, and not simply because of what had been accomplished before they began to seek the keys to these long-lost tongues.

Grotefend   A German, Georg Friedrich Grotefend, had tackled the top inscription directly below the sculptured relief on the Behistun Rock. This section was written in Old Persian and it was discovered that a single diagonal wedge mark formed a separation and acted as a divider between words. Working on this basis, it became evident that one of the words was repeated in almost identical cuneiform characters throughout the inscription. The positions of these characters led to the correct assumption that they were all the word for "king." This was checked against other Persian inscriptions and furnished a phonetic pronunciation of some of the single cuneiform characters that appeared in the names of King Xerxes and King Darius. These then supplied the alphabetical sound value of the same characters wherever they were used.

The first steps toward the decipherment of the Old Persian cuneiform had been taken, and it was then possible to ascertain a number of the cuneiform characters of the alphabet, but no further headway could be made. The puzzle awaited clearing up so that the language could be read in its entirety just as it had been written. The man who was to accomplish this was Henry Rawlinson, even though he knew nothing about the work of Grotefend and the others who had made some progress in decipherment.

Rawlinson   Henry Rawlinson undertook what was a physical task as well as a scholarly one. At great risk and with determined thoroughness, he not only climbed up the precipitous cliff to the inscribed rock face, but spent hours suspended there, carefully copying off the old cuneiform characters. Then he was ready to approach decipherment by using what knowledge of cuneiform he had already attained.

Rawlinson had previously compared, and found similarities in, two inscriptions in Old Persian that had been found elsewhere. By an intuitive, logical guess, he had arrived at the same conclusion Grotefend had. Although both inscriptions began with the kings and their names, this was only the entrance to a blind alley that remained dark and led no farther.

The Behistun Rock, however, gave him a wider scope for his

genius and further opportunity for comparison. By following a dialectic method of approach and standing firm in his belief that the cuneiform characters of the ancient Persian inscription were phonetic and alphabetical, he unsnarled the interwoven threads of sound. The sounds of the modern Persian dialects showed, by this system of comparative linguistics, that they were related. Eventually the alphabet of the ancient Persian stood forth and it was possible to transcribe and translate the old cuneiform characters.

Henry Rawlinson went through the same procedure twice again. The Babylonian inscription beside the sculptured panel yielded, as did the Susian below it. The relief section and the three inscriptions now told their messages—or single message, for they proved to tell the same story. The story itself had always been known, for the sculptured relief had been Darius' way of informing the illiterate both of his own times in the fifth century B.C. and of all future years —until Rawlinson's accomplishment presented it to the world in 1846.

Grotefend, Rawlinson, and other scholars—some working independently as did Rawlinson, some working with their colleagues—all deserve acclaim for their parts in the decipherment of cuneiform. Important as the translation of the inscriptions on the Behistun Rock was, it was only the key. When the key was turned, the lock opened up a whole storehouse of cuneiform writing and this was of the greatest value. The ancient peoples of western Asia—the vast region of Persia, Babylonia, and Assyria—could now speak for themselves through their own contemporary writings.

UR

Sumer and Ur   In ancient times the Tigris and Euphrates rivers did not join to form one mouth before they emptied into the Persian Gulf as they do now, but each ran its separate course from source to mouth. Between the two rivers lay extremely fertile land, which would easily support those who settled there to farm and raise their sheep. It was natural, therefore, that one of the oldest of all cities, Ur, was located in this desirable region and came into existence almost five thousand years ago. The land was known as Sumer and the people were called Sumerians. The great city of Ur rose up on the banks of the Euphrates River. It was built of sun-dried bricks, made from the clay found in abundance there. With these bricks the Sumerians built a city in keeping with their high state of civilization, which thrived for two thousand years or more. Ur saw the birth of Abraham and his departure for Canaan, well over three thousand years ago, and it continued to exist at least until the time of Alexander the Great, the fourth century B.C.

Excavation   Ur appears in history approximately five hundred years before the time of Abraham, according to evidence disclosed by excavations at the site. The earliest archaeological work at Ur was conducted in 1854 by a British official, J. E. Taylor, and excavations have continued into the twentieth century. Under the direction of the late Sir Charles Leonard Woolley, exhaustive excavations have brought forth enough remains and artifacts to provide ample witness to the scope of civilization and culture of the great age of Ur.

As with most sites inhabited for centuries, it is apparent that many of the larger buildings went through several phases of rebuilding, enlarging, and restoration. The smaller buildings were even more prone to destruction by the elements, and once a structure was abandoned the mud bricks disappeared from sight with relative speed, leaving little but the outer walls. It is, therefore, mainly from the temples and graves that archaeologists have gained most of their knowledge of ancient Ur. But enough remains of the houses to show that Ur inhabitants had fine, comfortable homes. The typical larger houses had open courtyards, with a number of rooms, each for its own separate purpose—cooking, sleeping, worship—so that there was a feeling of spaciousness.

Temple of Sin   One of Ur's best-preserved temples was built around 2000 B.C. to Sin or Nannar, the moon god. The whole sanctuary covered an extensive area, which was surrounded by a thick wall. Inside the walled enclosure were a number of buildings for secular or business activities. These, with the sacred edifices, formed a city precinct within the city. A great temple tower, or **ziggurat,** rose into the air to support the shrine of the moon god. A ziggurat, meaning "peak," was a Sumerian pyramid. It was constructed of brick, the native building material, on a square or rectangular base and ascended by terraces to a flat summit, where the shrine was encased. Each story or stage was smaller in circumference than the one below and steps that wound around the outside gave access to the top. The last king to restore and build in this temple enclosure was Nebuchadnezzar, at the beginning of the sixth century B.C.

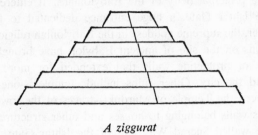

A ziggurat

Crafts The people of Ur buried their dead in graves or tombs and deposited both necessities and luxuries in them. The finds that excavations of these burial places have turned up make it possible to ascertain from the quality of workmanship and types of artifacts that Ur reached a high point of culture and maintained this advanced civilization over many centuries. Carvings, statuettes, and mosaics tell of their fine arts. Beautifully and delicately wrought jewelry shows that the Sumerians used precious and semiprecious stones— chiefly lapis lazuli and carnelian—as well as gold, silver, and copper.

BABYLON

Babylon, the magnificent capital of the ancient Babylonian Empire, was located on the Euphrates River and commanded a position of importance in trade. The history of Babylon, as far as we know it from archaeology and other sources, began in about the second millennium B.C., and her kings built a mighty city of brick through the centuries. Babylon reached its height of fame and grandeur under King Nebuchadnezzar, who ruled from 605–562 B.C. Nebuchadnezzar undertook the reconstruction of Babylon to make it a city worthy of the powerful Babylonian Empire. A new royal palace was erected, a larger city wall was built, and temples were reconstructed.

Processional Road and Ishtar Gate The Sacred or Processional Road was a brick-walled way. The walls were decorated in relief, with sculptured animal figures and ornamentations. These were of glazed brick, colored to suit the subjects they depicted, and enough of the walls with their sculptures still remains to tell of their former magnificence. The Processional Road was sacred to Marduk, the sun god, the principal deity of the Babylonians. It entered the city through the Ishtar Gate, a huge entrance dedicated to Ishtar, the Great Mother, the supreme goddess in the Babylonian religion.

Excavations on the site of ancient Babylon have brought to light the remains of protecting walls that extended for more than two miles around the city. Other ruins include temples—one of which may have been the Temple of Marduk—traces of the lower courses of numerous walls belonging to houses and other structures, and the ruins of the walled Sacred Way and of the Ishtar Gate. Otherwise nothing remains of the once-famous city that fell before the onslaught of other conquering empires, except for references to it and accounts of it found in the writings of ancient authors.

THE DEAD SEA SCROLLS

A Bedouin went into a cave near the northwest edge of the Dead Sea in 1947 and became the first man to discover the scrolls that had been hidden there for almost two thousand years. He became the first in a long succession of Bedouins, trained archaeologists, and others who brought forth numerous scrolls and fragments from several caves in that area. These Dead Sea Scrolls contain biblical and other religious material. As the writings of ancient authors have often given the archaeologist a light on the classical past, the Dead Sea Scrolls have made available valuable manuscripts written at the beginning of the Christian Era. Opened, pieced together, and read by archaeologists and other specialists, they have added greatly to our comparative and historical interpretation of the writings contained in them.

Khirbet Qumrān The men who produced these manuscripts—some of them original writings related to their own religious sect, but most of them copies of holy scripture—lived in a monastery at Khirbet Qumrān, about a mile from the Dead Sea and not far from the caves where the scrolls have been found. Several ancient writers, among them Philo of Alexandria and Pliny the Elder, describe a philosophical sect of Jews called Essenes, who lived in a community close to

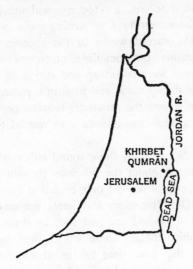

KHIRBET
QUMRĀN

JERUSALEM

JORDAN R.

DEAD SEA

Site of the Dead Sea Scrolls

the Dead Sea. There they studied ethics and the Bible; they taught a love of God, of virtue, and of man; and they preached a gospel of peace and freedom.

Excavation on a large scale under G. Lankaster Harding and Père Roland de Vaux was undertaken in 1951 and the monastery of the Essene community was unearthed. By piecing together all that the excavations reveal and supplementing this evidence from the writings of their contemporaries, archaeologists can get a good picture of the people who lived at the Khirbet Qumrān monastery.

The Essenes The Essene sect, with the Pharisees and Sadducees, probably originated during the second century B.C. and gained strength during a period of more than two hundred years, in which its members followed a communal way of life in their monasteries under natural and holy law. Worship, work, ritual bathing for purification, discipline, simplicity, and abstinence formed the daily routine of the Essene monks. They were also sworn to preserve the Essene scriptures. The excavated monastery at Khirbet Qumrān shows us a central building, covering an area of over one thousand square yards, built high on the cliffs overlooking the Dead Sea. Beyond the sea lay a flat plain, which the monks probably farmed.

Their living quarters centered around four courtyards, from which opened storerooms, kitchens, a refectory, and other rooms. In the central part was the scriptorium, or writing room, where the scribes carefully copied the sacred works of the Essenes on long scrolls made usually of leather, but sometimes of copper. When the scrolls were completed, they were rolled up and stored in tall earthenware jars, which were probably made and fired in a pottery workshop not far from the room where the manuscripts were copied. The scrolls were then readily available to anyone who wanted to read or study them.

From the Dead Sea Scrolls, those found either whole or in fragments, we learn much about the religious thought of the Essenes. The monks in the scriptorium not only copied in Hebrew or Aramaic the books of the Old Testament and wrote commentaries on them but also copied other sacred material such as Psalms and rules for their own community living. These works shed light on the Old Testament and at the same time tell us about the principles and lives of the Essene monks who lived and worshiped together, following their Teacher of Righteousness.

The Scrolls   Among the scrolls found to date are the *Book of Isaiah,* in Hebrew, complete on one scroll and in part on another; comments on the *Book of Habakkuk;* a version of the *Book of Genesis* in Aramaic; *Psalms of Thanksgiving,* which resemble those in the Bible; a story of war between right and wrong or good and evil, called *The War of the Children of Light Against the Children of Darkness;* and *A Manual of Discipline,* describing and explaining the rules of the Essene order and the punishments for breaking these rules.

Dating Evidence   When a time of danger threatened Khirbet Qumrān, the monks placed the manuscripts not already in clay jars for storage into other jars, sealed them, and then hid them in the nearby caves. The final disaster came with a destructive fire, which probably coincided with Jerusalem's capture by the Romans in A.D. 70. Evidence for this date, or one not more than a few years earlier, comes chiefly from carbon-14 testing, the dating of Roman coins unearthed at the site, palaeographers' dating of the script or handwriting in the scrolls themselves, and the dates revealed by fragments of pottery found during excavations at the monastery. Similar evidence places the date of the scrolls in the first century B.C.

Reading the Scrolls   Since the first scrolls were brought from their cave hiding places into the light of modern scholarship, a steady stream of scrolls and fragments has come forth, as a direct result of archaeologists' searchings or more deviously from the hands of Bedouins, who are ever eager to exchange ancient fragments for modern coins. This is how many untouched—or almost untouched—scrolls and innumerable fragments from scores of scrolls have found their way from the caves to scholars in places as widely separated as Israel, the United States, and England.

By concerted patient effort the mystery of the Dead Sea Scrolls is being unraveled. Much has been solved by the excavation of the monastery at Khirbet Qumrān and by the work done on the scrolls so far. Much remains to be done in the way of interpretation and study. The most difficult part, however, has been accomplished. This was the gigantic task of piecing together the countless fragments so that they could be read by specialists in ancient Hebrew languages. This was accomplished by groups of scholars from various countries working together in Jerusalem.

The seven leather scrolls presented almost no problem, as they had been wrapped in linen before they were placed in the jars by the Essenes and could be unrolled by painstaking modern hands. The two copper scrolls posed a puzzle that at first appeared insurmountable, because, while the jars had preserved the leather scrolls and time had broken into fragments those not in jars, corrosion had sealed the metal, apparently in a solid mass not to be unrolled. In England, Professor H. Wright Baker of the University of Manchester, working with great care and skill, was finally able to cut the copper roll into fine strips with a precision saw and then piece them together again for photographing and study.

Much interpretation of the Dead Sea Scrolls remains to be done in the light of former knowledge and biblical study. There also remains the possibility and hope of discovering additional scrolls in the Dead Sea area or in other parts of ancient Judaea.

HEINRICH SCHLIEMANN

Although Heinrich Schliemann followed Winckelmann by a century, archaeology was still in the early stages of its development as a science during his time. Thus he, too, helped to give it momentum by the greatness and number of his accomplishments and by his colorful life, both of which caught the attention of Europeans and Americans alike. His belief as a boy that Homer's *Iliad* was based on factual knowledge, his ambition to accumulate wealth enough to follow the rainbow of buried cities whose names were almost forgotten, and the realization of his dreams of Trojan and Mycenaean treasures have become legendary in archaeological biography.

Schliemann's Early Life Born in Germany in 1822, Schliemann shared with Winckelmann the background of birth into a poor family and an early and enduring interest in the peoples of ancient times. As a boy, he was stirred by the myths and tales his minister-teacher father told him. At an early age he decided that Homer's Troy was not a legendary place but a real one, which he himself would one day find and reveal to the world. Unlike Winckelmann, however, he received little formal education, and his schooling ended when he was apprenticed to a grocer at the age of fourteen. This apprenticeship, amazingly enough, provided the first in a series of events that were to lead him finally to the goal toward which all his efforts were directed. A young man who frequented the shop, usually in a drunken state, recited line after line of Homer's *Iliad* to the spellbound Heinrich Schliemann. This served to fortify Schliemann's hopes and plans for seeing Homer's Troy one day with his own eyes.

As a very young man, he began to teach himself Spanish, and while working for a merchant in Holland he studied not only Dutch but also French, Italian, English, Portuguese, and Russian to supply himself with useful linguistic tools. Schliemann was only twenty-four when he was sent to Russia on business by his employer, and it was not long before he started on the road to the riches necessary for his Trojan venture.

Schliemann's Later Life In 1869, after an unsuccessful marriage in Russia was terminated by divorce, Schliemann married a young Greek girl who shared all his enthusiasm about ancient Troy. They set out together in the following year for the Troad, as the region of Troy is called, and for twenty years shared archaeological activities and interests.

Heinrich Schliemann was a trail blazer in the field of archaeology because he believed in the writings of classical Greek authors as guideposts and found them to be full of reliable information rather than pure fantasy, as his fellow archaeologists thought.

In 1890 Schliemann died in Naples, and did not live to learn that the Troy of Homer's *Iliad* was the seventh city from the bottom and not the second or third, as he believed. But he had found its exact location and had excavated nine cities in all on the site, whereas others had thought that, if there had really been a Troy, it was at a spot a number of miles away. He relied heavily on practical evidence, such as findings of pottery that could be used in dating the various strata at which they were found, and thus introduced to archaeology a systematic means of dating.

In his eager haste he destroyed much material that was irreplaceable, but he found a far greater number of items of archaeological value than any one man before him. He made the mistakes that were common in archaeology's childhood, as well as other errors, but he forged ahead independently to bring forth new methods that were to lead archaeology into its adulthood. He had had little formal education, but he changed the entire focus of historical studies by correlating the tangible facts discovered by archaeologists with other types of historical research.

Perhaps Schliemann's most important contribution to archaeology was his world-wide fame. He was received and honored by leaders in the many countries he visited, and the romance of his life brought archaeology's accomplishments and possibilities from the limited realm of scholars to the broader realm of the interested layman.

TROY

The Greeks fought for ten years at Troy to conquer Priam, whose son Paris had held Helen, wife of King Menelaus of Sparta, captive. Ancient Troy was kept alive after the Greeks sacked and burned it by the poetry of Homer and by the writings of other authors who followed him, including the geographer Strabo. In its physical aspect the city lay buried and forgotten, following its destruction at some point of time—now estimated to be about 1240 B.C. but more likely even earlier, possibly around 1480 B.C.

The Troad Until the latter part of the nineteenth century and the appearance of Heinrich Schliemann, it was assumed that the scene of the Trojan War was as much a product of Homer's imagination as were the gods and goddesses who in the *Iliad* and the *Odyssey* played parts no less prominent than those of the Trojan and Greek warriors. The region of Troy known as the Troad was located in the northwestern corner of Asia Minor close to the Hellespont, but after three thousand or more years had passed, its location was lost in the land now known as Turkey and lay buried under a settlement known as Hissarlik. Those few who wondered about the city of Priam believed it to be in the vicinity of the Turkish town of Bounarbashi, some miles to the south.

Excavations in the Troad   One day in the spring of 1870 Heinrich Schliemann, with his Greek bride, copies of Homer, and great faith, arrived in Asia Minor to pursue his boyhood ambition to bring ancient Troy back into the light of history. By the time Schliemann finished his excavations, he had realized his dreams and had contributed greatly to the new scientific methods of archaeology. He had unearthed a total of nine cities—one above the other—and had discovered a wealth of precious things in the ruins. His choice of the wrong city as Homer's Troy is but a small error when considered against the entire background of Schliemann's achievements.

Since the site of ancient Troy was believed to be near Bounarbashi, Schliemann went there first. When trial excavations there produced no evidence to support this theory, he quickly abandoned these efforts and turned back to Homer's descriptions of Troy and its surroundings. This took him to the Turkish settlement at Hissarlik where there was a mound about one hundred feet in height, covering an area approximating that around which the Greek warrior Achilles could have dragged the body of Hector, son of Priam, without undue difficulty. This hill, moreover, was situated about three miles from the sea, making it within the realm of possibility for the Greeks to go back and forth to their ships with ease. Early digging at the Hissarlik mound unearthed evidence of an ancient site below the surface. With this encouragement, Schliemann went on to unearth the remains of the nine cities that had been built almost in layers, each using the ruined foundations of its predecessor.

The Nine Cities   The ninth, or uppermost, city had thrived for well over six hundred years until it was overshadowed by its rival, Con-

1. The modern settlement of Kafr es-Sammân encroaches upon the ancient necropolis in the desert outside Gizeh where there were three "Great" Pyramids, eight smaller pyramids, and innumerable mastabas. *Trans World Airlines, Photo.*

2. The Sphinx, with a portrait of Khafra, was partly based on rock outcroppings and built partly of limestone blocks. The "Great" Pyramid of Khufu is directly behind. *Trans World Airlines, Photo.*

3. The hill of modern Hissarlik, Turkey, on which "legendary" Troy stood was continuously occupied from the Bronze Age through Roman times. Troy VII is probably the level of Homer's *Iliad*. *Turkish Government Tourism and Information Office.*

4. Most ancient fortified cities took advantage of high ground for easier surveillance of the approaches. Marlowe's references to the "topless towers of Ilium" described Troy's hilltop location. *Turkish Government Tourism and Information Office.*

5. Minoan palace at Cnossus associated with the legend of King Minos and the Minotaur, Crete. *Greek National Tourist Office.*

6. Delphi, regarded as the center of the earth by the ancient Greeks, is located on the slopes of Mount Olympus, believed to be the dwelling place of the ancient gods. *Greek National Tourist Office.*

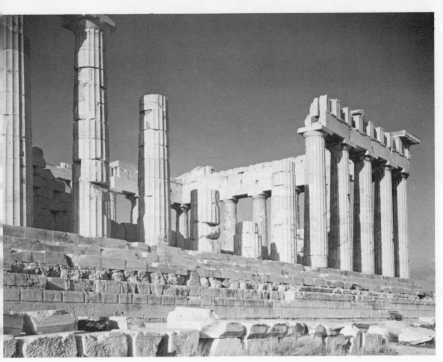

7. The Parthenon, the temple built in the Age of Pericles in honor of Athena on the Acropolis, Athens. *Trans World Airlines, Photo.*

8. The theater in Delphi, along the Sacred Way, seated about 5,000 spectators. *Greek National Tourist Office.*

9. View of the Theseum seen from the Agora or central marketplace of ancient Athens. *Greek National Tourist Office.*

10. View of the ancient Roman forum and the Palatine Hill. *Trans World Airlines, Photo.*

11. The theater in Pompeii which was destroyed by the eruption of Mount Vesuvius in A.D. 79. *Trans World Airlines, Photo.*

12. The best-preserved Roman aqueducts are in the old Roman provinces in France (Gaul) and the one shown here in Segovia, Spain. *Trans World Airlines, Photo.*

13. When Emperor Hadrian visited Britain around A.D. 120, an earthen wall, later of stone, was built in Northumberland to hold back the northern tribes. *British Overseas Airways Corporation, Photo.*

14. The famous hot mineral springs from which the City of Bath takes its name first attracted the ancient Romans who built thermae and temples there. They are now the finest Roman ruins in Britain. *British Overseas Airways Corporation, Photo.*

stantinople, across the Hellespont. Below that was a city which had endured for a similar period of time, but appeared to have been relatively unimportant. Next came a city with great fortress walls and evidences of destruction by extensive fire. An earthquake brought an end to the sixth city (the fourth from the top) which had many pretentious homes and palaces with artifacts of an advanced civilization. The three settlements below this belonged to people of some time before the second millennium B.C. and were not extensive, nor were the artifacts of these cultures especially noteworthy.

The second city from the bottom, with its massive walls, palace, countless artifacts and valuables, and evidences of destruction by fire, led Schliemann to the conclusion that his city, rising upon the ruins of the earliest settlement, was the Troy acclaimed by Homer. He felt that this deduction was corroborated when he discovered a hoard of treasures hidden in the walls. Here were articles of jewelry and adornment, cups and bowls—gold, silver, ivory, and jewels—of untold beauty and price, almost without number.

Dörpfeld and Blegen Following Schliemann's death, his work at Troy was carried on by Dr. Wilhelm Dörpfeld, who had been helping him in his excavations and studies for almost a decade. In the twentieth century more conclusive research has been carried on by Dr. Carl W. Blegen and his staff. As a result of these efforts, it is now accepted that there were settlements at Troy, with only brief intervals between each, from about 3000 B.C. until well into the Christian Era, and that it was the seventh Troy from the bottom and not the second, as Schliemann had thought, of which Homer sang.

Schliemann's Contribution Although a slight error in judgment— tinged no doubt by the gleam of gold—served to guide Schliemann to the wrong decision as to which of the nine entanglements of wall strata belonged to Homer's Troy, the conclusions of archaeologists on this subject could not have been established without Schliemann's work. It was his belief in the validity of Homer's narrative that led to unearthing the nine Troys, spanning more than three thousand years.

More than that, Schliemann laid the foundations for study and classification of pottery types in relation to other objects found at the same level of excavation. In this way he established a criterion for accurate, scientific conclusions in all aspects of archaeology, especially chronology. Later research brought about only a reassessment of Schliemann's great work, with some corrections in his dating and assigning of the stonework maze to its proper levels.

CHAPTER SEVEN

Early Greece

IMPORTANT DATES IN GREEK HISTORY

c. 2500 B.C.	Settlements in Greece
c. 1500–1200 B.C.	Mycenaean Age
c. 1240 B.C.	Trojan War
c. 1200–800 B.C.	Age of Kings
c. 1100 B.C.	Dorian Invasions
c. 1000 B.C.	Beginning of Iron Age
c. 800 B.C.	Homer
c. 800–650 B.C.	Age of Nobles
c. 776 B.C.	First Olympic Games
c. 650–500 B.C.	Age of Tyrants; Pisistratus
c. 624 B.C.	Draco's Code of Laws
594 B.C.	Reforms of Solon
492–479 B.C.	Persian Wars
490 B.C.	Persians defeated in Battle of Marathon
480 B.C.	Greeks defeated in Battle of Thermopylae; final defeat of Persians in Battle of Salamis
461–404 B.C.	Supremacy of Athens; Athenian Empire; Pericles
459–404 B.C.	Peloponnesian Wars
404–371 B.C.	Supremacy of Sparta
371–362 B.C.	Supremacy of Thebes
338 B.C.	Greece conquered by Philip of Macedonia
336–323 B.C.	Rule of Alexander the Great
146 B.C.	Greece conquered by Romans

Map of Early Greek World

SIR ARTHUR EVANS

Arthur John Evans was born in Hertfordshire, England, in 1851, with all the advantages of birth and background that would make the path to future success a smooth one. He was the first son of Sir John Evans, an eminent archaeologist and the author of several books on the ancient Britons.

After a traditional English education at Harrow and Oxford, Evans studied at Göttingen University, making frequent trips to the Balkans, Finland, and Lapland to pursue his interest in history and folk customs. In 1875 Evans returned to the Balkans for a longer period to study archaeology. His visit, which lasted about seven years, terminated with his imprisonment on charges of involvement in an insurrection in Dalmatia. In 1884, not long after his return to England, he was made keeper of the Ashmolean Museum at Oxford.

Evans' interest in ancient writing, especially hieroglyphics, led him to Cnossus on Crete, where he carried out extensive excavations. In 1911 he was knighted in honor of his outstanding contributions to the field of archaeology. Sir Arthur Evans spent most of his remaining life studying the highly developed civilization he uncovered in Crete and writing authoritative accounts of his discoveries, dealing especially with the script, religion, and culture of the Minoan civilization. In 1922 he published the first of a series of four highly detailed volumes called *Palace of Minos*. Sir Arthur Evans died in England in 1941 a few days after his ninetieth birthday.

CNOSSUS

Mythological Background One of the most familiar classical myths is the story of Theseus and Ariadne. According to the tale, Ariadne was the daughter of Minos, a king of Crete in the legendary times of prehistory. Minos was said to have built an extensive labyrinth in which a monster, half bull and half man, called the **Minotaur** (from Minos and *tauros,* "bull") lived. Because his son had met death while visiting in Athens, Minos demanded from that city a yearly tribute of seven boys and seven girls to be consumed by the Minotaur. To end this sacrifice, Theseus, son of the Athenian king, went to Crete. There he killed the Minotaur and escaped from the labyrinth with the help of Ariadne, who traced the way out for him by a thread she laid down. In this way Theseus and Ariadne, now lovers, both escaped successfully.

The City For some years the presence of ancient ruins at a place near Heraklion (the modern Candia) in Crete had been known, and Evans was able to acquire the property in the last decade of the nineteenth century. He started excavations there in 1900, and soon uncovered the palace at Cnossus. For the next eight years he spent considerable time and money excavating the site.

We know now that the site of Cnossus was inhabited as far back as the Neolithic Age and that from about 2500 B.C. it had been the home of a highly civilized culture which made its influence felt throughout the eastern Mediterranean during the thousand or more years of its existence. Constant trade and commerce with Egypt and the Near East had brought Crete into contact with the high civilizations existing in those areas and gave the island's inhabitants a great deal of wealth with which to pursue their luxurious way of living. The people who reached this lofty development seem to have been more closely related to the Near East than to any other culture and may have come originally from Asia Minor.

The Palace The palace unearthed by Sir Arthur Evans was erected in its earliest form about 2000 B.C. and underwent a number of building periods. Additions and enlargements were made from time to time, and around 1700 B.C. an earthquake necessitated the rebuilding of a large portion. The palace was destroyed some three hundred years later by fire—probably during the course of invasion —and was suddenly abandoned not long after that, perhaps because of an overwhelming catastrophe such as famine, earthquake, or plague.

In the course of its existence, architectural changes had created a structure covering between five and six acres of ground and rising several stories into the air. Due to its massive size and the confusion resulting from its final destruction and collapse, the plan and various parts of the palace could be brought forth only by the most careful excavation work and note taking. After accomplishing all this, Evans set forth his discoveries for all to see by reconstructing the palace on the scientific basis of the great mass of evidence at hand.

Since the palace at Cnossus had been built in different stages, there was no established architectural plan, although later building phases had been adapted to fit it with the earlier. Throughout its existence, however, the chief aim was to make the palace not only a livable home for the royal family and those connected with the household but also an organized administration center for the many affairs of the empire. To conduct the life of the court in an efficient way it was necessary to have a large number of people, from the highest officials to the lowliest servants, housed under the palace roof. They may have totaled more than a thousand persons. In addition a city of some size, possibly seventy-five thousand or more, was around the palace proper.

The visitor to the site of Cnossus is struck almost immediately with several impressions. First he is amazed at the vast extent and massiveness of the palace buildings. A closer examination shows that there are countless rooms of all sizes—many of them connecting—and numerous terraces and passageways, as well as a large number of corridors. This method of construction resulted in a true labyrinth of masonry in which it is difficult to find one's way.

A second feature is the use of courtyards, the central and largest measuring about 180 by 90 feet. These courtyards served both to unify the various rooms opening off them and joined together by corridors and to separate the great bulk of the structure into smaller parts. Thus the central courtyard was the focal point of the entire palace, but also divided the buildings into the court and administrative chambers to the west, and the living quarters of the royal household to the east.

A third feature is the use of several stories and levels—sometimes two and even four, or possibly more. These were connected by stairways, usually broken gracefully by landings. The stairways furnished access to the different levels and sections of the palace and at the same time supplied them with a feeling of spaciousness and with ample light and air through the colonnaded flights of steps. Additional wall shafts admitted light and kept out the summer's heat and winter's cold.

Western Section of the Palace   Most of the western section of the palace, which opened off the extensive West Court, was devoted to the working and administrative chambers. On the lower floor was a long corridor. From one side of this gallery a series of approximately twenty narrow rooms opened. In these were many storage vats and jars, some set below the pavement, others standing in rows. Those sunk below the stone flooring show, from remains of their lead linings and the gold and inlaid work found inside a number of them, that this was a storage place for treasures. Traces of grain, wine, and oil found in the jars give evidence that they held these basic commodities of trade and taxes. Many of the jars stand as tall as a man, or even taller, and are provided with a number of handles at various heights, so that several men could take hold of the vessels and tip them in order to empty their contents as the level of whatever was stored in them became lower.

Throne Room   From the central courtyard there opens an anteroom with stone benches on two walls and a reproduction of a wooden throne that apparently stood there. The actual Throne Room opens off this anteroom and contains the throne itself. It was a high-backed chair made of gypsum, with a fresco painting behind it and a stone

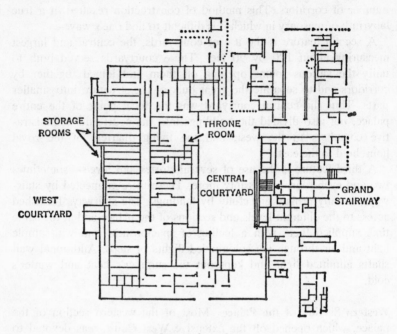

Plan of the palace

bench on the wall opposite. Steps lead to a small area that was probably used for purification purposes in connection with the person who was seated upon the throne. This was the king or a priest, or possibly a priest-king embodying the powers of both.

Eastern Section of the Palace The domestic apartments and quarters were approached by a broad stone stairway with several flights and landings flanked and supported by wooden columns, as is typical of all the palace stairways. The wooden columns were shaped like an inverted tree trunk—narrow at the bottom and widening toward the top. The entire column was simple, with a characteristic large rounded capital, and rested on a stone base.

The Grand Staircase formed a dignified and impressive means of ascent to, and descent from, the royal apartments. The king's apartment is the larger, but the queen's—with its stone benches, light wells, dressing room, bathroom with its terra-cotta tub, and a gay fresco of dolphins and marine life in the main hall or **megaron**—

makes fewer demands on the modern visitor's imagination, because it is so well preserved.

The Double Ax As one approaches the palace from the south, a great double ax becomes visible. The double ax is another distinctive feature of the palace at Cnossus and took several forms. The

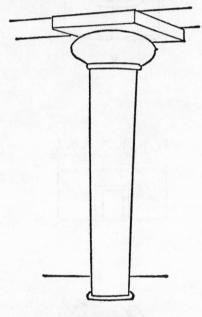

Minoan column

double ax itself was often cut out of stone and used as an architectural entity. It was sometimes set upon a stand beside an altar and used in conjunction with religious ceremonies. Several were used in a series to form a decorative edging, as above the **architrave** over a doorway. At other times the double ax was cut into stone to serve as a type of mason's mark. In this case it took a stylized form so that it might be incised more easily.

Cuttings of this type are found in the storerooms of the west section, in the king's megaron—usually referred to as the Hall of the Double Axes—and on stone blocks and pillars elsewhere in the palace.

The Minoan Age Whether King Minos was a real character or merely a legendary figure, or whether there were several kings by

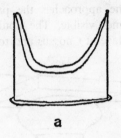

a

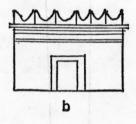

b

c

The double ax

that name, or whether the word Minos itself meant "ruler," like the word pharaoh, it is quite certain that a ruling king lived in the palace at Cnossus and that a dynasty or series of kings occupied it for over a thousand years. Sir Arthur Evans needed some consistent, workable term in order to classify the history and culture of the civilization he brought to light, and decided to use the term "Minoan," from Minos, the king in the myth of Theseus and the Minotaur. Therefore "Minoan Age" refers to the history, and

"Minoan culture" or "Minoan civilization" to the life of the people of Crete of that period. The whole period was subdivided into three parts, called Early Minoan (3500–2100 B.C.), Middle Minoan (2100–1550 B.C.), and Late Minoan (1550–1100 B.C.), usually abbreviated EM, MM, and LM respectively.

Since each period covered a number of centuries, the chronology was broken down into three further classifications and each was given a Roman numeral. Thus there are nine divisions in all: EM I, II, and III; MM I, II, and III; and LM, I, II, and III. This scheme furnished a broad and a more accurate method of describing and classifying the development of Crete's civilization from the end of the Neolithic Age to the decline of Crete and the rise of Greece.

The great work of Sir Arthur Evans and his staff in excavating and partially reconstructing the tremendous expanse of the site at Cnossus, and in studying and interpreting all the evidence brought to light, have given archaeology both the visible remains of the Minoan civilization and the less tangible record of the life and culture of the Minoan Age.

MINOAN WRITING

Minoan Script The people of the Minoan Age in Crete left behind no mass of written records in the form of historical accounts, as did their contemporaries in Egypt and Mesopotamia. During excavations, however, a large quantity of written documents came to light. It is fairly certain that Crete, especially Cnossus, controlled a good part of the shipping between the islands and mainland of the eastern Mediterranean. For this reason it was essential that business records and accounts be kept. In addition government transactions had to be recorded. As with other civilizations, the earliest Minoan writing was a type of picture writing or hieroglyphics, which later, when more speed and ease of writing were demanded, became modified and conventionalized to a much simpler script and a cursive style of writing. This has been given the name **linear script.** The writing material was clay, which made it necessary to adapt the script form for use on clay tablets.

Linear A and Linear B Scripts Linear script falls into two groups. Linear A script made its appearance during the Middle Minoan period, but, although it was widely used throughout the island of Crete, very few examples of it were found at Cnossus. Linear A has not been deciphered, but it is composed of simplified signs or symbols showing the transition from picture writing to the representation of syllables.

In contrast, Linear B script appeared on clay tablets found by the hundreds at Cnossus and also found later at Mycenae and Pylos in the Greek Peloponnesus. The locations in the palace where the tablets were found at Cnossus gave a clue to their context. Large numbers of them were found inside, or near, storage chests in rooms obviously used to store archives or records. This implied that the tablets were used primarily to keep lists and invoices dealing with trade, business, government administration, or the countless housekeeping details of the palace. The link with the Greek mainland documents, which could be dated at about 1200 B.C., pointed to Linear B as an inflected language related to Greek.

MICHAEL VENTRIS

Like others who have successfully deciphered previously unknown scripts and languages, Michael Ventris, an Englishman, showed an interest in foreign languages and ancient systems of writing at an early age. Born in 1922, Ventris became fascinated by hieroglyphics when he was barely of school age.

As Schliemann had before him, Ventris displayed native ability and a quick mind for languages, and he developed proficiency in a number of tongues by attending school in Switzerland and by travel in Europe. He rapidly mastered the various languages he was taught and learned others by himself. He did not, however, aim to make an academic career his life's work, but turned to architecture. Ventris served in the R.A.F. during World War II and finished his architectural studies in 1948. He continued to follow a parallel avocation—the study of Cretan scripts—with the same eagerness and skill that he applied to his profession.

Michael Ventris pursued a steady course, which gradually focused on the script of the ancient inhabitants of Crete, and in the end he unraveled the tangle of Linear B to reveal that the Minoan language was indeed a close relative in the family of Greek languages. Michael Ventris' double careers, architecture and palaeography, were tragically cut short when he was killed in an accident in 1956—his accomplishments great, but just beginning.

Ventris' findings appeared in *Documents in Mycenaean Greek,* a volume written in collaboration with John Chadwick and published shortly after Ventris' sudden death.

WILHELM DÖRPFELD

Wilhelm Dörpfeld was born in Germany in 1853, the son of an educator. Dörpfeld became an architect and soon directed his attentions to archaeology. Because of his training, he brought exactitude and a scientific approach to his work in that field.

Dörpfeld was fortunate enough to take part in the excavations at Troy, Mycenae, and Tiryns with the great trailblazer Heinrich Schliemann. From 1877 to 1881 he worked on the excavations at Olympia in the Peloponnesus. Dörpfeld married the daughter of Friedrich Adler, who was also an architect and one of the men in charge of the excavations undertaken by the Germans.

Dörpfeld's achievements in archaeology, which also included study and research on the Acropolis at Athens, won him deserved acclaim. He was made secretary of the German Archaeological Institute at Athens and held that position for thirty years.

Wilhelm Dörpfeld died in 1940 on Leukas, an island in the Ionian Sea just off the Greek mainland. His life had spanned the century from the budding of the new science of archaeology to its full bloom, to which he himself contributed greatly.

MYCENAE

Location The main road from Athens across the Isthmus of Corinth and down the eastern side of the Peloponnesus to the south runs close to the site of Mycenae. The ancient road probably passed between the hills and across the Argive Plain, following the contour of the land three or four thousand years ago much the same as it does today. Mycenae was situated on an almost triangular ridge of rock that rose more than nine hundred feet above the plain. It was set back some distance from the road and was protected further by a deep ravine, which fell sharply on the far side and rose again to the neighboring mountains towering more than two thousand feet above the city.

History of Mycenae The stories about Mycenae and its founding go far back into legend and tradition. Homer tells us that it was the home of Agamemnon, brother of Helen's husband, Menelaus, and it already enjoyed a prosperous and well-developed civilization by the time of the Trojan War. According to archaeologists' finds, people were living there at least as early as 2500 B.C. Jewelry, pottery, and other objects turned up in the course of excavation as well as the general plan of the palace suggest that Mycenae may have been a colony established by Cretans or that it was in close enough contact with Crete to import many items from that island and to be influenced by its culture. Excavations at the site have also revealed that Mycenae reached its height about the fourteenth century B.C. and was inhabited as late as the second century A.D.

Cyclopean Walls Mycenae was built on an **acropolis**—a high, fortified place. The word acropolis comes from the Greek words *akros,* meaning "high," and *polis,* "city." Unlike Cnossus, however, Mycenae was in constant danger of invasion by land, so the protection afforded by its natural position was further reinforced by **cylopean walls** which formed a stronghold against attackers advancing across the broad plain of Argos. The name "cyclopean" owes its derivation to the fact that the Greeks, who invaded and overthrew the Mycenaeans about 1200 B.C., could not believe that anyone but the giant Cyclopes could have erected walls of such size and proportions. From that, the term is applied to masonry of a massive type built with huge stones fitted together to form a strong wall. The stones in the walls of Mycenae's citadel were hewn to a fairly regular shape, but those of most other cyclopean walls were rough and irregular in

Cyclopean walls

shape. When we consider the length of the walls at Mycenae, approximately 4000 feet, and the weight of the stone blocks, a good many of them weighing several tons, we can understand why they were thought to be Cyclopes' work.

Walls of Mycenae The massive defense walls of Mycenae were not only cyclopean but were strengthened further at the main entrance by a bastion. This made the area of approach narrower and forced attacking soldiers to expose their unprotected right flank to the defenders. Also the soldiers inside the fortification could, because of the outward projection of the bastion, attack from above before an advancing enemy reached the entrance gate.

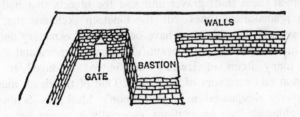

Walls of Mycenae

Lion Gate The main entrance to the acropolis was through the Lion Gate, constructed of four monoliths forming the threshold, jambs, and lintel. The name Lion Gate comes from the stone piece placed above the center of the lintel. A hollow space was created by the

Lion Gate

builders to relieve the pressure of the weight of the stone blocks upon
the lintel. The function of the carved triangular piece was to fill in
the empty space, and it was decorated on the outer side with ornamental sculpture. The carving shows two lions standing and looking
toward each other, with their front paws upon a pedestal that sup-
ports a column rising toward the apex of the triangle. The column, in
the style of the columns at Cnossus, is narrower at the bottom.

Grave Circle   Just to the right inside the gate is a double circle of
thin, upright stones enclosing a necropolis or cemetery. The graves of
this Grave Circle were of the shaft type, dug vertically deep into the
ground, and were marked by grave **stelae,** or stones. When Schliemann opened these shaft graves and saw the objects that had been
buried in prehistorical times with the nineteen skeletons that were
found, it seemed that this must have been a royal cemetery and that
the gold masks and cups, the beautifully carved ornamental figures,
and the many items of jewelry had indeed belonged to King
Agamemnon and members of his family. One of the death masks is
still popularly designated as Agamemnon's Mask, as Schliemann
called it, although later excavations, especially in recent years, have
disproved his enthusiastic and hasty conclusions in regard to the
Grave Circle. Even so, the gold and silver cups, the skillful designs
and lovely decoration of gold, silver, and bronze objects, the rings
and necklaces, the beautiful bronze daggers inlaid in gold and silver
with hunting scenes and the like, the items of jewelry, and many
utensils and other articles found in the shaft graves served to re-
create for archaeologists the civilization of the citadel of Mycenae
during its height.

Palace   The palace was built at the top of the acropolis, and a ramp
and staircase were constructed to facilitate the ascent from the Lion
Gate. The palace was entered through the **propylaea** (from *pro,* "in
front of," and *pyle* "gate"), a colonnaded vestibule type of entrance.
From the ruins, archaeologists have determined that the entire structure closely resembled the Minoan palace at Cnossus. Remains of
stairways and passageways indicate that two or more stories existed
before the building fell into ruins and parts of it collapsed toward the
deep ravine to the south and west. The megaron, or Great Hall
bore frescoes on its stucco walls, and a painted hearth still stands in
the center, as do two bases of the four columns that originally encir-

cled the round fireplace. The remains of a large courtyard, of a portico and vestibule in front of the megaron, and of a throne room with its anteroom, as well as of domestic chambers and storage rooms, give further details of the palace and furnish additional comparison with Cretan structures.

Beehive Tombs During the later Mycenaean Age, a group of kings known as the beehive-tomb dynasty ruled. They lived on the peak of the rocky hill in the palace, which was rebuilt during their era to equal the luxurious and grand living scale of the contemporary culture. The beehive tomb associated with these kings derives its name from the shape of the main room, which was circular and topped with a dome resembling a beehive in its proportions. Each beehive or **tholos** [round] **tomb** was built into the side of a hill, and after the rock had been hollowed out to the desired dimensions, the entire underground area was lined to the top of its vaulted roof with hewn stones. Not only were most of the stones hewn, but they also had to be shaped to fit the circular curve of the tomb—no easy task.

View inside a beehive tomb, looking out

The tomb was approached by a long rock-lined passage that started from the outer base of the hill and led to the entrance doorway. After each burial, this passage could be filled with dirt to give the appearance from the outside of a natural, solid hillside. This was apparently done to forestall robberies, since many valuable items were buried with the dead. These objects, however, are lost to archaeology, since they were stolen long ago.

Two of these beehive tombs are representative of the nine that have been discovered. These two are outstanding because of their size and the technical skill involved in their construction. They are the so-called Tomb of Clytemnestra and the Treasury or Tomb of Atreus.

The larger of the two is the Treasury of Atreus. By the skill of its masonry, its dimensions, the great size and weight of some of the stones used, and the remarkable state of its preservation, it furnishes

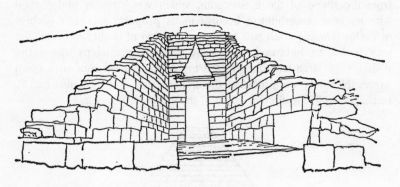

Entrance to a beehive tomb

archaeologists with an excellent example of the beehive tomb. A long avenue leads through the side of a hill to its great doorway, formed of massive stones, and above the lintel is a triangular hollow that was created, as in the Lion Gate, to relieve the stress of weight. Its high, vaulted dome, a little less than the tomb's diameter, stands about forty-three or forty-four feet above the floor level.

Chamber Tombs There are other tombs at Mycenae cut directly into the hillside and called chamber tombs. These rectangular chambers were probably sepulchers of the wealthy and noble personages of about the same period as the royal beehive tombs and have also yielded information of archaeological importance.

Excavations of Mycenae Schliemann carried on excavations at Mycenae between 1874 and 1876 and uncovered not only the city, with its palace and tombs and all they contained, but also the civilization of the Mycenaean Age—one contemporary with and similar to that of Crete. The objects found, whether gold and silver treasures, paintings, or pottery, were the tools used for reconstructing Mycenaean culture. We must remember that Sir Arthur Evans' excavations at Cnossus were not started until twenty-five years later, so that no basis for comparison existed at the time Schliemann undertook his work at Mycenae and interpreted his finds. Since that time continued excavations by German, British, and Greek archaeologists have brought to light a comparatively exact and detailed knowledge of the Mycenaean Age.

TIRYNS

Location In contrast to Mycenae, Tiryns was not fortified by its natural location, but stood little more than fifty feet above the Plain of Argos. Because of the broad, flat land around it, however, Tiryns commanded a view of the surrounding countryside and of an approaching enemy, and the rocky acropolis on which it was situated was well fortified by cyclopean walls. The blocks of stone in these walls were shaped, although somewhat roughly and irregularly in most places, and many of them weigh ten tons or more. According to legend, these massive cyclopean ramparts were adequate to hold the great Hercules, imprisoned by King Eurystheus, who forced him to undergo many difficult labors. According to the evidence of excavation, the citadel was complete with walls, entrance, palace, and all the necessities of royal habitation by about 1400 B.C.

History of Tiryns Archaeological research reveals that the site of Tiryns was inhabited as early as the third millennium B.C. by people whose chief building material was mud brick. Traces of mud-brick houses and other buildings dating from this period have been found, as well as a large circular building that stood at the summit of the hill. This structure measured about ninety feet across and was apparently roofed over—possibly with wood covered by tile, from the evidence of tiles that were discovered at the spot.

The later settlement at Tiryns may have differed in some respects from its neighbor, Mycenae, ten miles away, but excavation and research show that the two sites shared the same high civilization and characteristics of construction during the Mycenaean Age. We have already mentioned the existence of cyclopean walls and ramparts in both. In addition Tiryns' main entrance gate, measuring about the same as the Lion Gate, was also protected by a bastion. A ramp was built outside the gate to make the approach by horse or chariot easier. The protective walls were broken at several points by **postern gates,** and the west postern gate was reached from above by a long stairway that winds through the wall and gives a realistic idea of the immense proportions of the walls and the huge stones of which they are built.

The Palace   Excavations unearthed the well-defined plan of the palace that was erected at the top of the rocky citadel during the thirteenth century B.C. It consisted of a great hall, or megaron, large and small courtyards, colonnades, connecting passages and corridors, stairways, entranceways, vestibules, and columns—all reminiscent of the attractive, comfortable living quarters at Cnossus and Mycenae. The decorations, too, remind us of Crete, since not only were frescoes employed but the patterns and scenes show similar animals, people, sports, and floral and marine life. On the practical side, resemblances appear also in the presence of cisterns, baths, and drainage systems.

The Vaulted Gallery   An interesting feature at Tiryns is the vaulted or covered gallery. Galleries of this type are found on the south and east sides and were composed of a series of rooms and a corridor

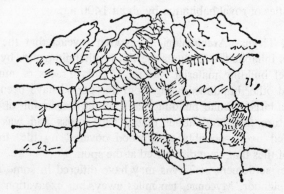

The vaulted gallery

constructed within the wall. They were used in ancient times as storage places and were supported on the outer side by casements.

Excavations at Tiryns Excavations were carried on at Tiryns in 1884–86 by Schliemann and Wilhelm Dörpfeld. The latter continued work at the site until the beginning of the twentieth century and others have since taken over the investigation, the study of finds, and the task of reconstruction, to make the picture of ancient Tiryns ever clearer. Several palaces, constructed at different times, have been uncovered and are dated from about 1500 to 1200 B.C. There were two parts to the ancient city. The northern part was lower, and those living on the lowlands around the citadel could go there for protection in troubled times. The southern section included the remainder of the citadel with the palace and related buildings.

CHAPTER EIGHT

Athens

Location Nature gave Athens an almost perfect setting. Located near the end of a peninsula, it had easy access to the sea and the excellent port of Piraeus only a few miles away, but it was far enough inland to be protected from enemies approaching by water. Its position on the plain of Attica offered sufficient room for city expansion and the cultivation of fields, while the mountains which surrounded it on almost all sides supplied fine stone quarries and pro-

Map of Later Greece

tection from land attacks. Mt. Hymettus, rising to the east, was the
source of travertine, a hard, gray-blue stone used widely for building
and sculpture. Mt. Pentelicus, farther to the north, yielded an excellent pure white marble, called **Pentelic marble,** which was used in
all the best buildings of Athens. Streams and springs supplied water,
making the Attic plain fertile. In an imposing and strategic position,
the Acropolis, upon which Athens was built, rose more than two
hundred feet into the air, providing a naturally fortified place from
which the inhabitants could defend themselves.

Map of Attica

The Areopagus and the Pnyx To the west lay a smaller and
rounded rocky hill, named the Areopagus, or Hill of Ares, god of
war. Here, in ancient times, the Senate of the Areopagus met. This
body acted as both a governing council and a court of justice. When
St. Paul addressed the Athenians, he probably did so from the Areopagus.

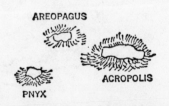

Location of the hills of Athens

Beyond the Areopagus was a rocky slope called the Pnyx, which rose gradually in the shape of a crude semicircle. The north slope of this hillside made an excellent place for the citizens of Athens to meet and hold their democratic assemblies. There were no seats, but the people sitting on the hill could easily see and hear the speaker who stood on the terrace below them. The Pnyx was used as a meeting place throughout the fifth and most of the fourth centuries B.C.

Excavations at Athens Through extensive excavations at Athens most of the ancient city's remains have been uncovered and reconstructed. As a result, the visitor has little difficulty in picturing for himself the city as it was in ancient times. He is aided, too, by the Acropolis, which serves as an excellent vantage point from which to view the important points of interest, the circling mountains, and the harbor of Piraeus, all spread out before him in a panorama. Almost every archaeological institution and most archaeologists have played a part in excavating, studying, and interpreting the ancient city of Athens. The Greek Government and a number of archaeological schools from various countries have done the major work of separating the old Athens from the new, and Wilhelm Dörpfeld, of the German Institute of Archaeology, and B. W. Hill, of the American School of Classical Studies, are among the many outstanding scholars who have contributed to our knowledge of ancient Athens.

HISTORICAL SKETCH OF ATHENS

Because a primary function of archaeology is to bring history out of past ruins, a description of Athens' archaeological remains will be clearer with some understanding of the background against which that city played her part in ancient times.

Early Athens Archaeological evidences of primitive hut dwellings in the vicinity of the Acropolis indicate that the earliest habitation occurred around and on the Acropolis in the Neolithic period. Dating the early history of Greece depends to a large extent upon potsherds. Fragments of pottery found in wells and graves suggest that northern invaders came into Athens and other parts of Greece at the beginning of the Bronze Age and that the two races then mingled. Not more than a thousand years later another race of invaders came into Greece. This invasion, called the Dorian Invasion, swept over the

Greek mainland and on to Crete and Asia Minor. The intermingling
of the Dorians with the peoples they conquered resulted in the race
of Greek people who did most of the building in Greece with which
we are primarily concerned.

Age of Kings The period following the Dorian invasions is generally referred to as the Age of Kings, since the people of each community were under the rule of a king, and their houses were clustered
around his palace. Our best sources for this Age of Kings are the
poems of Homer, who lived about 800 B.C.

Age of Nobles When the nobles became greedy and powerful
enough, they overthrew their kings. The Age of Nobles lasted until
about 650 B.C. During this time some of the cities, including Athens,
grew powerful enough to rule over the entire district surrounding
them, and were therefore known as **city-states.** By the eighth century
B.C. the appearance of the alphabet on inscriptions and on objects
from Egypt and the entire eastern Mediterranean indicates that there
was fairly wide contact and trade between these places and Greece.
In the following century the introduction of coinage shows that the
increase in commerce brought about a need for this medium of exchange. The coins and pottery found in many widely separated parts
of Greece and the eastern Mediterranean world indicate the extensive export trade carried on by the Greek city-states at that time.

Age of Tyrants The Age of Tyrants came next and lasted from approximately 650 to 500 B.C. A tyrant was one who seized the power
in a city-state. Many of the tyrants were excellent rulers and encouraged the economic and cultural growth of the city-states under
their control. One such was Pisistratus, who fostered the development
of Athens in many ways in the sixth century B.C. This, as archaeologists have demonstrated, was one of the great periods of building and
artistic creation at Athens.

Persian Wars A series of reforms and changes throughout the sixth
century led to a democratic form of government in Athens, giving
the citizens a large measure of control over their rulers. As a result
of this strengthening, the Athenians were able to meet Persian attacks in the Persian Wars of 492–479 B.C. and to bear the brunt of
repelling the invaders and finally defeating them.

Golden Age The long period of peace in the fifth century following the Persian Wars was the Golden Age of Athens. Now the city was under the wholly democratic rule of its citizens. Peace brought prosperity and the greatest of Athens' building periods—based on civic pride, the means and desire to beautify the city, and a need to rebuild after the destruction caused by the Persian Wars. The fifth century B.C.—the Golden Age, or Age of Pericles—saw Athens at the height of her glory.

Decline of Athens As Athens became more powerful, so did the other city-states of Greece. Always independent in spirit, the Greeks jealously guarded their independence and defended it when necessary. Growing rivalry led to the leaguing of one city-state with another in an attempt to gain more power and wealth. In the end, war between Sparta and the city-states allied with her, and Athens and her allies broke out. These **Peloponnesian Wars** lasted from 459 to 404 B.C., with intermittent periods of truce between the three wars. Sparta emerged victorious from the long conflict. Athens did not recover from the blow. Her army and navy were destroyed, her treasury empty, her spirit crushed. Nor did the other city-states survive for long. Sparta was supreme in Greece for a little more than thirty years. Then Thebes gained leadership and held it for less than ten years. In 338 B.C. Philip of Macedonia conquered the weakened and disunited Greeks. Two years later his son Alexander the Great succeeded him. Alexander strengthened his hold over the Greek world. Greece never recovered, and fell easy prey to the Romans, who conquered it in 146 B.C. The Romans held the entire Mediterranean area under their control for the remaining time with which archaeology is most concerned—that is, until all declined into the Dark Ages.

THE ACROPOLIS

The Early Acropolis The Acropolis dominates the landscape of Athens and grips the minds of all who see it, just as it has for countless generations. It was a natural fortress, a plateau of rock which stretched approximately 150 yards from north to south and more than 300 yards from east to west. It was high enough and large enough to accommodate with some safety the inhabitants of Athens in the earliest times. It was there that the kings had their palaces. Additional protection and fortification were gained when the Acropolis was walled at some time before the Dorian invasions, probably in the thirteenth century B.C. A temple to Athena, patron goddess of Athens, was also built during this period and was of poros, a type of limestone widely used in early Greek buildings. Traces of this temple existing today testify to the durability of the building methods.

As Athens became stronger and the fear of attack grew weaker, the inhabitants moved their dwellings from the Acropolis and placed them in more easily accessible positions around the foot of the citadel and in the more level areas surrounding it. The fortification walls, however, remained and were rebuilt or strengthened from time to time so that the people could take refuge within them when danger threatened. The top of the Acropolis remained sacred to Athena throughout ancient Greek history, and was given over to buildings dedicated to the gods when it no longer held the dwellings of kings and lesser men.

After the Persian Wars During the Persian Wars, the Athenians barricaded themselves atop the Acropolis and were able to resist Persian attacks for some time. The determined Persians, however, finally forced their way in through the stone stairway, still visible on the north side, which had been built to give the Greeks access to their water supply near the base of the hill. Plundering and burning followed. The walls, the temples—already built or under construction—the entrance gates, the shrines, and everything else in the path of the invaders received a share of the destruction. Shortly afterward the Greeks defeated the Persians on land and sea, and emerged victorious from the contest. All this took place in 479 B.C.

As soon as the Athenians recovered sufficiently, they started the great task of rebuilding their city. Houses and walls came first. Archaeologists find it difficult to reconstruct the buildings belonging to the period before the Persian Wars because the Athenians, in their haste to rebuild the Acropolis walls, used whatever building materials were closest to hand. Stone of all kinds, whether from temples or statues, went into the walls. That is the answer to questions of visitors today who look up at the outer wall on the north side, or see it from closer range atop the Acropolis, and notice a number of drums from columns set into the wall. These still make a strong fortification, just as they have for almost 2500 years.

By the middle of the fifth century B.C. Athens had achieved great wealth and prestige. Under the leadership of Pericles the Athenian Empire entered its Golden Age, and most of the buildings on the Acropolis as we know it today were constructed at this time. The greatest architects and sculptors and the best workmen available were employed to create monuments that would be artistically worthy of a city at the height of its power and cultural development.

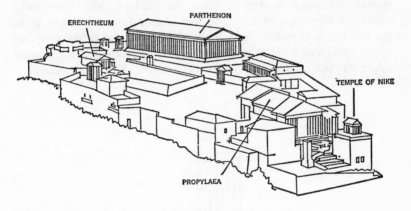

The Acropolis

COLUMNS

The Three Orders of Columns There are three basic styles of columns, each of which developed over a long period of time from the earliest type—a tree trunk, rather short and sturdy, and usually inverted so that the wider part bore the main burden of support. Wooden columns were used throughout the eastern Mediterranean, especially in Egypt, Mesopotamia, and Crete, until the use of stone by the Greeks led to the three orders of Greek architecture: the **Doric, Ionic,** and **Corinthian,** each characterized by its columns.

Parts of a Column A column is composed of three main parts: the capital, the shaft, and the base. Each of the three orders had standard specifications for each part of a column. The **capital,** from the Latin word *caput,* meaning "head," is the top part of the column. The body of the column is the **shaft,** which forms the long central section. This may be made of one solid piece or may be constructed of a series of drums or cylinders. The outside of the shaft is generally hollowed from top to bottom in grooves, called **flutes** or **fluting.** The **base** on which the shaft is mounted is the third feature of a column.

Doric Order   The Doric order began in Greece and was the first to appear. Its name is derived from the Dorians, who were early settlers in Greece, and its shape and simple form are taken from the tree trunk. It consists of a plain capital, rounded below a square upper part, and a fairly wide shaft, either smooth or with shallow ridges of fluting, usually twenty in number. It stands without a base.

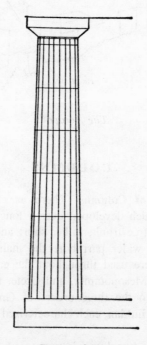

Doric column

Ionic Order The Ionic column bears the name of its place of origin, Ionia, in Greek Asia Minor, where it appeared about the seventh century B.C. The capital of an Ionic column is identified by a version of the lily pattern, found on earlier wooden columns, which gradually became stylized to form **volutes** or spirals in the four corners. Its shaft was more slender than the Doric and was generally given twenty-four flutings, which meant that the grooves were closer together. The Ionic column has a base.

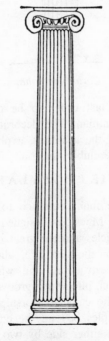

Ionic column

Ionic Order The Ionic

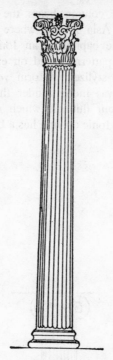

Corinthian column

Corinthian Order The last order to be developed, a century or two later, was the Corinthian. The decoration of its capital is derived from the leaves of the acanthus, a plant found in Greece. In other respects it closely resembles the Ionic order.

THE PROPYLAEA

In the Golden Age the main entrance to the Acropolis was the Propylaea. The architect Mnesicles designed an imposing building as befitted the plans of Pericles and the great buildings to which it was a gateway. It was built on the west side, where the earlier Propylaea had stood before its destruction, and was approached over the rocky incline of the citadel, into which grooves had been cut to afford a foothold for people who came to worship and for the animals to be sacrificed at the temples beyond the entrance. Its large central doorway was flanked on either side by two smaller ones. The outer colonnade was in the Doric style, and the inner columns, framing the view of the top of the Acropolis, were Ionic. For one reason or another—lack of funds, internal dissension, or growing threats to Athens' security—the Propylaea was never completely finished. The gateway stands today much as it was in the fifth century B.C. That some of the stones, all of fine Pentelic marble from nearby Mt. Pentelicus, were never smoothed off, or that the final ornamental sculpture was not added, or that there are a few other minor signs of incompletion, does not detract from this impressive porticoed entrance to the wonders of the Acropolis.

TEMPLE ARCHITECTURE

A temple was the home of the god or goddess to whom it was dedicated. For this reason it was not only designed as a suitable dwelling place for the deity, but the style of its architecture underwent changes during the course of time to keep it a fit residence for so important a figure. A temple was not necessarily large, since only the priests and a few selected individuals commonly entered it. Everyone else had to remain outside to make sacrifice and worship, or to look and admire.

The Tholos Some temples were round, but they were exceptions. A circular temple is generally given the name **tholos.** It was built on a simple plan, with columns circling the entire building.

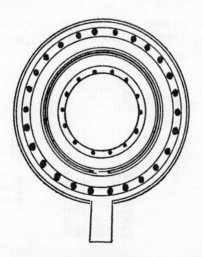

The tholos

Rectangular Temples The majority of temples were rectangular. The main body was called the *naos* in Greek, or the *cella* in Latin. A vestibule in front, formed by the extension of the walls, was called the **pronaos,** meaning "in front of the naos." Rectangular temples are classified according to their general plan, especially in regard to the position and number of their columns.

In antis designates a temple whose side walls are brought forward and have two columns situated between these projections of the walls, called **antae,** and in front of the entrance.

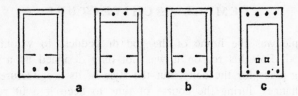

*Temple styles: a–*In antis. *b–Prostylos. c–Amphi-prostylos*

A similar type is the **prostylos,** with four columns forming a porch. The cella walls are sometimes extended as well.

Amphiprostylos means that the arrangement of four columns is repeated at the back of the temple to make another porch. *Amphi* means "both."

A further development and enlargement led to the **peripteros** temple, the most widely used form. In this type the entire temple

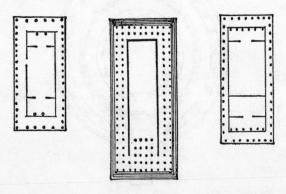

Peripteros type

is surrounded with an outer continuous row of columns, or colonnade.

An adaptation of the peripteros type is the **pseudoperipteros,** or "false" peripteros. This type was employed frequently by the Romans. The columns of the colonnade do not stand free, but are "engaged," meaning they are attached to the cella wall.

Ornamentation of a Temple All temples were set upon foundations and were reached by a series of steps, generally three. The outer columns supported the main crossbeams or stone blocks called the **architrave.** Above the architrave came the **frieze,** usually decorated with sculpture. The frieze of a Doric temple was composed of **triglyphs** and **metopes.** The triglyph appeared above each Doric column and between every two columns. It received its name from the three (*tri-*) channels (*glyphs*) or half channels that were hol-

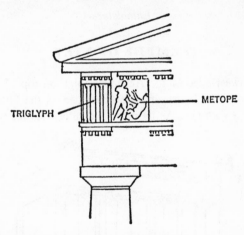

Triglyph and metope

lowed out vertically to decorate the rectangular space. The metope is the sculptured square that appears alternately between the triglyphs.

When the triglyph and metope were not used, the frieze consisted of a continuous band of sculptured relief. The **cornice** rested upon the frieze. The roof of a rectangular temple formed a triangle between the cornice called the **pediment.** This was generally decorated with sculpture, the central figures being upright and larger, with the others graded in position and size to fit logically into the triangular space. The architrave, frieze, and cornice together are referred to as the **entablature.**

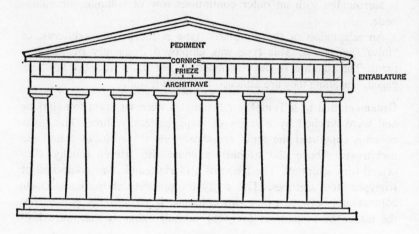

Entablature

TEMPLE OF NIKE

On the southwest edge of the Acropolis, high on top of a bastion to the right as one climbs toward the Propylaea, is the little Temple of Athena Nike (Victory). As its name indicates, this temple was dedi-

Nike Temple

cated to Athena in gratitude for victories won by the Athenians. It was built of Pentelic marble with an Ionic porch of four columns at each end, in the amphiprostylos style. Its sculptured frieze shows scenes of Greek battles and deities. The statue of Athena in the temple is wingless. The architect of the Temple of Nike was probably Callicrates, one of the most notable architects of the fifth century B.C.

STATUE OF ATHENA

The famed sculptor Phidias created several statues of Athena. One of these stood on the Acropolis in a commanding position facing the Propylaea. A cutting to support its foundation, a fragment of marble that probably belonged to its pedestal, and many legends and accounts of it have come down to us. We know that it was a colossal bronze statue, towering thirty to fifty feet high. Athena was dressed in armor. Her shining helmet could be seen from Piraeus and the sea, giving protection and comfort to sailors as they traveled in and out of the port. The statue was paid for by the booty gained when the Greeks defeated the Persians at the Battle of Marathon in 490 B.C. The huge bronze statue was thus another symbol of the link between the patron goddess and the victories of the Athenians.

PARTHENON

Under Pericles the architects Ictinus and Callicrates and the sculptor Phidias were employed to erect a temple on the Acropolis that would be worthy of the goddess Athena. The Parthenon was constructed in less than ten years, from 447–438 B.C., and to this day remains unsurpassed in grace, beauty, and perfection of design. The Greek word *parthenos* means "maiden" or "virgin." Actually the Parthenon is the Temple of the Maiden or Athena.

Architecture of the Parthenon The Parthenon was built of Pentelic marble in the Doric style. There is a colonnade on all four sides, with eight columns on the east and west ends and fifteen columns (seventeen including the columns at the corners) on each side, making forty-six in all, each about thirty-five feet in height. The cella, or walled main chamber, was not quite as high and had six columns at the ends. The cella walls projected forward *in antis*. The cella itself consisted of two sections. The western part, called the Parthenon—from which the entire temple gets its name—was somewhat smaller than the eastern.

Statue of Athena   The eastern part of the cella held the cult statue of Athena enclosed within its long and lofty colonnade of Doric columns. This great statue, the work of the incomparable sculptor Phidias, has completely disappeared, but literary evidence furnishes archaeologists with a description of it. It was made of gold and ivory and was a colossal statue, standing at least thirty feet high. This type of statue is called **chryselephantine,** from the Greek *chrysos,* "gold," and *elephas,* "ivory." The name is derived from the use in such statues of ivory for the skin and pure gold, probably laid over wood, for the rest—garments, hair, and the like. In addition, paint was used to give further realistic effects. Chryselephantine statues were popular among the Greeks and were employed especially in portraying the deities. In the chryselephantine statue of Athena on the Acropolis, the protecting goddess was represented with a helmet, the aegis (breastplate), a Nike or Winged Victory in her right hand, and her shield and lance at her left side.

Birth of Athena   There are various versions of the legend of the birth of Athena, or Pallas Athena, as she is sometimes called. The most commonly accepted one is that she was brought forth full-grown and in armor from the head of her father Zeus, who had consumed his wife lest she produce a son who might overpower him. Athena gave her name to Athens, the chief city of the ancient region of Attica, and protected it with the power over war and victory (or nike) that was always closely associated with her. The maiden Athena was the exemplification of all the womanly virtues, but was also a warlike goddess and a goddess of victory. She was usually clothed in armor, wore a helmet, and carried a spear or lance. She used the storm-producing aegis or goatskin, with its snake-encircled Gorgon's head in the center, as a shield or breastplate. Throughout their history the Athenians worshiped Athena not only as the protective deity of their city and a goddess of victory but as a patroness of peacetime arts and of all good things to which they aspired.

Contest of Athena and Poseidon Athena was not, however, the reigning deity in Athens at the very beginning. There was a time when Poseidon, god of the sea, claimed that honor. A contest between Athena and Poseidon followed, which was judged by the gods on the basis of which one could give the more valuable gift to the people of Attica. Poseidon offered power over the sea, his special province, and in proof of this he pierced the earth with his **trident,** the three-pronged spear—symbol of his rule of the seas. Athena's gift to the people was the olive tree of peace. For this she won the contest and the control of Attica.

Parthenon Pediments The pediments, or triangular sections below the roof at each end of the Parthenon, were filled with monumental high reliefs, composed and shaped to suit the allotted spaces and the entire theme of the temple. We have few remains of these, but we do have literary descriptions by ancient authors. The east pediment depicted in marble the birth of Athena, rising from the head of Zeus. On the west pediment was depicted the contest between Athena and Poseidon to win possession of Attica.

Panathenaic Festival In honor of Athena and her many favors to the people of Attica, the Panathenaic festival was established. This took place every year, with more elaborate celebrations every four years. As the name shows, it included all the Athenians, and it took the form of competitive contests in athletics and music. Athletes entered horse and chariot races and the more usual foot races, javelin throwing, jumping, wrestling, and boxing. The winners were given prizes of olive leaves and vases of oil, in commemoration of Athena's gift to Attica. Archaeologists have uncovered many jars and fragments of pottery in different parts of the Greek world which show that athletes traveled great distances to compete in the Panathenaic festivals. These vases depict for us the festival scenes just as they were in ancient times, with the winner's sport on one side and the image of Athena on the other.

Panathenaic Procession After the contests, the great Panathenaic procession wound its way up to the summit of the Acropolis to do honor to the goddess Athena. Since sacrifice was an important part of all religious ceremonies, animals—cows and sheep—to be killed before Athena's altar were led in the procession. A feast was held after the rituals and sacrifices had been completed. The worshipers in the procession formed a cross section of the Athenians and all those under their domination: boys and young men on horseback or carrying vessels and vases, old men bearing olive branches and presents to the goddess, girls and women with gifts, four-horse chariots, musicians, and many groups of people, all playing their part to make the festivities a success. The climax of the Panathenaic procession was the presentation of a **peplos** (robe) to Athena. Each year selected Athenian girls worked hard and long to weave and embroider a new peplos to clothe the statue of the goddess. The peplos was presented to Athena's priest and priestess in the presence of the Greek gods.

Parthenon Frieze The subject of the frieze that runs around the upper part of the Parthenon's outer cella wall is the Panathenaic procession. It is carved in low relief and its entire length, over five-hundred feet, is filled with the action, motion, and life of the procession. Along the longer sides (the north and south walls) are depicted the numerous citizens and worshipers who approach in an uninterrupted stream to bring votive offerings, carry out the sacrifices, and present the new peplos. The presentation of the peplos takes place at the temple's east end and that section of the frieze is filled with two groups. There are the figures in the center who are receiving the peplos and, on either side of them, the gods and goddesses, in whose presence the presentation takes place, but who look toward the procession approaching along the north and south sides of the frieze. The group of figures at the west end consists of riders and their mounts, who form part of the procession. The entire frieze is not only well thought out and extremely suitable, but is outstanding for the variety of poses, the naturalness of movement, the unity of composition, and the artistic technique of execution.

Parthenon Metopes On the outside of Doric temples, around the top above the achitrave, there usually was a frieze of triglyphs and metopes. On the Parthenon, the rectangular metopes that alternated with the triglyphs were covered with sculpture. These carvings —ninety-two in all—were in high relief. They showed scenes of mythological contests and battles, and many of them are still in place.

Details and Refinements Greek architects realized that it was necessary to compensate architecturally for differences between line effects produced by inanimate stone and lines as seen by the human eye. Thus optical illusions of many kinds were built into the Parthenon to create a perfect whole. Its tall Doric columns narrow gracefully and imperceptibly—but in a slight and gentle curve instead of a straight line—and they also tilt inward as they rise. Otherwise the columns would not appear to be even and straight. This architectural refinement—making a column curve slightly in a convex arc so it appears to taper in a straight line—is called **entasis.** For the same reason, the columns at the corners are somewhat larger and more closely spaced. This makes them look as though they were the same size and measurement as the others, and gives them the appearance of standing straight in the correct vertical proportions. The eye is also tricked by the horizontal lines, which curve slightly upward and outward at the middle of the building, as may be seen quite easily by looking closely at the lines of the steps. As a result of this constant use of curved lines to produce an illusion of straight lines, complexity of execution brings the simplicity of perfection to the eye of the beholder.

Later History of the Parthenon During the Christian Era the Parthenon was converted into a church and underwent a number of architectural changes. One of these was the addition of a tower. In the fifteenth century A.D., when Greece was under Turkish rule, it became a mosque. Later it was used as a storehouse for powder during the Venetian attacks on the Turks, and was destroyed in 1687 by an explosion when gunfire touched off the powder.

Early in the nineteenth century the Turkish Government gave Lord Elgin, a British diplomat, permission to remove much of the Parthenon sculpture to the British Museum. Almost all of the surviving pediment sculptures, many of the metopes, and sections of the frieze are on view there (where they are known as the

"Elgin Marbles"), and for many years a controversy has raged as to whether they should be kept in Britain or returned to their original setting in Greece. Considering how quickly the Parthenon fell into disrepair and became a target of plunder by tourists in the last century, however, it would be hard to prove that Lord Elgin did not preserve the marble pieces that he moved from their unprotected position in Athens to the safety of London.

The Parthenon exemplifies the spirit of the ancient Greeks by its symmetry and grace, balance and beauty. Its fine white Pentelic marble was painted to relieve the sun's glare and to accent the decorative carvings and ornamental sculpture. Among the many achievements of the architects and sculptors who worked on the Parthenon, one of the most remarkable was the balance between mathematical precision and artistic refinement. The Parthenon's restoration according to existing archaeological evidence is currently taking place, for this temple is still one of the greatest of man's works and a lasting example to the future.

ERECHTHEUM

Erechtheus One of the earliest mythical figures connected with the legendary history of Athens was Erechtheus. He was said to have been a king of Athens and to have been instrumental in establishing Athena's popularity as the city's patroness. As time passed, Erechtheus himself appears to have been worshiped as a deity, or at least to have become closely associated with the other deities especially favored in Athens—Athena and Poseidon.

Early Temple An early temple was built on the Acropolis near the north wall. This sanctuary may have been built by Erechtheus or to him, but in any case it came to be shared by Athens' three chief deities: Athena, Poseidon, and Erechtheus. Obviously from the latter came its name, the Erechtheum.

Erechtheum After the earlier temple was destroyed during the Persian Wars, the present Erechtheum was constructed as part of the general rebuilding in Athens that followed the wars. The new temple, built at the end of the fifth century B.C., is one of the best examples of Ionic architecture.

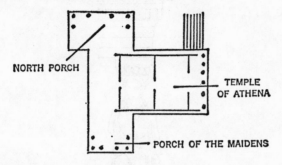

NORTH PORCH

TEMPLE
OF ATHENA

PORCH OF THE MAIDENS

Plan of the Erechtheum

Actually several temples, each a unit in itself, were gracefully and beautifully combined to make up the Erechtheum. The section dedicated to Athena contained a cult statue of the goddess facing toward the east. This section was entered through a porch of six tall, slender Ionic columns. Behind this were two other temples containing altars and quite probably dedicated to Erechtheus and Poseidon. Another deity was also worshiped here—Hephaestus, god of fire and, according to some mythological sources, father of Erechtheus.

At the Erechtheum's western end is a row of seven Ionic half columns along the wall. On the north side is a portico, also with Ionic columns, four in front and one on each side of the porch. This was the entrance to the small chamber of the western section. The north porch has an opening in its ceiling and a corresponding one in its pavement—both said to have been made by a thunderbolt of Zeus or by Poseidon's trident.

Porch of the Maidens On the western chamber's other side is the well-known Porch of the Caryatids or Maidens. Caryatids were sculptured female figures dressed in long, flowing garments and used instead of columns to support the entablature. This probably originated from depicting in stone statues the girls who took part in sacred ritual dances at the festival of Artemis. One of the caryatids from the Porch of the Maidens is now in the British Museum and has been replaced at the Erechtheum by a reproduction.

Caryatid

The Erechtheum is a gem of Ionic architecture. Its Ionic columns have never been surpassed in workmanship. The carving and ornamental details, especially in the moldings and bases of capitals, show great refinement and skill.

THEATERS

The theater, in both its literary and architectural forms, held an important position in the Greek and Roman worlds. When the great religious festivals and games were held in Greece, theatrical performances became a part of them. They were attended by thousands, who watched them with the same keen interest as they did the athletics and the other events. To accommodate the spectators and make the performances as perfect as possible, theaters were carefully designed and well built. Later the Romans constructed their theaters on the Greek models. We now have a fairly detailed knowledge of ancient theater construction, gained from the writings of classical authors as well as from archaeological excavations and research.

Seats It is quite possible that at first the spectators stood or sat on natural hillsides to get a better view of the performers on a level space below. In any case, the Greeks used such slopes when they began to build permanent theaters, first of wood and then of stone. Actually the sides were built out from the slope so that the seats were arranged in a semicircle. In the beginning most of the seats were formed by simply cutting them out of the stone and earth of the hillside. It was a logical step to make these seats more comfortable by covering them with wood, and then finally to construct them of stone, especially marble. The seats were deep so that each spectator could place his feet on the seat below him and still leave sufficient room for the person occupying that seat.

The spectators entered from either side and climbed up to their seats. Important persons—such as magistrates and other officials, visiting dignitaries, or priests—occupied the first rows. These seats were reserved and were often specially constructed individual seats, usually having backs and sometimes arms for the added comfort

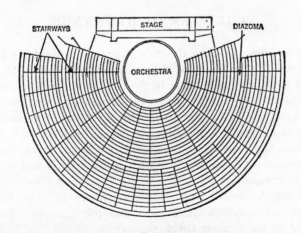

Greek theater

and honor of their occupants. The general seats were approached by steps and aisles that divided the theater into wedge-shaped sections. When the size of the theater warranted it, a further division was made by horizontal aisles running parallel to the rows of seats. This method of facilitating the entrance and exit of large audiences is familiar, for it is still used in most theaters and stadiums today.

Orchestra The orchestra was a flat, open, usually stone-paved area where dancing, singing, and some acting took place. It was located in the ring formed by the semicircular tiered seats. This made it possible for performers to enter and leave from either side and to make themselves easily heard. In some theaters, as at Epidaurus, the shape of the hill and the architecture of the seats and orchestra resulted in nearly perfect acoustics. In that theater it is possible to hear clearly from any location words spoken in a whisper by someone standing in the center of the orchestra.

Stage Most of the actors performed on the stage, which was situated behind the orchestra and approached by steps. Since little scenery and a minimum of props were used, the stage was built to serve as a background for many settings. Doorways, columns, and statues could represent houses, temples, and palaces equally well for most situations. This permanent scene also screened the dressing rooms and the actors offstage.

THEATER OF DIONYSUS

Festival of Dionysus The theater's origins lie in the great festivals of Dionysus. In the spring of each year a feast was held to Dionysus, god of wine, for his share in the fertility of the land and vineyards. Singing and dancing, a part of the festival, took place on flat ground marked off in a circle to form an orchestra. Soon the addition of seats and a stage formed a theater, and as speaking parts became more important than the sacred chorus, the drama arose. Gradually plays became a part of the Dionysian spring festival and were presented in competition for prizes in the Theater of Dionysus at the foot of the Acropolis. Here Athenian citizens gathered to watch tragedies and comedies. Here they were privileged to witness the works of all the greatest Greek playwrights—Aeschylus, Sophocles, Euripides, Aristophanes.

Theater of Dionysus The first permanent Theater of Dionysus was built on the south slope of the Acropolis in the fifth century B.C. Circular tiers of seats were cut out of the natural hillside rock and were covered with wood. The orchestra, however, was not paved. During the fourth century B.C. the need for a theater built entirely of stone led to new construction, and a fine structure arose.

The construction of this new theater closely followed the general pattern of classical Greek theaters. It is believed to have had a seating capacity of about fifteen hundred spectators, but some estimates place the number much higher. When the wooden seats were replaced by stone ones, the first-row seats were made of marble. These had backs and were intended for persons of position and honor—the priest of Dionysus in the center, with other priests, magistrates, and dignitaries occupying the remaining marble chairs. Inscriptions on the seats of honor have left archaeologists a written record of their occupants. At various times after that the theater underwent changes and alterations until after the Roman occupation of Greece.

Archaeological excavations at this theater site were carried on in the second half of the nineteenth century, largely under the direction of Wilhelm Dörpfeld. This work was continued into the twentieth century to restore the ancient Theater of Dionysus as it once was.

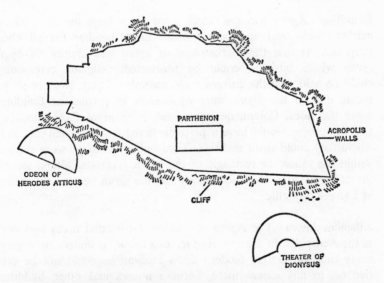

Location of Theater of Dionysus and Odeon of Herodes Atticus

ODEON OF HERODES ATTICUS

Herodes Atticus was an extremely wealthy man who lived in the second century A.D. He was born in Attica and spent a good deal of time in Athens, where he had a wide reputation as an orator. He spent vast sums of money on public buildings and other benefits for his fellow Greeks. When his wife Regilla died, he had an **odeon** erected in her memory. An odeon was a concert hall built like a theater, but smaller and more confined in shape, and designed to furnish the best acoustics possible. The Odeon of Herodes Atticus was built about 161 A.D. against the southwest side of the Acropolis. It had a rather narrow stage, with a high back wall. The semicircular tiers of seats rose sharply along the base of the Acropolis and could accommodate over five thousand persons. According to ancient literary evidence, no other odeon was bigger or more elaborate than the Odeon of Herodes Atticus. Today the building has been reconstructed and is still used for concerts.

AGORA

Definition *Agora* was the Greek word for a large flat area where markets were held and people could meet together for all civic purposes. At first the marketplace or agora was simply an open space where business could be transacted, religious ceremonies could be held, and the citizens could assemble. Later, rows of shops facing out on the agora were established in permanent buildings along the sides. Colonnades were built in front of these shops so that the people would have a place sheltered from the sun and rain where they could stroll and talk. Then public buildings were erected within the square or rectangle of the agora. Temples, altars, monuments, and statues were also added and the agora became the center of a Greek city's life.

Athenian Agora The Agora of Athens was located north and west of the Acropolis. In the course of its long history it underwent a great many changes. During modern times excavations could not be carried on to any extent there, because houses and other buildings covered the site, and the expenses involved made it prohibitive to do

15. Aerial view of the excavation site of Khirbet Qumrān, on the shores of the Dead Sea, near Jericho in Israel. *Georg Gerster / Rapho Guillumette.*

16. The so-called "Monastery" at Petra in Jordan, carved out of the pink and rose to brown colored stone. It became an important Middle Eastern caravan route of the Nabbateans whose "carved architecture" reflected some classical Greek and Roman elements added to the native motifs. *British Overseas Airways Corporation, Photo.*

OPPOSITE
18. The amphitheater at Petra was built by the Romans and seated about 3,000 spectators. After the Moslem conquest, Petra was abandoned and forgotten for centuries. *British Overseas Airways Corporation, Photo.*

17. The ruins of one of the buildings at Masadah in Israel, above the Dead Sea, which was once fortified by King Herod. *British Overseas Airways Corporation, Photo.*

19. Detail of window in the megalithic wall, shown opposite, with a view of the Andean peaks for which the prehistoric Peruvian settlement was named, Machu Picchu. *British Overseas Airways Corporation, Photo.*

20. Because of its precipitous location, Machu Picchu was never fortified, unlike most ancient cities. *British Overseas Airways Corporation, Photo.*

21. Stonehenge in Wiltshire, England, although having an entirely different purpose from those of the Incas, reveals monolithic forms that are evidence of extraordinary engineering skills found in many early cultures. *British Overseas Airways Corporation, Photo.*

22. The Mayan pyramid-temple of Kukulkan was called "El Castillo" by the Spaniards who visited Chichén Itzá, Yucatán, in the early sixteenth century. *Mexican National Tourist Council.*

OPPOSITE
24. Underwater exploration in progress of the sacred Mayan well (*cenote*) at Chichén Itzá. *Mexican National Tourist Council.*

23. This photo shows the Ball Court and "El Castillo," at Chichén Itzá, before the restoration of the monuments. *Mexican National Tourist Council.*

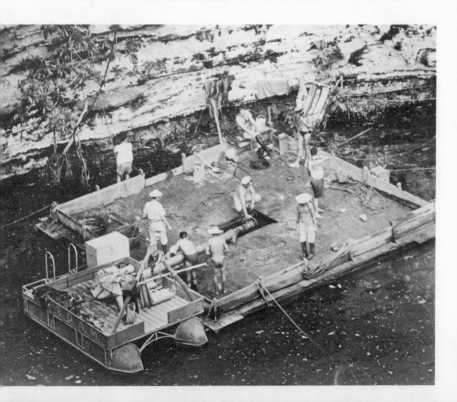

25. View of the Pyramid of the Sun and the Avenue of the Dead at Teotihuacán, a great center of the Toltec civilization. *Mexican National Tourist Council.*

26. The Pyramid of Quetzalcoatl, the plumed serpent, is a pyramid within a pyramid. The outer, later, pyramid, seen at the left, was relatively plain. Inside is the earlier, more ornate structure. *Mexican National Tourist Council.*

much digging. In the interests of archaeology, however, the Greek Government and American funds enabled archaeologists to start work on the site in the 1930s. Interrupted by World War II, the excavations were later continued and gradually the Agora of ancient Athens has emerged.

The discovery of foundations and other sections shows that there was a covered portico, called a **stoa,** on each side of the square. The entire east side was taken up by a stoa two stories high, which was built by Attalus II, a very wealthy king of Pergamum in the second century B.C. This large stoa has been restored by the American School of Classical Studies and now houses the museum of the Agora. On the opposite side stood the buildings concerned with the political life of Athens—the **metroon,** where the public records were kept; the **tholos,** a round building which held the dining and sleeping quarters of the chief magistrates; and the Senate House or **bouleuterion.** A large Doric temple dedicated to Ares and an odeon built by the Roman Marcus Agrippa under the Emperor Augustus stood in the Agora's grounds. The Panathenaic Way also crossed the Agora.

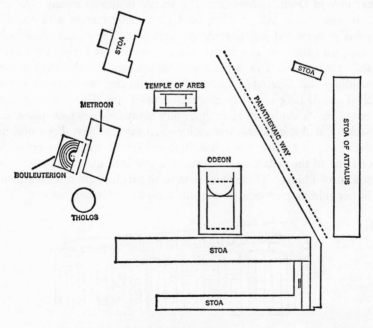

Plan of the Agora

THESEUM

Dedication of the Temple On the top of a low hill that rises to the west of the Agora stands a temple popularly known as the Theseum. The reason for this name is that visitors in the last centuries of the Middle Ages mistakenly identified it as a sanctuary of Theseus, because the deeds of this great Athenian hero were sculptured on some of the temple metopes. Modern archaeological research, however, has connected it instead with Hephaestus. As god of fire, Hephaestus was closely associated with the pottery makers and other craftsmen who used fire in their work. Thus it was natural that a temple was dedicated to Hephaestus, on whom the Athenians so depended for aid in their workshops.

Theseum The temple of Hephaestus, or the Theseum, was erected in the fifth century B.C.—Athens' great building period. Its remarkable state of preservation furnishes archaeologists with an excellent example of Doric architecture. The temple is approximately 100 feet long and almost half as wide, built of Pentelic marble with six columns at each end and thirteen on each side. The construction is *in antis,* with two columns at the east and west ends between the cella wall projections. The ornamental decorations on the ceiling and moldings still bear many traces of the paint that was applied in ancient times. Like so many classical temples, the Theseum was converted into a church in later times and many changes took place, especially in the interior. Archaeologists, however, have been able to determine that there was originally a colonnade within the cella. At one end of the cella stood two statues, executed by a sculptor in the school of Phidias. These statues were of Hephaestus and of Athena in her role as patroness of the city's crafts and manufacturing. Un-

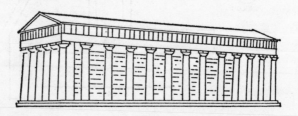

The Theseum

fortunately the Doric entablature of triglyphs and metopes is not well preserved, but remains show that the carvings represented the exploits of two legendary heroes, Theseus and Hercules. The Theseum, closely overlooking the Agora, formed an important adjunct to that Athenian marketplace.

ROMAN FORUM

When the Romans conquered Greece and occupied Athens, they introduced many of their own customs and ways. As a result, they established an agora of their own east of the Athenian Agora. In time, this Roman Forum, although smaller and less pretentious, also became an area of permanent buildings and marble decorations. It was a large rectangular court, about three hundred feet long, with shops and Ionic colonnades along its sides in the manner of the neighboring Agora.

At the end of the first century B.C. a great entrance gate or Propylaea was constructed at the Roman Forum's west side. This was made possible by the Roman Emperor Augustus, but it was dedicated to Athena. The Propylaea consisted of a wide center arch for carriages, and smaller arches on each side for foot traffic. Its porches were formed by Doric columns. The gate made a fitting entrance to the impressive courtyard and buildings of the Roman Forum. The information gained by archaeologists through excavations has been supplemented by a number of inscriptions found in the Roman Forum. From them archaeologists are told when and by whom a number of the Forum structures were erected.

HADRIAN'S LIBRARY

Beyond the Roman Forum to the north was Hadrian's Library. This building was constructed in about the same proportions and manner as its neighbors. A square central courtyard was surrounded on all four sides by a colonnade. Excavations have resulted in restoring the plan of Hadrian's Library, and archaeologists are again aided by descriptions of ancient writers. We know that there were one hundred columns of the peristyle and that they were made of marble. The main entrance was from the west side, corresponding to that of the Forum, and remains of its fine marble façade show it once had columns of the Corinthian order. On the east side was the main part of the library, where there were reading rooms and where the books, written on long scrolls, were kept safe in containers stored on shelves. The far wall of this section, with six Corinthian columns on its outer side, still stands. Certainly Hadrian's Library, with its quiet reading rooms and attractive peristyle, must have been an extremely pleasant place for browsing.

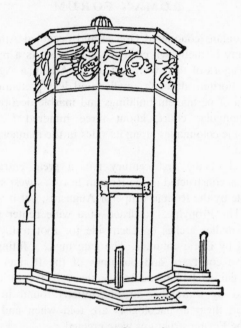

Tower of the Winds

TOWER OF THE WINDS

Southeast of the Roman Forum and adjacent to it lies the Tower of the Winds. This is a small eight-sided structure, about thirty feet wide and forty feet high, built of marble. It is in a good state of preservation and enables us to imagine quite clearly how it worked in ancient times. Among other things, it was a water-powered clock. Water, brought to it by an aqueduct, flowed into the clock's octagonal interior. There the hydraulic mechanism responded to the amounts of water fed to it from a storage place built against one side.

The tower roof is also eight-sided, and in ancient times had a weather vane on its peak. Doorways located in its two northern sides were reached by steps and small Corinthian porches. Each side of the octagonal structure faces a point of the compass, and long ago a sundial on each wall below the frieze was set to tell the time from each direction. Today we can still see the frieze around the upper part of the tower. The sculptured figures are extremely realistic and depict in stone the winds representing the eight compass points. Each figure is shown with his characteristic attributes and the entire frieze has great variety of expression and motion.

HADRIAN'S ARCH

The section of ancient Athens that lay beyond the walls built by Themistocles in the fifth century B.C. was built and ornamented by the Romans after they conquered the Athenians, and came to be

Hadrian's Arch

known as the City of Hadrian. Between the old and the new city a large gate, about sixty feet high, was erected. It had a wide arch set in a wall and edged on each side by an engaged Corinthian column. Above this rose a portico formed of Corinthian columns. The entire structure was of Pentelic marble and was originally decorated with statues and other sculpture, but these have disappeared. Inscriptions appear on opposite façades of the frieze. The one facing toward the Acropolis reads, "Here is Athens, the old town of Theseus." On the other is written, "Here is the town of Hadrian and no longer that of Theseus." It is from these inscriptions that the gate is commonly called Hadrian's Arch.

TEMPLE OF ZEUS

Early Temple Beyond Hadrian's Arch near the River Ilissus stood a sacred precinct where the Temple of Olympian Zeus was located. In the sixth century B.C., during the Age of the Tyrants, a temple to Zeus was begun on this site. It was planned in the Ionic style and was to have two rows of columns as an outer colonnade. The building material was tufa, a porous stone. Fragments and traces of this early temple have been found, but when the tyrants were overthrown, work on it was stopped before it had risen much above the foundations.

Temple of Olympian Zeus When Antiochus, ruler of Syria, undertook the completion of the temple, he planned an edifice on a grander scale to be built of Pentelic marble in the Corinthian style. He did not live to see this temple finished, however. It was the Roman Emperor Hadrian who saw the Corinthian temple completed and was present at its dedication in 132 A.D. Its columns were over fifty-six feet high and numbered 104 in all. They were set on a foundation of three steps. At each end were twenty-four columns in triple rows. There was a double row of columns on each side. In the cella was a chryselephantine statue of Zeus.

The Temple of Olympian Zeus has fallen prey to the vicissitudes of time. It was used as a stone quarry, as were many other ancient structures. Only fifteen of its graceful Corinthian columns now remain in place. One column was overturned in a tornado and lies where it fell. On the basis of what remains, however, and with the help of literary evidence and excavation it is possible to reconstruct the great temple as it was during Hadrian's time.

Remains of the Temple of Olympian Zeus

STADIUM

Location of the Stadium   The Panathenaic Stadium was built and used for the purpose implied in its name—the athletic competitions in the Panathenaic festival. Since it was necessary to have a large flat area where athletic contests such as running, javelin hurling, and wrestling could be held and watched comfortably by a great many people, a place was selected southeast of the Ilissus River and outside the city walls, almost a mile from the Acropolis. The main reason for this choice was that a ravine made a natural slope against which the tiers of seats could be constructed without having to build up the sides entirely with fill and retaining walls.

Construction of the Stadium   The stadium was built between the two sides of the ravine in a narrow horseshoe shape. The racecourse was almost seven hundred feet long, a distance greater than that required for foot races. The entrance was on the north side, and spectators reached their seats through a wide passage that ran around the lower part of the Stadium and was divided from the actual track by a low marble wall. The tiers of seats were separated into sections by twenty-nine flights of steps leading from the passage at their base. Approximately seventy thousand spectators could be accommodated in the Stadium.

Reconstruction of the Stadium   Although the Stadium was used at least as early as the fourth century B.C., it was not until the second century A.D. that Pentelic marble was used to build the fine permanent tiers of seats. This was done through the generosity of Herodes Atticus, who did so much to beautify Athens and other parts of Greece. When the Olympic games were revived in modern times, the Stadium was restored by another wealthy Greek, George Averoff. It was used when the games were held in Athens in 1896, with nine countries competing in the athletic contests.

CHAPTER NINE

Other Greek Cities

DELPHI

Location   Delphi is located in one of the most spectacular and beautiful spots in all Greece. Situated almost two thousand feet up the south side of lofty Mt. Parnassus, it is surrounded by rocky crags and deep ravines. Far below, the Pleistus River flows through a gorge between the mountains to empty into the Gulf of Corinth at Itea, called Cirrha when it was Delphi's ancient port.

Early History   In ancient times Delphi was important for a number of reasons. There is archaeological evidence that the site was used for religious purposes as far back as the Mycenaean Age. It was believed to be the center of the earth and was sacred, during its earliest period, to both Poseidon, god of the sea, and a divinity named Ge-Themis, representing the Earth and Justice. At that time it was known as Pytho. According to legend, a son of Ge, the Earth, was Python, a dragon or serpent. From the time of its early history there was an oracle at Pytho and the priestess of the oracle (originally a maiden but in later years a succession of older women) was called Pythia. When sailors from Cnossus came to Greece, they brought with them the dolphin god of Crete, Apollo Delphinius. The people of Pytho took up the worship of Apollo, who was said to have killed the dragon Python. The god was thereafter known as Pythian Apollo and the town was renamed Delphi. The priestess of the oracle then became the priestess of Apollo, although she continued to be called Pythia, and the prophecies she uttered as she sat on her tripod, where vapors arose from the ground through cracks in the rock, were believed to come from the god Apollo himself. Over the years people came from all parts of Greece, and from even greater distances, to consult the oracle. As a result, Delphi came to have great influence politically and in secular interests, as well as in religion, and grew in size and wealth as its prestige increased.

Pythian Games Because of Apollo's victory over the dragon Python, a festival in his honor was held at Delphi late in the summer. This festival took the form of the Pythian games, held every eight years, or, during some periods, every four years. Delegates from the Greek city-states came with offerings and gifts. Sacrifices were made in honor of Apollo's victory, and the killing of the dragon was re-enacted in a religious drama. Contests in song and on musical instruments celebrated the arts sacred to Apollo. At a later time dramatic contests in tragedy and comedy were included in the performances. Competitions in the various sports included chariot races. In order to accommodate adequately the spectators and many contestants for the laurel wreaths which were awarded to the winners, suitable buildings were erected. The remains of the Gymnasium, Palaestra, and Bath on the south slope, and of the Stadium and the Theater on the north slope have been excavated.

Gymnasium The Gymnasium was the place where the athletes trained. It was built in the fourth century B.C. on the upper of two man-made terraces which furnished level stretches of ground. A covered portico—almost six hundred feet long—made it possible to practice for foot races in bad weather. In front of this colonnade was an open racecourse of about the same dimensions. The Gymnasium proper was built around a courtyard with a portico.

Palaestra and Bath The Palaestra, where the wrestlers trained and practiced, was built on the terrace just below the Gymnasium. It consisted of a central courtyard with a colonnade around all four sides and nearby rooms where the wrestlers were anointed with oil, kept their clothing and equipment, or rested. Adjacent to the Palaestra was a circular pool for cold baths. This was supplied with running water, as were the wash basins set in a wall.

Temples of Athena The south slope was not devoted exclusively to athletics. Here there were also two rather small temples, both dedicated to Athena, one belonging to the end of the sixth or the begin-

Plan of the south slope

ning of the fifth century B.C., and the other to the fourth century B.C. Near the later temple is a charming piece of architecture, a tholos, built in the fifth century B.C. for a purpose that is not known. There were engaged Corinthian columns in the interior of the cella. The outside was surrounded by twenty columns in the Doric order.

Stadium The Stadium was built at the uppermost point of the ancient site—no mean climb for the athletes. This location was probably chosen because it offered both flat ground for the track and an embankment from which the tiers of seats on the long north side and the short west side could be hollowed out. A retaining wall was built on the south side to support the seats there. Except for the rows of seats on the south side, the Stadium is in a good state of preservation.

The Stadium was reconstructed during Roman times by Herodes Atticus, who rebuilt it in stone and added a triumphal archway at the entrance, which was located in the southeast corner. The racecourse was almost six hundred feet long and was marked off at each end by strips of marble to show the starting and finishing lines. The Stadium had stone seats, separated by stairways into sections, for about seven thousand persons. The north side had the greatest number of seats, since it had twelve tiers, as against six tiers on the west and south sides. The judges of the athletic contest sat on the north side in reserved seats with backs.

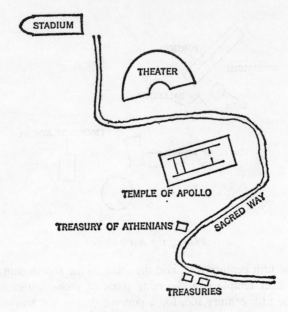

Plan of the north slope

Theater The Theater was erected on a terrace to the southeast of
and somewhat below the Stadium. It was built in the fourth century
B.C. and was later restored more than once. The Theater was reached
from below by a stone stairway, which remains in place today. Nothing remains of the stage's superstructure, but the tiers of white stone
seats are still in good condition. This auditorium could seat about
five thousand spectators.

Sacred Way The Sanctuary, or sacred precinct of Apollo, occupied
most of the steep hillside's north slope. It was a walled enclosure
with a number of entrances. The main entrance to the sacred enclosure was at the southeast. From this point the Sacred Way began its
ascent. It wound upward in a course of turns and bends to the Temple of Apollo. On either side of the Sacred Way were numerous terraces supported by retaining walls, to create spaces for buildings and
monuments of all sorts. The monuments were mainly votive and
thank offerings. Many of the monuments were dedicated for victories
in war. There were also numerous statues erected along the Sacred

Way. A number of these monuments bear inscriptions, which are helpful to archaeologists in identifying and dating them.

Treasuries The treasuries were built in the form of small temples, usually in the Doric style of architecture. They were erected chiefly to hold the wealth dedicated by the various city-states to Apollo. The Treasury of the Athenians, to the northwest of one of the bends in the Sacred Way, has been reconstructed and shows how this small but beautiful building looked in ancient times. It was erected by the Athenians as an offering of thanks after their defeat of the Persians at Marathon in 490 B.C. and was paid for out of the spoils of the battle. The Treasury is in the Doric order and has two columns at

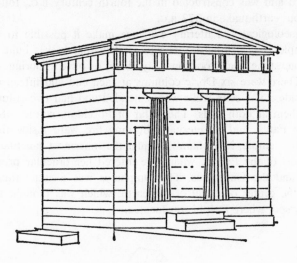

Treasury of the Athenians

the entrance. Its sculptured frieze depicted the deeds of Theseus and Hercules, a favorite subject of the Athenians.

Delphic Oracle Pythia, the priestess of Apollo, set forth the prophecies of the god and told the future. She did this from her seat on a tripod in the hall or innermost sanctuary of the Temple of Apollo, after having purified herself with sacred waters. Vapors and fumes contributed to her state of trance. She then uttered answers, generally ambiguous in nature, to questions put to her by individuals of all types who came to hear Apollo's prophecies. The questions usually had to do with everyday affairs, but as the Pythia's fame grew, she was often consulted on matters of state.

Temple of Apollo   The Temple of Apollo was used as a quarry and destroyed by earthquakes in ancient times, leaving very little to posterity but the foundations and some of the southeastern columns, none of them complete. The temple was built on a great terrace, which was supported by a huge polygonal retaining wall on the south and west sides. The first temple erected was burned in the sixth century B.C. It was rebuilt within fifty years. The present temple was the third and was constructed in the fourth century B.C., following a disastrous earthquake in 373 B.C.

Archaeological and literary evidence make it possible to describe the temple as it was before its final destruction. It was built of tufa, or porous stone, and stood on a **stylobate,** or paved flooring, of three steps. There were six Doric columns at each end and fifteen on each of the sides. The cella walls were extended and had two columns between them at both ends. The Altar of Poseidon, statues of Apollo and the Fates, and an eternally burning fire were inside the cella. Inside the temple, in a chamber under the innermost sanctuary, were the tripod of the Pythia, where she uttered her oracular pronouncements, and the Omphalus. The Omphalus was a stone that represented the center or navel of the earth, which was thought to be at the very spot where Delphi was located.

The Omphalus

Delphic League Following the Mycenaean Age, the Greek cities formed religious leagues. These grew, just as the town of Delphi did, to be motivated not only by religious but by political and commercial interests. One such league, composed of about twelve neighboring city-states which met at least once a year at Delphi to discuss matters of mutual importance and benefit, was the Delphic League. The Delphic League furthered the growth of Delphi, which continued to grow and to be beautified in tribute to its wide influence and that of Apollo throughout the history of ancient Greece. Some of the monuments and buildings were destroyed by earthquakes, so prevalent in that area, or by fire, or were plundered from time to time. In the fourth century A.D. the Roman Emperor Theodosius prohibited all cults and worship except the Christian religion, and Delphi fell into decline as a result of this edict.

Excavations at Delphi The work of nature—especially earthquakes—through the centuries covered up the remains of ancient Delphi. In modern times another town grew up on the site. Some excavation work was carried on by both German and French archaeologists in the nineteenth century, but was greatly hampered by the presence of the town of modern Delphi. By the end of the nineteenth century the French School of Archaeology undertook extensive excavations that necessitated the removal, at great expense, of modern Delphi to a position about a mile to the west, and the difficult task of carting away the rubble and dirt as digging to expose ancient Delphi extended far into the steep mountainside.

EPIDAURUS

Location Ancient Epidaurus was situated on the coast at the northeastern corner of the Peloponnesus. About six or seven miles from the sea was the sanctuary of Aesculapius, as famous in modern times as it was in antiquity. This great sacred precinct lay in a valley wide enough to accommodate its numerous buildings easily and comfortably. The hills surrounding the plain afforded protection from the elements and also presented a natural setting for the theater. The port of Epidaurus made the nearby sanctuary of Aesculapius easily accessible, and the two were connected by a beautiful and dignified Sacred

Way, along which pilgrims from all parts of the Greek world journeyed back and forth as they came to worship and seek new health.

Aesculapius Aesculapius was the Greek god of medicine. A number of myths and legends have survived through the ages, and, although versions vary in many details, all show that Aesculapius was the son of Apollo. His mother, Coronis, was generally believed to have come from Thessaly, but did not live to bring up her child. Instead he was said to have grown up in the mountains, where he learned the skills of medicine and curing human illnesses with the help of Apollo. Aesculapius met with such success in his healing that he was made a god, and numerous shrines and temples were dedicated to him after his death. One of the most important of these was the temple at Epidaurus, around which an extensive sanctuary was built.

Temple of Aesculapius The Temple of Aesculapius was designed by the architect Theodotus and was erected during the first part of the fourth century B.C. It was built in the Doric style and had six columns at each end and eleven on each side. Many pieces of sculpture from the temple have been found, making it possible to reconstruct a picture of the whole as it existed in ancient times, before the tiled wooden roof fell into decay and the painted and decorated entablature, pediments, and ornamental statues broke into fragments. We know that the statue of Aesculapius was bigger than life-size and was chryselephantine.

Other Buildings of the Sanctuary The length of the journey to the sanctuary of Aesculapius and the time it involved required that most visitors spend at least one night in the sacred precinct at Epidaurus. A large two-story hotel with about 150 rooms was built for this purpose. Another building of importance and one essential to the process of healing, was a portico called the **abaton.** It was here that the invalid slept, hopeful of the cure that would be brought to him while he was asleep, in the form of a dream or the appearance of the god Aesculapius himself. A large number of inscriptions found on the site attest to numerous cures of all sorts. Whether the healing was real or not, the sanctuary of Aesculapius was effective and its reputation and size continued to grow over a long period of time, covering the full era during which Greece was at her height.

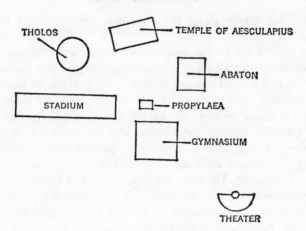

Plan of Epidaurus

Theater Perhaps the best known of all the structures in the sanctuary of Epidaurus is the great theater, and rightly so. Not only was it the most impressive and perfect of all ancient Grecian theaters, but it has survived through the centuries and gives archaeologists an excellent example of its type. The theater was built in the second half of the fourth century B.C., and its remarkable state of preservation as well as the perfection of its form and acoustics are more than a credit to the architect Polycleitus. Of the stage only the foundations

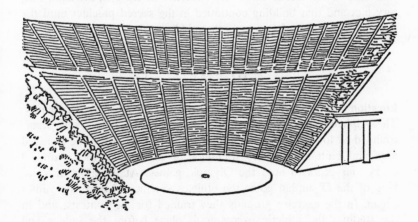

Theater at Epidaurus

remain, but almost all of the seats and stairways have been preserved.

The plan of the theater was at once simple and beautiful. The orchestra is a perfect circle. A person standing in the orchestra and speaking in a normal tone, or even in a whisper, can be heard clearly and perfectly from any seat in the theater. Some rebuilding of the outer and upper sections of seats has been necessary, but for the most part this area of the theater, like the orchestra, is well preserved—probably because neighboring peoples did not need it as a quarry. The theater is in use today and its seating capacity is about fourteen thousand. The seats are arranged in two sections. The lower thirty-four tiers of seats are divided by stairways into twelve wedge-shaped sections. A broad aisle or **diazoma** forms a passage in front of the upper twenty-one tiers of seats, which are partitioned by stairways into twenty-four sections.

Excavations at Epidaurus　　In 1881 the Greek Archaeological Society began excavations on the sanctuary of Epidaurus. Most of the remains have now been unearthed, but reconstruction work and research are still going on. All that has been excavated to date bears witness to the fame and importance of the site. Archaeologists are supplied with a fine example of a typical sanctuary of Aesculapius and the visitor can see before him the plan of the various buildings connected with healing the sick. Excavation has revealed that the sanctuary at Epidaurus came into existence as early as the sixth century B.C. and that building continued in the sacred precinct until the Roman occupation of Greece in the middle of the second century A.D.

OLYMPIA

Location　　The location of Olympia is one of great scenic beauty. The Alpheus and Cladeus rivers run through a broad valley surrounded by low-lying hills. Here the ancient Greeks set aside a sacred area and built a sanctuary in honor of Zeus. Here they gathered every four years to hold the Olympic games. At the altar of Zeus, king of the Olympian gods, the athletes sacrificed before the games began. In the exercise grounds they trained for the contests, and in the stadium the athletic events took place before the judges and spectators.

Olympic Games In the year 776 B.C. the first Olympic games were held at Olympia. They took place every four years after that until the end of the fourth century A.D., when the Roman emperor brought them to an end. These athletic contests were local at first, but later included all the Greeks of the Hellenic world. That the Olympic games were of great importance is shown by the Greek system of dating. The year of the first Olympic games was taken as a starting point in the chronology of the ancient Greeks. Each four-year period was called an Olympiad. Further division of time was made possible by designating the first, second, third, or fourth year of a given Olympiad. On the basis of inscriptions, literature, and other evidence archaeologists have been able to figure out that the first year of the first Olympiad corresponds to the year 776 B.C. in our reckoning.

The Olympic games were held every four years in the summer during a full moon. The organization of the festival and the nature of the events changed from time to time during the long history of the games, which included almost three hundred contests in ancient times. A description of the games as they existed when Greece was at the height of her power gives, perhaps, the most comprehensive picture. At all times the games had a religious significance combined with a desire to please the participants and spectators as well as the gods with a demonstration of the best features of a highly trained body, mind, and spirit. Those who entered each event had developed their individual skills to the point where they represented a peak of perfection worthy of their gods and their fellow citizens. The men who competed had not only to be pure-blooded Greeks, but honorable and upright of character. When the dates of the Olympic games were announced, a sacred truce or cessation of hostilities was proclaimed at the same time. This made it possible for all who were to take part in the games, either as competitors or as spectators, to make the journey from all parts of the Greek world to honor Zeus and the other gods at Olympia.

After an oath was administered to all contestants, the competitions began. Among the athletic events were foot races as well as horse and chariot races. One of the outstanding events was the **pentathlon,** or series of five athletic competitions. These were jumping, javelin throwing, a foot race, discus throwing, and wrestling. Boxing matches were held, in which the boxers had leather straps, called **cestuses,** wound over their fists and wrists to serve as boxing gloves. Events were also held in some of the arts, such as poetry, music, and drama.

An olive branch and a palm branch were presented to the victors, as well as all the honors accorded to heroes.

Altis   The sacred grove of Olympia is called the **Altis.** In this walled enclosure were located all the buildings connected with the worship of Zeus. Of those in existence today, the building considered to be the oldest is a temple dedicated to Hera, wife of Zeus. This temple was Doric and had six columns at each end with sixteen on each side. The Temple of Zeus was also Doric in style, but considerably larger than Hera's Temple. It, too, had six columns on the front and rear porches, but only thirteen on each side.

The Temple of Zeus was erected during the middle of the fifth century B.C. Enough fragments of the great sculpture that adorned the temple have been found to reconstruct some of the scenes that were depicted in stone. On the east pediment was a mythological scene: the preparation for a chariot race between Pelops and Oenomaus for the winning of the latter's daughter, Hippodamia, with Zeus as the central figure. On the west pediment another legend, the battle between the Centaurs and the Lapithae, was sculptured, with Apollo in the center. Fragments of the metopes show that these bore sculptures of the Labors of Hercules. In the temple was one of the Seven Wonders of the Ancient World, the throned statue of Zeus. All that remains of this statue is the literary evidence of ancient writers. It was a huge chryselephantine statue, created by the superb craftsman Phidias. We know that the statue was burned in a fire in A.D. 475, shortly after it had been taken from Olympia to Constantinople, which had then been for many years the western capital of the Roman Empire.

On the north side of Olympia rises a cone-shaped hill called Mt. Cronion, which was sacred to Cronus, father of Zeus. The hill of Cronus is a gentle, pine-covered slope about four hundred feet high. At its base, along the side of the Altis, the Greek states placed their treasuries. These treasuries, like those at other sacred enclosures, were built both as offerings to the gods, especially for victories in the games, and to hold in a safe place the wealth of gifts brought by Greek citizens to be dedicated to their deities.

The treasuries were all very similar in construction and were built side by side on a terrace. They were in the shape of small Doric temples, with one large room for storing the offerings. An entrance porch was supported in most cases by two columns, although some treas-

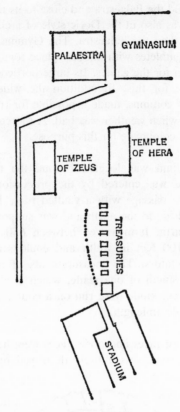

Plan of Olympia

uries were larger and had four columns. There were originally twelve treasuries in all, as we know from contemporary literary evidence and from the remains of the foundations. Fortunately, enough fragments of a number of them are left to make it possible for archaeologists to reconstruct a clear picture of this row of buildings.

Palaestra Outside the sacred precinct and to the northwest stood the Palaestra. This consisted of a large open courtyard with colonnades all around it. Each side of the Palaestra measured over two hundred feet, and rooms on all four sides of the building opened through the Doric portico onto the courtyard. The Palaestra was built in the third century B.C. and here the athletes who were to compete in such events as jumping, boxing, and wrestling trained and exercised.

Gymnasium   Beyond the Palaestra and close to its north side was the Gymnasium. This was also in the Doric style of architecture, but was considerably larger than the Palaestra. The Gymnasium's chief function was to provide athletes with another place for training and exercising in preparation for the games. Its large porticoed courtyard furnished ample space for this. In addition the wide porticoes, with their double rows of columns, made it possible for runners to practice in a sheltered place when weather was bad. A racecourse was marked off under the roofed colonnade for this purpose.

Stadium   The Stadium was located beyond the treasuries on the hill of Cronus. This was entered by the procession of competitors through a long stone passage with a vaulted roof. The Stadium was built against the hillside to the north and was supported on the other sides by built-up earth. It measured between 650 and 700 feet in length and about 100 feet in width and could seat approximately forty thousand spectators. The measurements of a Greek stadium were based on the length of one **stade,** which is about six hundred feet. Races of different kinds were run on a course that was a stade, or multiples of a stade, in length.

Hippodrome   Chariot races and horse races were held in the Hippodrome. The Hippodrome was entirely destroyed by flooding of the

Entrance to the stadium

Alpheus River over the centuries, but in antiquity it stood south of the Stadium.

Excavations at Olympia The site of Olympia gradually became buried by centuries of deposits, especially those left when the nearby rivers overflowed. Extensive excavations were carried on by German archaeologists, directed by Ernst Curtius, at the end of the nineteenth century and have been continued in the twentieth. Work is currently in progress to excavate the Stadium more completely and to restore it where possible.

DELOS

Location There is a rocky island in the middle of the Aegean Sea, one of the Cyclades group. Although the tiny island is only about a mile square, it rises sharply toward the east to the peak of Mt. Cynthus, 350 feet high. According to mythical legend, Leto gave birth on Delos to twin children of Zeus. They were Apollo and Artemis, who shared many attributes, among them hunting and singing. The island of Delos became sacred to both Apollo and Artemis, and an annual festival was celebrated there in antiquity.

History From archaeological evidence something of the island's history is now known. Delos was probably settled by people from Asia Minor, who established colonies on many of the Aegean islands for purposes of trade. Traces of dwellings belonging to this period of prehistory have been found on Mt. Cynthus and are dated as early as the second millennium B.C. Delos appears to have been an important religious and commercial center, and for these reasons attracted visitors and settlers in increasing numbers. By the third century B.C. a large and prosperous town had grown up on Delos. The archaeological remains of the religious, commercial, and residential buildings that are seen on the island today belong chiefly to that period and the following centuries. As was the case with all the parts of Greece that fell under Roman domination by the end of the second century B.C., a certain amount of rebuilding was carried out on Delos by the Romans. By the following century, however, the prosperity and wealth of Delos fell prey to the pirates who roamed the Aegean Sea and plundered what they saw. As a result, Delos gradually declined until it was important only for religious reasons. When the worship of the ancient gods was prohibited by the Roman emperors in the fourth century A.D., Delos no longer had anything to support her existence and so fell into ruins.

The Port   The ancient port, on the west side of the island, was used by pilgrims coming to the island for religious purposes and by traders who came only for commerce. Accordingly, the harbor was in two sections. The ancient sacred harbor was toward the north, close to the sacred precinct and more important shrines. Toward the south was the commercial harbor, fringed with the wharves, warehouses, shops, and similar business buildings of the area devoted to commerce and trade.

The City   The residential area was located to the south and east, beyond the commercial quarter. Paved streets with a good system of drainage are lined on both sides with houses, many of which are in a good state of preservation. Their owners' wealth is manifested in the large size and fine construction of a number of the houses. Colonnaded courtyards, beautiful mosaic pavements, flights of steps that led to upper stories, graceful columns, wall paintings, statuary, and ornamental decoration all contributed to the beauty of these houses.

The Greek House   The private dwellings of the Greeks varied somewhat with the size of the house, but were built according to a common general plan. The Greek house was usually built close to the street to be easily accessible to those who came on business. The front door opened directly into a vestibule. On either side of the vestibule were the porter's room and the rooms where the master of the house conducted his business. These chambers might be where a lawyer met his clients, or a merchant had his shop, or a landowner saw his tenants. In some cases additional shops facing on the street were rented out to shopkeepers of all kinds, selling wine, bread, oil, pottery, or any one of countless products.

Beyond the section that faced on the street was the main part of the house, where the family lived. The vestibule opened onto a large open courtyard, with columns surrounding it and forming a portico. In the center there often stood an altar to Zeus, guardian of family life. The living quarters were built around this central rectangular court and consisted of the bedrooms, dining room, living room, and the like. The slaves' quarters were generally in the back part of the house. The house usually had a garden in the rear, and larger homes often had a second courtyard, called a **peristyle,** with columns on all

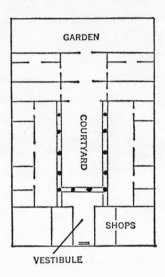

Plan of a Greek house

sides, plantings, fountains, statues, and other decoration, which made it a pleasant outdoor gathering place.

Many of the houses had an upper story with additional rooms corresponding to those below. Decorative mosaic pavements, wall paintings, graceful furniture, beautiful pottery and household utensils made the homes of the Greeks, especially those of the wealthy, very pleasant places in which to live.

Theater A theater was built in the residential quarter of Delos during the first part of the second century B.C. Unfortunately it is not in a good state of preservation, but we know that the stage was approximately fifty feet long and built in the Doric style with engaged columns and a row of triglyphs and metopes above. On the metopes were sculptures of tripods and the heads of bulls.

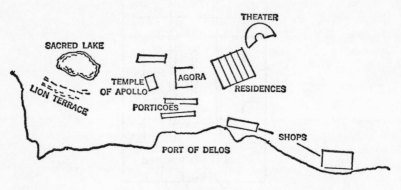

Plan of Delos

Sanctuary The religious sanctuary of Delos covered most of the area northeast of the port and parts of the slope and summit of Mt. Cynthus. The approach from the sea was a colonnaded one, through long porticoes and the Propylaea. The Temple of Apollo, located within the sacred precinct, was close to one hundred feet long and built of local marble. There were six Doric columns at each end and thirteen on each of the sides, with two columns *in antis* at each end of the cella. This Temple of Apollo was started during the fifth century B.C. Work began on the temple when the Delian Confederacy was established. This was a union between the Athenians and the Greeks of the Aegean area, formed after the Persian Wars for mutual protection, and was supported by contributions of ships and money from its members. Delos was chosen as the place for the safekeeping of the money, and the treasury was in the Temple of Apollo. Near the temple, the base and fragments of a colossal statue of Apollo were discovered. Inscriptions tell archaeologists that the marble statue was erected in the sixth century B.C. as a votive offering from the people of Naxos.

Within the sacred precinct of Artemis was a temple dedicated to the goddess. This was in the Ionic style and was rebuilt in the second century B.C. Ivory figures of animals and humans in relief sculpture have been found in the sanctuary's vicinity and are dated from the Mycenaean Age.

North of the Temple of Apollo was a row of small templelike treasuries, and a long portico was erected behind them. Beyond this was the Sacred Lake. Here the sacred swans of Apollo are supposed to have been kept. On the west side of the Sacred Lake was the Lion Terrace. This had a row of nine lions on pedestals facing toward the Sacred Lake. They were carved in the archaic style, of marble from Naxos. The terrace was over 150 feet long, and five of the great lions can still be seen.

Lion Terrace

Mt. Cynthus   Near the summit of Mt. Cynthus were the sanctuaries of foreign gods. These temples and shrines were erected on terraces and were dedicated to the deities of the Syrians and Egyptians. At the peak was a sanctuary of Zeus and Athena.

Excavations at Delos   The French School of Archaeology undertook excavations on Delos in the second half of the nineteenth century. Work has been carried on by the French since that time, with only a few interruptions. At present the site has been quite extensively excavated, and with the help of the Greek Government an excellent museum has been built to house the numerous artifacts brought to light in the course of excavation. The excavations as a whole can be divided roughly into three categories, according to the use to which each area was put in ancient times—the commercial, residential, and religious, each with its distinctive buildings, as we have described above.

CORINTH

Location Ancient Corinth was located on the Isthmus that lies between the Gulf of Corinth to the west and the Gulf of Athens to the east. Situated more than a mile inland from the Gulf of Corinth, at the foot of an acropolis called Acrocorinth, which rose almost two thousand feet above it, the ancient city was well protected. By its situation on a fertile slope not far from its ports on the Isthmus, Corinth could support a population of farmers and traders and could command land traffic moving between northern and southern Greece and sea traffic moving from east and west.

History Traces of habitations dating from about 4000 B.C. have been found by archaeologists, but the earliest inhabitants were apparently overwhelmed by invaders. The site was resettled by Greeks after the Dorian invasions. This settlement of the first millennium B.C. grew steadily in importance and size, due mainly to its very favorable location. Pottery, bronzes, and tiles were among the articles made at Corinth and shipped to many parts of the Greek world. In exchange, many items of necessity and luxury were brought back to the city, which became increasingly wealthy. As the population and trade of ancient Corinth expanded, colonists were sent out and colonies established in many parts of the eastern Mediterranean. By 600 B.C. there was growing rivalry with Athens over trade, especially over pottery exports. The strength of Athens weakened that of Corinth, and, although Corinth recovered periodically and temporarily from the vicissitudes of wars and commercial struggles, she fell under Roman domination by the beginning of the second century B.C.

In the year 146 B.C. Corinth was burned and destroyed as a result of her rebellion against Rome's power. The men of the city were killed, and the women and children were sold as slaves. A century later, Julius Caesar rebuilt the city and Romanized it. About A.D. 50 St. Paul lived in Corinth for more than a year. Corinth gradually experienced a revival of her former power during the first and second centuries A.D., until she again became a great and thriving city, a center of commerce and culture. A period of invasions and earthquakes through the third, fourth, and fifth centuries A.D. led to decline from which ancient Corinth never recovered.

City Walls The walls of ancient Corinth, which stretched for approximately ten miles, protected the city over the distance from Acrocorinth to its main port on the Gulf of Corinth. Roads entered the city from the direction of its ports and from the overland highway. A road led into the Agora from the north from the port of Lechaeum on the Gulf of Corinth; from the south from the port of Cenchrae on the Gulf of Athens; and from the west from the town of Sicyon.

Lechaeum Road The Lechaeum Road was a broad, paved street bordered by sidewalks and colonnades leading into rows of small shops. It was the main entrance to the Agora from the busy port of Lechaeum. Remains of baths belonging to the second century A.D. have been found on the east side, and a fifth-century B.C. market was found on the west side of the Lechaeum Road, but excavations have been hampered because structures belonging to various building periods have been superimposed on each other. At the end of the

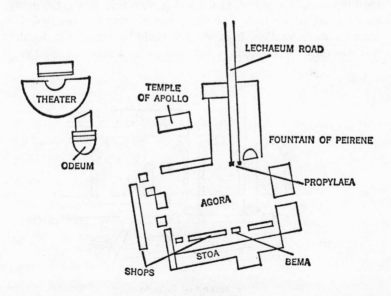

Plan of Corinth

Lechaeum Road flights of marble steps and a monumental gate, or
Propylaea, made an imposing entrance to the Agora of the ancient
city.

Agora   Changes and rebuilding in the Agora during Roman times
created a complexity of buildings that largely erased the appearance
of the marketplace as it was before the Romans arrived to destroy
it and reconstruct it as a Roman market. Excavations have unearthed
a long Greek **stoa** on the south side. This was a colonnade with
front columns in the Doric order and Ionic columns on the inner
side. There were two rows of shops behind this stoa and opening
from it.

Bema   In front of the south stoa was another long row of shops,
in the center of which was a **bema,** or speaker's platform, from
which people assembled in the Agora could be addressed. The marble of the bema was highly decorated with sculptured ornamentations, but these have almost entirely disappeared. It was from this
bema that St. Paul spoke to the Corinthians.

Fountain of Peirene   The Fountain of Peirene lay to the east of
the Propylaea. The waters of the spring were held in a great storage
area cut out of the rock. The water flowed from this reservoir into
three basins or sections, from which it could be drawn. The fountain
was decorated by a façade, which underwent a series of changes in

Fountain of Peirene

the course of Corinth's history. An Ionic portico at one time, it became a large ornamental arcade when the Romans occupied Corinth.
A fine, walled courtyard with a basin in the center and ornamented
with mosaics and statuary was built of marble in the second century
A.D., quite probably by the famous benefactor Herodes Atticus,
making the Fountain of Peirene a truly beautiful structure.

Temple of Apollo Seven columns of the Temple of Apollo to the
northwest of the Agora still stand in place and dominate the landscape of ancient Corinth. The Temple was erected about the middle
of the sixth century B.C. The Doric columns are heavy and archaic
in shape, measuring less than twenty-four feet in height. The column
shafts are monoliths, each cut with twenty flutings, and there were
originally six columns at each end and fifteen on each side of the
Temple.

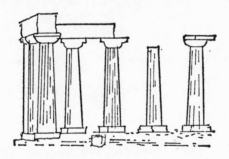

Temple of Apollo

Theaters The smaller of the two theaters situated beyond the
Temple of Apollo is an odeon cut out of the rock of a hillside. It
held approximately three thousand people and was built in the first
century A.D. The Odeon was rebuilt in marble by Herodes Atticus
and underwent changes several times after that. The larger theater
nearby was built as early as the fourth century B.C., but was replaced by a Roman structure. When the Odeon was beautified by
Herodes Atticus, a colonnade was built to join it to the Theater. At
one period the Romans converted the Theater into an arena, and
although it was used for theatrical performances after that, the
Theater fell into ruins during the general decline of ancient Corinth.

Excavations at Corinth   Excavations were undertaken at the site of ancient Corinth at the end of the nineteenth century by the American School of Classical Studies and have been continued since that time without interruption except during wartime. Excavation, study, and research have brought to light most of the ancient Agora, the Theater and the Odeon, and many pieces of sculpture and other artifacts that enable archaeologists to re-create the appearance and life of the ancient city.

Colonists from Corinth and from numerous other Greek cities settled throughout the Mediterranean world. They took with them the traditions and culture of their homeland and kept them alive. In turn, all those with whom the Greek settlers came in contact felt the glory and splendor of the Greek civilization, absorbed it, and made it their own. Thus the grandeur of Greece was not extinguished with the past, but helped to kindle the flame of the future.

CHAPTER TEN

Early Italy

Geography Civilization did not come to the Italian Peninsula until the peoples of the eastern end of the Mediterranean had well-advanced cultures. This late development tended to make the inhabitants of Italy copiers and imitators rather than creators, and the Romans, therefore, came to direct their energies more toward power and conquest than toward cultural and intellectual activities. This was partly due to Italy's location and to the geography of the Italian Peninsula. The Apennine Mountains, running down the middle of the peninsula, made a division that separated the more desirable west coast from the east and forced the people to look more toward the west than toward the civilized east. Its strategic location at the center of the Mediterranean gave Italy a tremendous advantage in trade and control of the seas. This led the Italians to develop a taste for expansion and domination.

Early History There was probably habitation in Italy as early as 3000 B.C. Archaeological study of the remains of pottery and implements dating from that period indicates that the earliest inhabitants led a primitive but settled type of life, similar to that of other Mediterranean peoples of the Late Stone Age. By the next millennium settlers came into Italy from both the eastern Mediterranean area and the north, bringing with them the use of bronze. During the Bronze Age the inhabitants of the Italian Peninsula were divided into many separate groups or tribes, all having many characteristics in common, but differing in the dialects they spoke and the sections of Italy in which they lived. Among the more important groups of people were the Oscans in the coastal regions of the south, the Samnites in the mountains, and the Latins in the central plains of the west coast.

Map of Italy

Etruscans Another group of people arrived in Italy at some time following the Trojan War. It is quite possible that they came from Asia Minor. They settled on the western coast along the Tiber River and reached a high point of civilization and influence. These people were called the **Etruscans** and the region in which they lived was known as **Etruria.**

Magna Graecia Not long after the arrival of the Etruscans, Greek colonists established settlements on the island of Sicily and all along the southern coast of the Italian Peninsula. These settlers from Greece came primarily for purposes of trade, but they brought with them all the characteristics of Greek civilization, and the area they occupied was known as **Magna Graecia,** or *Great Greece*. From about

800 B.C. onward the influence of Magna Graecia was strong and continued to grow until about the third century B.C., when the Romans conquered and absorbed the area.

ETRURIA

Almost all that is now known about the Etruscans has come down to us through the resources of archaeology. The people of ancient Etruria built with stone and so it has been possible to unearth the remains of their cities. They also had a deep concern with, and belief in, a future life, and the detailed preparations they made for a life after death have provided a rich source for archaeologists, who can look back over more than twenty centuries and re-create the characteristics of the lives and culture of the Etruscans and their history.

Excavations in Etruria As early as the sixteenth century statues and some other traces of the Etruscans were found, and during the eighteenth century some excavating was done by the Italians. It was not until the latter part of the nineteenth century, however, that large-scale and systematic excavations were carried on. The new impetus that has been given to archaeological methods in recent years by the use of aerial photography has been especially helpful in locating Etruscan tombs and in determining which among the vast number of tombs might be worth further investigation. With the invention and use of a tiny camera device that can be lowered into a tomb and can actually photograph the interior, much time and expense can be saved. Effort can be devoted to those tombs which the photographic plates indicate as potentially most worthwhile and rewarding.

Etruscan Language Some explanation of what is not known about the Etruscans may give a better idea of some of the problems and many unsolved mysteries confronting archaeologists. The Etruscan language—with the exception of some proper names and a few of the more common words—has not yet been deciphered. The Etruscans did, however, leave behind them a vast amount of material, chiefly inscriptions, for palaeographers and specialists in linguistics to puzzle over, and it is possible that these will eventually yield fresh clues leading to decipherment. In the meantime, work is hampered by the brevity and similarity of the inscriptions, since most of them deal with burial or religion and are not long enough or sufficiently varied to be of real help. It has been determined that the Etruscans took the Greek alphabet and adapted it to their own use, with changes and modifications in accordance with the differences between the two languages and the needs of their own. To date, it seems that Etruscan is not related to other known ancient languages. It is hoped that a text which is bilingual, possibly Etruscan and Greek or Latin, may be found.

Etruscan Cities Relatively less is known about Etruscan cities than about those of other ancient peoples because, although built in stone for the most part, much has been destroyed and very little has reached us across the centuries. Not much is visible above the ground except foundations. From these, however, and from countless architectural fragments it is possible to visualize and reconstruct the plans and even the buildings themselves. There are also sections of city walls with their gates and towers still standing in many places. Those cities that have been discovered and excavated give us considerable general information and some details.

The Etruscans built large towns and located them on hills when feasible. Cities were fortified and protected by walls and towers. The chief deities corresponded to Jupiter, Juno, and Minerva. At the highest point in each city was a temple, usually built of wood or sun-dried brick, with two columns on the porch, and terra-cotta ornaments. In the square interior there was always a statue of the deity to whom the temple was dedicated.

Among the more important cities were Tarquinia, Caere, and Veii. We know, also from excavations, that the Etruscans settled close to the sea and the Tiber River along the west coast of Italy in a section stretching about two hundred miles in length. The first settlements were probably made at the beginning of the first millennium B.C. Evidence indicates that the early inhabitants settled along the coast, no doubt for purposes of trade, and that the population later spread inland as farming gained in importance. The Romans called these people to the north Etrusci or Tusci, a name that has survived in the Italian district of Tuscany. They were called Tyrrhenians by the Greeks and gave that name to the sea along their coast.

Map of Etruria

Etruscans and Romans By the time the Etruscans were at the height of their power, during the sixth and fifth centuries B.C., there was enough contact between them and the Greeks and Romans for the latter to leave us some literary evidence about the Etruscans. At the same time, the Etruscans left a definite imprint upon Roman civilization. We, therefore, find among Roman remains tangible evidence that can be traced back to the Etruscans. The Etruscans influenced the Romans in architecture, by giving them the round arch and the principle of the keystone and vault; in methods of fighting, especially the use of the two-wheeled chariot; in religious beliefs and many of the attributes of their deities; and in the arts, primarily sculpture, painting, and metal work.

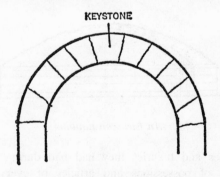

Arch and keystone

The Etruscans had been conquered during the period of Roman expansion throughout Italy in the third century B.C. and the two peoples mingled, with the result that many Romans were of Etruscan blood. Etruria, however, declined after she lost her power, and her influence had merged with Rome and disappeared as a separate entity by the first century B.C.

Etruscan Tombs An Etruscan necropolis was quite literally a city of the dead. The cemeteries were built outside the city walls, as was customary in ancient times, and everything about them indicated a strong belief in a future life. They were laid out with streets that were generally paved, and the tombs flanked the streets like houses. The earliest tombs, dating from about the eighth century B.C., were trench tombs, but by the seventh century B.C. a tomb had two or more underground chambers. In other ways, too, the **tumuli** (plural of **tumulus,** the burial mound) took on the appearance of subterranean houses. They were cut into the natural rock, which in that area was tufa, and were entered by means of steps leading down from a doorway or street entrance. The part of the structure that was aboveground was a circular stone base with an earthen mound on top. The rooms were large and arranged as those in a house would be. Niches for funeral urns and stone couches where the dead were laid the only indications that it was not the home of the living.

The sepulchral chambers of the Etruscans act as documents which can be studied and interpreted by archaeologists to explain the civilization represented by them. The dead were supplied with the

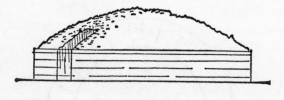

An Etruscan tumulus

same necessities and luxuries they had had during life. Furniture and all kinds of possessions and articles of everyday use were buried with the dead. Although in many cases looters in ancient times removed a great deal from a number of the tombs, enough remained untouched and intact and can now tell archaeologists many details about the Etruscans' civilization and life.

Etruscan Art Many works of art have survived from the ancient Etruscans. These show that they were skilled craftsmen who directed their taste for luxury toward creating objects of beauty. They also made good use of the mineral resources of that section of Italy, which yielded an excellent supply of iron and copper. Other materials came to the Etruscans through trade. We have numerous pieces of jewelry, finely wrought in gold, and a large number of ivory objects. Etruscan pottery shows the strong influence of imported Greek vases, but also had its own individual characteristics. Made by hand, it took a wide variety of forms and shapes and was richly decorated. Etruscan pottery was predominantly black in color, called **bucchero** ware, but other colors—especially browns, reds, and yellows—were also used. A large quantity of Etruscan bronzes has come down to us. Many of these had to do with fighting and include such items as bronze chariots, helmets, and shields. Bronze was also used extensively for statues, mirrors, lamps, and cinerary urns. Urns and statuettes were also frequently made of terra cotta, as were the ornamentations of temples and other buildings.

Inside the chamber tombs, mural paintings and relief sculptures abound and are fine examples of Etruscan art. They, too, tell us the story of the activities, appearance, and even the ideas of the ancient Etruscans. The frescoed scenes painted on the walls of the chambers offer a rich variety in both subject matter and execution. Most of the paintings depict scenes from life. Hunting and fishing; athletics and sports, dancing and music are represented. Animals and humans, flowers, birds, and fish are brought to life and have their places, as do geometrical patterns. Other wall paintings tell something of the Etruscans' thoughts about death, their belief in a future life, and their deities and myths. Supplementing the store of information that can be gained from the polychrome-frescoed walls is that furnished by the sculptured bas-reliefs. These cover a wide range of items that were in common use. A vast assortment of household objects—such as a coil of rope, an ax, or a kettle—is represented. Pets and domestic animals also appear in the relief sculptures.

No one can walk among the remains of ancient Etruria, especially the elaborate cities of the dead, without sensing the high point of culture and civilization the Etruscans attained during the centuries in which they flourished, and the permanency, vividness, and superior technique of their artistic creations.

CHAPTER ELEVEN

Rome

IMPORTANT DATES IN EARLY ITALIAN AND ROMAN HISTORY

c. 3000 B.C.	Habitation in Italy
c. 800 B.C.	Greek Colonies in Magna Graecia
753 B.C.	Founding of Rome
753–509 B.C.	Rule of Kings
509–27 B.C.	Roman Republic
390 B.C.	Rome sacked by Gauls
350–265 B.C.	Roman expansion over Italy
264–241 B.C.	First Punic War against Carthage
218–201 B.C.	Second Punic War
149–146 B.C.	Third Punic War
146 B.C.	Carthage and Corinth destroyed
44 B.C.	Assassination of Julius Caesar
27 B.C.–A.D. 14	Rule of Augustus
27 B.C.–A.D. 476	Roman Empire
A.D. 117	Roman Empire at greatest extent, under Trajan
A.D. 307–337	Rule of Constantine
A.D. 410	Rome sacked by Goths
A.D. 476	Fall of Western Empire

Location At the beginning of the first millennium B.C., the earliest settlers chose a place along the Tiber River about fifteen miles upstream from the sea to establish a village that was to become Rome. There were seven hills in the vicinity and the valley near the river was swampy. The valley was bordered by the Capitoline Hill on the west and by the Palatine Hill on the south. To the east was the Esquiline Hill, and to the north the Quirinal Hill. The first settlement was quite probably on the Palatine Hill, above the valley.

Founding of Rome   The traditional date given for the founding of Rome is 753 B.C. Nevertheless, there undoubtedly were people living along the Tiber Valley in the period of prehistory which preceded that date. The region south of the Tiber River was known as **Latium**

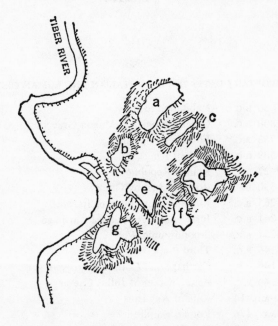

The Hills of Rome: a–Quirinal. b–Capitoline. c–Viminal. d–Esquiline. e–Palatine. f–Caelian. g–Aventine

and the people were called **Latins.** Rome was ruled by kings from the time of its founding until the end of the sixth century B.C., or approximately 509 B.C., according to modern calculations and reckoning of time. During the last century of that period, Rome was under the domination of the Etruscans, who conquered and ruled the city. When the Etruscans were overthrown, Rome became a republic.

The Roman Republic During the time of the Roman Republic, Rome was a democracy under the control of her citizens—although citizenship was limited at first to the upper class. The powers of the king were placed in the hands of two consuls, who were elected annually. About 390 B.C. the Gauls entered Rome and sacked the city, but were driven out shortly afterward. During the four centuries of its existence, the Roman Republic came to include all classes of citizens in the government. Toward the end of that period, however, greed for power led to dictatorships and rule by one man, and ultimately to the establishment of the empire under Augustus in 27 B.C.

Punic Wars While these changes in government were occurring, changes were also taking place in the political power of Italy. Rome began to subjugate her neighbors in the fourth century B.C., and her power steadily expanded to include all of Italy a century later. When Rome had subdued the Greek cities of southern Italy and eastern Sicily, she ran into conflict with Carthage—which had colonies in western Sicily—over control of that section of the Mediterranean and its commerce. The struggle between the two cities broke into a series of wars, the Punic Wars, which lasted from 264–146 B.C. with intervals of peace between, until Rome emerged from the long contest victorious and powerful. Her territory then included Italy, Sardinia, Corsica, Spain, and northwestern Africa. In addition, she had gained supremacy over Macedonia and Greece through wars fought in retaliation for Macedonia's aid to Carthage during the Punic Wars. Both conflicts ended in 146 B.C. when Rome destroyed both Carthage and Corinth.

Provinces By the second century B.C. the Roman Army had become a highly organized and well-trained body, under the leadership of skillful generals. Each conquered territory was ruled by a governor, who was appointed to govern the civil and military affairs of his province. He was backed up by units of the army that were stationed in each province to keep the peace and to speed the process of Romanization. Meanwhile soldiers and generals alike, realizing their contribution to the power of Rome and Rome's resulting dependency upon them, demanded and gained more and more benefits and rights. The republican form of government grew weaker

during the last part of the second century B.C. as the law and the
constitution were disregarded and democratic methods were replaced
by riots and force.

Dictatorship In the first century B.C. one leader after another set
himself up in power—seized through military strength and mob popularity—and became a dictator. Julius Caesar, fresh from his conquest of Gaul and his invasion of Britain, entered Rome with his
army in 49 B.C., seized power, and was soon the undisputed dictator. By that time Rome was without a rival in the Mediterranean
world. Many of the reforms introduced by Caesar and laws passed
under his rule were needed and beneficial. Caesar's success, nevertheless, created enemies and he was assassinated in 44 B.C.

The Empire By 31 B.C. Octavius, Caesar's nephew, had defeated
his political rivals, and in 27 B.C. he established a new type of
government. Octavius took the title and name of Augustus and became the first Roman emperor. The framework of the constitutional
government was retained, but the powers of the officials were weakened and finally absorbed completely by the emperor, who thus
became an absolute ruler. The reign of Augustus was one of peace
and prosperity. When Augustus died in A.D. 14, he left behind a well-
established monarchy and a beautiful city.

The emperors who followed Augustus varied greatly in ability
and accomplishments, but the Roman Empire continued to grow
in strength and size. Throughout the next century frontiers were
fortified, laws were made uniform, and government administration
was improved. On the other hand, the Christians were persecuted
and Jerusalem was destroyed. By A.D. 117, at the end of Trajan's
reign, the Roman Empire reached its greatest extent geographically.
Its borders stretched from the Atlantic Ocean to the Caspian Sea
and from England to Egypt. The emperors of the second century
A.D. are known as the "good emperors." The empire was unified
and solidified, largely by the extension of citizenship to people in
the provinces and the Romanization of the provinces.

Fall of Rome Internal and external forces were at work, however,
even when Rome was at the height of her power, and these eventually
brought about her downfall. Waste and luxury led to extrava-

gances and a decline in the value of money. Growing discontent among the underpaid soldiers caused the army to put its own favorites into power. By the third century A.D. the rulers, with only a few exceptions, had little competence or interest in the government. In the meantime, barbarians from the east and north were attacking the frontiers and making successful inroads in a number of places. For a short time under Diocletian, who was emperor from A.D. 284–305, good government and peace were restored. Constantine further benefited the falling empire by an efficient reign, from A.D. 307–37. He reorganized the government and created an Eastern Empire, with its capital at Byzantium, which was then renamed Constantinople. The Western Empire grew steadily weaker and ceased to have an emperor after A.D. 476.

ROMAN FORUM

A description of the archaeological remains of Rome must begin with the Roman Forum, since the first settlements were made in that section and it was from the Forum—center of Roman civic, business, and religious activity—that the power of Rome later radiated out to control the entire Mediterranean world and ultimately to influence all Western civilization.

Necropolis The earliest datable relics that have been unearthed were found in the necropolis, an archaic cemetery belonging to the Iron Age period. It was in use from approximately the ninth to the seventh century B.C. and was probably used by the Latin settlers who lived in huts on the surrounding hills, and who buried their dead below in the valley that was later to develop into the Roman Forum. In the necropolis there were graves for burial and small pits for cinerary urns. Bronzes and pottery vases found in the necropolis help in the dating.

It was not long before the inhabitants began to build their huts or houses in parts of the valley. This is the time taken as the traditional founding of Rome. The date, according to our method of reckoning time, was about 753 B.C. The Latin village was under the rule of kings and nobles, and the period 753–509 B.C. is known as the **Period or Rule of the Kings.** During this time the Etruscans conquered Rome and inhabited it for about two hundred years. The Etruscans brought with them their superior civilization and made a great contribution in art and architecture to the future of Rome. Two among the last kings to rule Rome were quite probably Etruscans, or of Etruscan origin. Under them the marshes were drained to make habitation of the whole valley possible. This was accomplished by building the Cloaca Maxima, a very large main sewer, which was constructed with a stone lining and through which the swamp waters emptied into the Tiber. A small circular shrine was erected to Venus for her help in the task of making the Forum habitable.

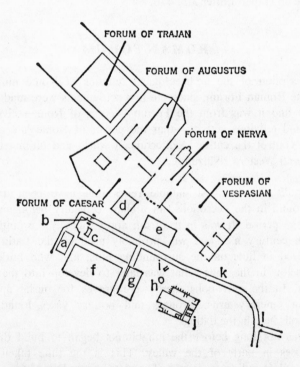

Plan of the forums: a—Temple of Saturn. b—Arch of Septimius Severus. c—Rostra. d—Curia. e—Basilica Aemilia. f—Basilica Julia. g—Temple of Castor and Pollux. h—Temple of Vesta. i—Regia. j—House of Vestals. k—Sacred Way. l—Arch of Titus

As Rome continued to grow so did the Forum, and many buildings and monuments were erected there. These were chiefly of a religious, commercial, or political nature, to fill the needs created by the activities that centered in the Forum. The Palatine Hill came to be the place where the homes of the wealthy citizens of Rome—and later the emperors' palaces—were located. At different times throughout its history the Roman Forum was destroyed by fire or covered with floods, necessitating rebuilding and reconstruction. During the Middle Ages widespread plundering and quarrying of the ancient monuments and buildings took place in the Forum, as elsewhere. In spite of these vicissitudes, however, enough has survived to make the Roman Forum a place of beauty and a well from which archaeologists can draw the materials of history.

Comitium Just to the west beyond one corner of the Forum proper was a level space where the assemblies of the people were held. These meetings took place in the open, and the space that was set aside for this purpose was called the Comitium.

Curia Close to the Comitium the Curia was built. This was the Senate House, where the senate generally held its meetings, although temples and similar buildings were sometimes used for a meeting of the senate. The senators sat on chairs which were placed on the three marble steps along both sides of the Curia. The platform or podium was at the far end. The Curia was reconstructed several times and was rebuilt as late as the fourth century A.D. under Diocletian. It is the restoration of this building that we see today. The fine bronze doors of the Curia are now the doors of the Lateran Church, another instance of the freedom with which antiquities were removed in the past from their original places.

Rostra On the other side of the Comitium was the Rostra, or Speakers' Platform, from which orators could address the people. The Rostra got its name from *rostrum,* meaning "beak" or "prow," because the prows of ships that were captured during the fourth century B.C. were attached to columns on the platform as decorations. The platform was mounted by steps at the back.

Regia The Regia was the residence of the chief priest, or Pontifex Maximus. In the course of its history it was rebuilt and enlarged several times. It was located toward the middle of the Forum on the *Via Sacra,* or Sacred Way, the road that passed through the length of the Forum from the southeast to the northwest, and along which religious and triumphal processions passed.

Temple of Vesta   Not far from the Regia were the Temple of Vesta and other buildings concerned with the worship of the goddess of the hearth. The entire group of edifices was connected with the religious life of the city. The Roman year began with a ceremony at the temple. A fire was lighted and kept burning continually throughout the year. The earliest Temple of Vesta was possibly a wooden hut with a roof of straw. When it was later built of stone and brick, it still kept the circular form, with a hole in the center of the roof

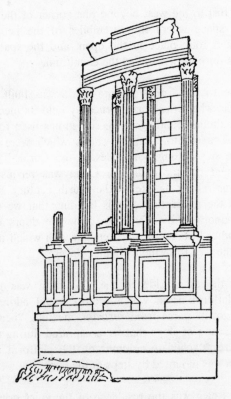

Temple of Vesta

through which smoke could escape. The temple was rebuilt a number of times following fires, until at least the end of the second century A.D. The structure we now see is a restoration based on evidence revealed by excavations, existing fragments, and reproductions on coins. The round tufa platform survived almost unharmed, and parts of the building above that have been reconstructed. The temple had a circular cella wall, surrounded by twenty tall Corinthian columns of marble. The roof apparently sloped upward toward the center opening.

House of the Vestals The priestesses who tended the fire lived in a house that extended to the south and east of the Temple of Vesta. The House of the Vestals was last reconstructed at about the same time as the Temple of Vesta. One group of the Vestal Virgins was always in charge of keeping the fire in the temple burning, while another group was being taught its responsibilities by those who had completed their term of active service. Because of the nature of their work and its deep religious significance, the Vestal Virgins were held in high esteem by everyone, and it was a great honor to be selected as a priestess. The house in which they lived grew to be a fine large edifice befitting their position. A large central court had fountains in the middle and was surrounded by a portico. Rooms opened on all sides of this courtyard and stairways led to a second story—and very likely a third. The Vestal Virgins were not only provided with a house worthy of their place in the community, but were given many privileges.

By the time the Rule of the Kings came to an end around 509 B.C. and the republic came into existence, there was quite a nucleus of structures in the Forum. Most of these were rebuilt and ornamented and many more were added during the time of the republic and in the period of the empire. As Rome grew, the architecture of the city was affected by contact with the peoples of the eastern Mediterranean, the Greeks in particular. Building was on a grander scale, and ornamentation became more varied and refined.

Temple of Saturn In the beginning of the fifth century B.C. an early temple dedicated to Saturn, god of the harvest, was built in the Forum. During an annual festival in his honor, sacrifices were made at the altar in front of the Temple of Saturn for the bounties bestowed by the deity. The temple was later rebuilt several times and the present remains are from the restoration of the fourth century A.D. The building was erected on a large rectangular platform with steps leading up to it. It was in the Ionic order of architecture and eight of its lofty granite columns still stand in place, supporting the entablature above.

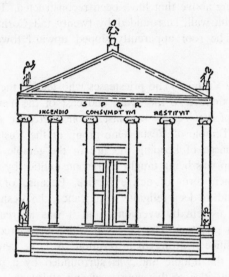

Temple of Saturn

Temple of Castor and Pollux   The Temple of Castor and Pollux was first dedicated early in the fifth century B.C. It was erected to commemorate the victory of the Romans over the Etruscans in 496 B.C. in a battle fought at Lake Regillus. According to the legendary account, two young men rode into the Forum and brought the good news of the battle's outcome to the people of Rome. After the disappearance of the horsemen, it was apparent that they had been the twin sons of Zeus, Castor and Pollux. The temple was built in their honor by the grateful Romans, who realized that the deities had assisted them in the battle of Lake Regillus. The temple, placed near the spring where the twin riders had watered their horses, was on a high platform and was entered by steps on either side. There are remains of several building periods, the last of which was in the first century A.D. There was a row of columns along both sides of the cella, and at one time a mosaic pavement. The three slender Corinthian columns of the Temple of Castor and Pollux, with their entablature in place, still stand near the Temple of Vesta, and the House of the Vestals, making one of the most impressive sights in the Forum.

Temple of Castor and Pollux

Basilica Although Roman buildings were in many ways influenced strongly by Greek architecture, the Romans made changes and modifications adapted to their own needs. One example of this is the Basilica, which was designed as a spacious building where financial and commercial business could be transacted and where civil law cases could be tried. The structure was in the shape of a large rectangle. The interior of a basilica consisted of a high central hall with columns on either side that formed side aisles. These columns also supported a second story, or gallery, above the aisles. There were some variations of this basic plan which could be altered by the decorations and materials employed, but any Roman basilica was of this general type.

The Christians, in turn, adopted the basilica form and modified it by rounding one end to make an apse.

The first basilica in the Forum was built near the Curia, but was not rebuilt after its destruction in the first century B.C. Remains of two basilicas can be seen in the Forum today. The Basilica Aemilia was built in the second century B.C. on the north side of the Forum. Existing fragments tell us it was ornamented with marble flooring and columns and with decorative sculpture. There was a row of shops in front of it, with a high porticoed entrance.

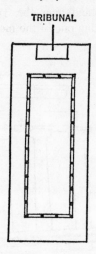

Plan of a basilica

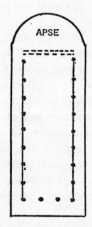

Plan of a church

The Basilica Julia stood on the south side of the Forum. Both edifices were reconstructed and restored a number of times during the period of the Roman Empire, after they had suffered damage and destruction by fire and the invasions of the barbarians. In the Middle Ages and Renaissance they were used as quarries. Enough remains of their foundations to visualize them—with the aid of the existing architectural fragments—as they appeared in ancient times.

Triumphal Arches Another kind of structure designed by the Romans was the triumphal arch, based on the principle of the rounded arch which the Romans had learned from their neighbors and conquerors, the Etruscans. The triumphal arch was a monument erected to honor a general who had won a great victory. Later, triumphal arches were also erected to emperors. The arch was highly decorated with engaged columns, detailed bas-reliefs and architectural sculpture, and inscriptions.

Arch of Septimius Severus The Arch of Septimius Severus was erected on the Sacred Way at the northwest end of the Forum in A.D. 203, in honor of victories won by the emperor over the Parthians. It has a large center arch flanked by two smaller arches. The engaged columns are Corinthian, and the sculptured scenes and figures have to do with the emperor's fighting and victories in the East. A great bronze **quadriga,** or four-horse chariot, with statues of Septimius Severus and his two sons, stood on top of the arch.

Arch of Septimius Severus

Arch of Titus At the opposite end of the Forum is the Arch of Titus, erected in memory of the emperor and his capture of Jerusalem in A.D. 70. The arch has only one passageway, and relief sculptures on the inner sides depict the spoils, including the seven-branched candelabra, being carried in a triumphal procession, and the Emperor Titus riding in triumph in his quadriga.

Arch of Constantine Outside the Forum stands the Arch of Constantine, built near the Colosseum in A.D. 312. This structure has three archways—a large central arch with a smaller one on each side—and was erected in celebration of Constantine's victory over paganism.

Arch of Titus

Arch of Constantine

Imperial Forums There were five other forums in ancient Rome, to the northwest of the Roman Forum. These are called the Imperial Forums, because they were built by five different Roman emperors to provide more space for business and legal activities in the ever-growing city, and to glorify themselves at the same time. They were all constructed with great colonnaded courtyards and temples, following a pattern similar to that of the Roman Forum, but on a smaller scale. Caesar's Forum was finished by Augustus, who then built one of his own, and Vespasian, Nerva, and Trajan each built a forum.

Trajan's Forum Trajan's was the biggest of the Imperial Forums. It contained a large basilica and two libraries. The Column of Trajan still stands there, where it was erected in A.D. 113. A spiral relief frieze winds for two hundred feet around the column and contains vivid, detailed scenes from the emperor's successful military expedition against the Dacians. The column is composed of a series of marble drums set on a pedestal and rising about 125 feet in the air. There was originally a statue of Trajan on the top, but one of St. Peter has stood there since the sixteenth century.

Amphitheaters An amphitheater was another type of edifice created by the Romans. It was an adaptation of the Greek theater form and had a complete circle or oval of seats to accommodate more spectators and to provide a central arena for gladiatorial combats and other spectacular exhibitions. The seats of an amphitheater rose in tiers on all sides of the structure and were divided by stairways. They were reached through entrances evenly spaced around the building. These passages opened off to exterior flights of steps.

The Colosseum The Flavian Amphitheater, popularly known as the Colosseum, was built during the rule of the Flavian line of emperors—Vespasian, Titus, and Domitian—who reigned from A.D. 70 to 96. The work was undertaken by Vespasian, dedicated in A.D. 80 by Titus, and finished under Domitian. The Colosseum was a massive stone structure, the largest of all the amphitheaters built by the Romans. Below the ground level was a huge basement with dens and cages for the animals and intricate machinery to raise them to the arena. The arena floor was a wooden one covered with sand, but it could be converted to hold water for naval battles. The great outer walls of the structure were almost 160 feet high and rose in four stages. The three lowest stages were in the form of arcades circling the building. There were eighty arcades in each story, and between each pair of arcades was an engaged column. The columns of the lowest arcade were Doric; of the second, Ionic; and of the third, Corinthian. The fourth and upper story was a solid wall with square windows, forty in all, in every other section. On the inside a high podium ran around the arena and held marble seats and boxes, which were reserved for the emperor, the chief officials, the Vestal Virgins, and other persons of honor. The Colosseum accommodated between fifty thousand and eighty thousand spectators. Masts fixed

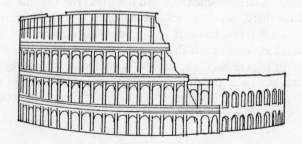

The Colosseum as it appears today

in the wall above the windows supported awnings that stretched out above the seats to protect the people from rain and sun. The fact that it was one of the most accessible and convenient places from which stones could be removed in later times accounts, to a large degree, for the Colosseum's appearance today.

Hadrian's Tomb   An enormous tomb was built by Emperor Hadrian on the bank of the Tiber River. It was built in the shape of a huge Etruscan tumulus. The circular lower part of the mausoleum was of stone, and the rounded top was filled with earth for the planting of trees. The upper part was later replaced by a papal fortress, but the remainder of the edifice is still well preserved.

Pantheon   The Pantheon stands today essentially as it was in the time of Hadrian—as far as the walls and the great domed roof are concerned. The inscription over the entrance tells us that the temple was built by Agrippa, the son-in-law of Augustus, in 27 B.C. It was reconstructed by Hadrian in the second century A.D. What we see today is a circular building with a height of close to 142 feet, equal to the diameter of the dome. The cupola was made of concrete, a bold architectural undertaking, and the hole at its top is a large one to admit light for the entire building. The columns of the front portico and those of the interior are Corinthian. In spite of the fact that the bronze roof tiles and some of the marble facings of the in-

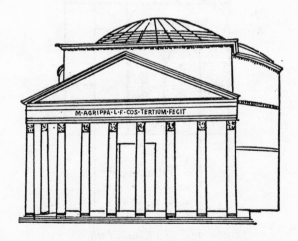

The Pantheon

terior were taken away in the past, the Pantheon remains as one of the most perfectly preserved of ancient structures.

Roman Baths The Roman **thermae,** or public baths, developed from fairly simple buildings to structures of huge proportions and great luxury, where people could meet not only for various kinds of baths—hot, cold, and steam—and swimming, but could take part in games, exercise, and other recreation or could read in the library or visit with friends in the courtyard. Time spent each afternoon at one of the numerous establishments of this sort came to be a popular and regular indulgence among the Romans.

The three most important rooms in a bath, one either in a private house or in a public establishment, were the **tepidarium,** the **caldarium,** and the **frigidarium.** These rooms and baths were heated by a furnace using wood or charcoal for fuel. Shovels made of iron for feeding the furnaces have been found. The furnace heated the water in storage tanks, and then pipes, generally of lead, carried the warm or hot water from the cisterns to the basins in the tepidarium and caldarium. The floors and walls of the baths were double. The two floors were separated by small square pillars of brick or stone about two feet high, called **pilae,** and the space between them formed an underground heating chamber. Heat ran from the furnace all through this area, called a **hypocaust,** warming it, and from there traveled into the hot-air passages between the walls.

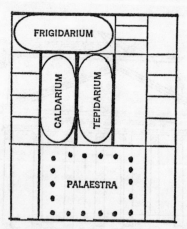

Plan of a Roman bath

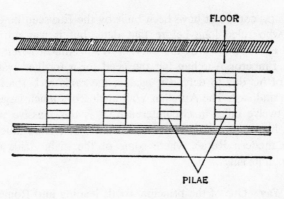

A hypocaust

After undressing in one of the rooms arranged for this purpose, the bather entered the tepidarium. This was a warm chamber adjacent to the caldarium or hot bath. The last bath was the cold bath in the frigidarium. This was often a luxurious swimming pool of extensive proportions. There were also rooms for steam baths, anointing with oil, and rubbing and massage, but the regular series of baths consisted of the three described above. When women as well as men were admitted, as was quite customary, a group of similar but separate rooms was provided for the women.

The first thermae were erected by Agrippa at the beginning of the first century A.D. As public baths increased in number, so did their size and splendor. They became most pretentious and elaborate. Of the many thermae in Rome, the Baths of Titus, constructed in the first century A.D., the Baths of Caracalla, built early in the third century A.D., and those of Diocletian, erected approximately a century later, are still standing, although in a ruined condition. These thermae were constructed on a gigantic scale. The Baths of Caracalla are now used as an outdoor opera house in summer, and the Baths of Diocletian, which could accommodate as many as three thousand persons, was an even more spacious and magnificent edifice.

Walls of Rome Not long after Rome was sacked by the Gauls in 390 B.C. and the invaders were driven out, a wall was put up, beginning at the Tiber River, to surround the city and protect it from further invasions of this sort. This defense wall, constructed of courses (layers) of stone blocks, was over five miles long and parts of it are still standing. This wall, which circled Rome in the fourth century B.C., could not have been built by the Etruscan king, Servius Tullius, who ruled long before that date, but it was attributed to him and is still known as the Servian Wall. Almost seven centuries later the Emperor Aurelian felt the need for a fortified wall around the city of his day to defend it against the raids of barbarians from the north and east. The Aurelian Wall enclosed a much larger Rome, close to twelve miles in circumference. It is this massive wall, over fifty feet high and more than ten feet wide, that is so much in evidence in modern Rome, where some of the main roads enter the city through its gates.

Appian Way One of the principal roads leading into Rome through one of the gates in the Aurelian Wall was the Via Appia, or Appian Way, which ran to Naples and then south to Brindisium. The Via Appia was constructed under Appius Claudius at the end of the fourth century B.C., although it did not reach its full length until much later. It was along this road outside the walls of the city that the Romans buried their dead, and the remains of the monuments that once lined both sides of the road may still be seen there. Those citizens who did not have a private or family tomb could be buried in one of the many large subterranean tombs. Some of these underground burial places, called **catacombs,** were cut into the natural rock. Others were chambers constructed below the ground. They were entered by a flight of steps, and the walls were covered with niches made to hold the funeral urns. Because of their resemblance to dovecotes, they were given the name **columbaria,** from the Latin word for "dove."

A columbarium

Roman Aqueducts Rome required a huge supply of water not only for ordinary needs but for the innumerable bathing establishments, which created an increasing demand. The Romans solved their problem by building aqueducts to carry water from its source—often a considerable number of miles distant—into the city, where it was stored in cisterns. The water was carried in lead pipes to the many fountains of the city, where it was available to all, and to public and private buildings. The aqueducts were built of stone and brick, sometimes with, and sometimes without, mortar and cement. Roman engineers made the fullest use of the principle of the arch. Tiers of arches supported the water channels at the top, so that the water supply could flow evenly and steadily to its destination over rough terrain and even underground through tunnels. The first aqueduct had been built several centuries before, but in the first century A.D. the Emperor Claudius built a vast aqueduct to transport water into Rome from the south. The aqueducts that crossed the countryside outside Rome were largely destroyed by the invading barbarians in the sixth century A.D. as a strategic measure, but they were too well built to be effaced entirely from the landscape, where stretches stand in position today as they did in centuries past.

Before we leave Rome and a study of its antiquities, it must be remembered that Roman architects and engineers designed and erected similar structures all over the empire. Wherever the Romans conquered and imposed their civilization, they and those who became Romanized under their influence built houses, theaters, aqueducts, baths, temples, and many other edifices in the same manner and style as those in the Eternal City. The physical ruins of these

An aqueduct

structures can, therefore, be seen in many places throughout the Mediterranean world and even in Britain. The cultural remains of the Romans can be seen in their effect on Western civilization and in many examples of later imitations and adaptations of the original Roman architectural plans.

CHAPTER TWELVE

Other Italian Cities

POMPEII

Eruption of Vesuvius On an August day in the summer of A.D. 79, Mt. Vesuvius began to erupt. From its peak almost four thousand feet above the Bay of Naples it showered small pumice stones and volcanic ash upon the land below. The inhabitants in surrounding towns, who were going about their daily business, were surprised and distressed when they saw the eruption. However, they were not overly alarmed at first, because the mountain was several miles distant, the pieces of pumice were small, and the fall of ash and dust was light. Moreover, the inhabitants of Pompeii, a nearby city of about twenty thousand persons, were still busy rebuilding their town following the widespread destruction caused by an earthquake more than fifteen years before.

It soon became apparent, nevertheless, as ashes and fragments of rock continued to reach Pompeii in increasing amounts through the clouds of smoke, that the eruption was a violent and damaging one. The people left their shops, their kitchens, the exercise grounds, the streets—whatever they were doing at the moment—and sought safety. Many of them fled to basements, where they were sheltered and protected from the volcanic rock. Others fled, or tried to flee, to places outside the danger zone. Those who remained behind and even many who had reached the roads beyond the city walls were overcome by the deadly sulfuric gases. Approximately one tenth of the population were killed by these unseen fumes. When it was all over, the survivors rescued what they could and abandoned the city.

Excavations at Pompeii During the intervening centuries Pompeii lay buried under layers of pumice and ash that were close to twenty

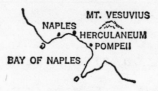

Map of the Bay of Naples

feet deep in many places. The city remained in an almost static condition, preserved very much as it was in the first century A.D. when the ashes fell and the people were suffocated. A few finds were made at the site and some unscientific digging was carried on before the eighteenth century to find objects, such as statues, that could be sold. By the middle of the eighteenth century, however, excavations were undertaken under the direction of French archaeologists for the purposes of research and study. These have been continued since the nineteenth century by the Italian Government. Everything uncovered at Pompeii shows that the tragedy which occurred there in the first century A.D. preserved a whole city and an entire way of life almost intact for future explorers to unearth, study, and observe. The past speaks to the present at Pompeii.

History of Pompeii   The area along the Sarnus River and on the Gulf of Naples that was to become the city of Pompeii was inhabited by the seventh or sixth century B.C. The earliest inhabitants were of Oscan and Etruscan origin and mingled with the Samnites, a tribe from the nearby mountains. Archaeologists have been able to trace the early history of Pompeii from literary evidence and from objects found in graves. Numerous inscriptions and bronze seals, on which the names of families were written, furnish further evidence. As the city grew in size, it became a center not only of farming but also of trade and industry because of its excellent location on Italy's west coast. By the first century B.C. Pompeii had been made a Roman colony and became Romanized, as had all towns under Roman control.

Plan of the City   The city walls of Pompeii still stand in many places and are in a good state of preservation. The walls were often fifteen to twenty feet thick and were protected at intervals by towers along the length, which extended for a little more than two miles around the city. Entrance to the city was through great gates at the ends of the roads leading from the port and the neighboring towns. There were eight gates in all. Two principal streets ran through the city from northeast to southwest, and another, the Via di Stabia, crossed these at right angles. This geometrical layout made the plan of Pompeii look much like that of a modern city. The streets were paved with lava blocks and were flanked by sidewalks on both sides. At the intersections, steppingstones facilitated pedestrian crossings but allowed room for the wheels of vehicles to pass. In many places deep ruts were worn into the pavement by the constant passage of vehicles in the streets. Fountains placed along the streets, generally at the corners, made it easy for the public to draw water and also acted as gathering places where the people could pause to talk.

A Pompeian street. Note the fountain and steppingstones in the foreground.

Forum The Forum, or marketplace, was located in the southwest section of the city, where the ground was level. It covered an area about 465 feet long and 125 feet wide and was the center of the city's activity. The public buildings concerned with business, government, and religion were built around this large rectangular space. The

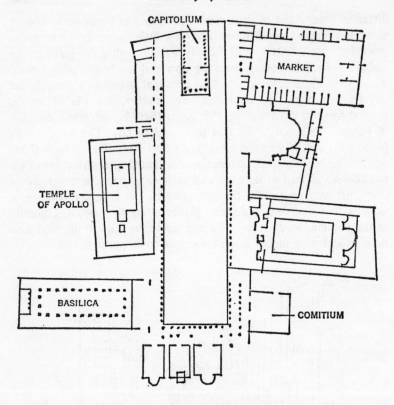

Plan of the Forum

Forum at Pompeii was one of the finest of its kind. A beautiful colonnade surrounded it on three sides, and in many places stairways led to a second story or gallery over the portico. Bronze and marble statues added to the Forum's decoration, making the whole impression one of architectural and artistic beauty.

Capitolium At the north end of the Forum was the Capitolium, or temple dedicated to Jupiter, Juno, and Minerva, usually called simply the Temple of Jupiter. It stood on a high platform and had six graceful Corinthian columns in front. Streets entered the Forum through monumental arches on either side of the temple. The Temple of Jupiter was one of the buildings of Pompeii that had been extensively damaged in the earthquake of A.D. 62 and had not been reconstructed by the time of the disaster of A.D. 79. The temple, therefore, appears today much as it did when Vesuvius erupted, but that condition is one of ruin.

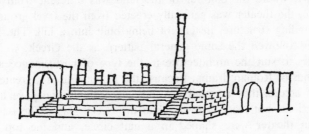

The Capitolium

Basilica In the southwest corner of the Forum was the great and imposing Basilica. This structure was erected in the second century B.C. as a place where commercial and financial matters could be transacted and court cases concerned with business and civil suits could be heard. The Basilica was built in the shape of a large rectangle, and the interior was divided into three sections or aisles by two rows of columns running down its length. There were engaged columns against the walls, and a second-story gallery along the two sides of the interior was supported by the rows of columns below.

Temple of Apollo The Temple of Apollo lies along the west side of the Forum. The entire sacred precinct was surrounded by a portico. The temple was built on a high platform reached by a series of steps, and was in the Corinthian order of architecture.

Market During the time of Augustus a large square building was placed on the northeast side of the Forum, across from the Capitolium. This was an enclosed market area for shops. It was entered from the street through a fine marble portico of Corinthian columns.

The whole magnificent Forum of Pompeii, with its rich architecture, fine sculptures, and wide expanse allowing for many vistas, all equally beautiful, must have been unsurpassed by that in any Roman city of comparable size.

THE ROMAN THEATER

In Italy, where the contour of the land was different from that of Greece, the theater was generally erected from the level ground as a freestanding structure, instead of being built into a hill. The Roman theater followed the same general pattern as the Greek, with some changes to suit the architecture to the type of performance and the demands of Roman drama. Because the Romans used a greater number of actors, they adapted the stage accordingly and gave it larger dimensions, but made it lower than the Greek stage. The seats of a Roman theater were shaped in a half circle, and the top of the

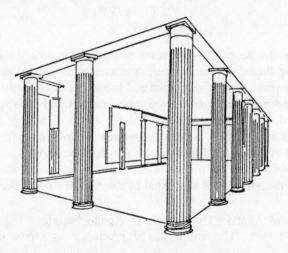

The Basilica

outer wall generally held a series of masts, which supported a large canopy that extended over the seats to shade the spectators.

Theaters The large theater at Pompeii was built during the second century B.C. and the Romans later reconstructed it into a more ornamental structure which could seat approximately five thousand spectators. It was built into the natural curve of a hill in the southern part of the city. A large square porticoed courtyard was added beyond the stage as a gathering place for the audience. A small theater

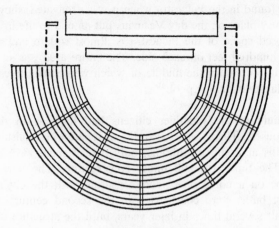

Roman theater

to the east is in a very good state of preservation. This was erected in the first century B.C. by the Romans, who colonized Pompeii at that time, and served as an odeum, or music hall. The small theater could accommodate not more than one thousand to fifteen hundred people and was small enough to be roofed over. It, too, had access to the adjacent colonnaded court.

Amphitheater   In the southeastern corner of the city, just inside the city walls, was the great Amphitheater, erected in the first century B.C. Archaeological evidence shows this to be the oldest amphitheater in existence. The arena seats were divided into wedge-shaped sections by stairways, in the manner of a theater. There were two large main entrances to the Amphitheater, but the upper tiers of seats could be reached more easily by flights of steps on the exterior of the edifice. As was customary in Roman amphitheaters, the officials, magistrates, and other important personages sat in special seats in the reserved lower rows. An estimated twenty thousand persons—or the entire population of the city—could be accommodated to witness the gladiatorial spectacles held in the Amphitheater at Pompeii.

Palaestra   The Palaestra, situated next to the Amphitheater, was an imposing structure in which the athletes trained, exercised, and competed in games and gymnastics. A number of skeletons of young men were found in the Palaestra when it was excavated, showing that it was a busy place on the day Vesuvius put an end to life in Pompeii. The enclosed space of the Palaestra is almost square and measures over four hundred feet on each side. The entire area was surrounded by an Ionic portico, in the middle of which were shade trees planted around a large swimming pool.

Baths Many of the wealthier citizens had thermae in their own private houses. There were also three separate establishments of public baths at Pompeii, although only two of them were in use in A.D. 79. The third was still under construction. The new thermae were to be on a noble scale, commensurate with the city's wealth. The oldest baths were constructed in the second century B.C. and were rebuilt several times in later years, until the structure ultimately became a magnificent one. It had a large porticoed courtyard, or palaestra, connected to it, and the thermae had separate sections for men and women, each with a complete series of the rooms common to all baths. Smaller thermae, located near the Forum, were built in the first century B.C. Some of the beautifully decorated rooms of this establishment have been exceptionally well preserved and are fine examples of their type.

THE ROMAN HOUSE

On the whole, the Roman home did not differ essentially from that of the Greeks. It, too, was built close to the street and around a court, called the **atrium,** into which the vestibule opened. In the older and smaller dwellings, the atrium was the center of the household and the living quarters opened from it. There was usually a mosaic floor and the walls were painted or were of marble. Later, as was also true of the Greek houses, a colonnaded peristyle was added at the back. One different feature was the roof. The roof on most Greek houses was flat, but on Roman dwellings it sloped down and in toward the courtyard. The roof was open above the court, furnishing ample light and allowing rain to fall below into a sunken rectangle, usually paved in mosaic. This shallow pool was called the **impluvium** (from *im-*, "in" and *pluere* "to rain") and had an outlet through which the water drained into a storage cistern underground or in the basement.

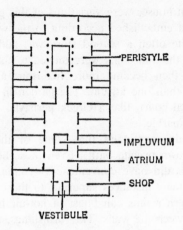

Plan of a Roman house

In both Greek and Roman cities there were buildings very similar to present-day apartment houses. They were usually quite large, sometimes taking up an entire block, and were several stories high, averaging about four or five floors, although some were even higher. Because these structures were isolated units, the apartment-house type of dwelling was called *synoikia* (from *syn,* "with" and *oikein,* "to inhabit") in Greek, and *insula* ("island") in Latin.

Pompeian Houses The houses of Pompeii furnish us with examples of many kinds of dwellings. We can see them standing as they appeared in the first century A.D., lining the streets on both sides. Excavations have unearthed their balconies and courtyards, their floors and roofs, their decorations and furniture almost intact and, except for the destruction wrought by time and decay during the intervening centuries, almost as they stood when they were overwhelmed by the eruption of Vesuvius. Walking the streets of the now-abandoned city, one can easily picture it filled with the activity of its citizens.

The typical home in ancient Pompeii opened directly on the sidewalk and was entered by several steps leading to a vestibule. The atrium, or main courtyard, was roofed with tiles, except for the **compluvium,** or central opening, through which rain fell into the pool below. The living quarters of the family were in the rooms opening from the atrium. In back of the atrium was a walled garden, generally ornamented with fountains and statuary.

Other Pompeian houses were variations of this general plan. They were enlarged and embellished according to the wealth and taste of their owners. Quite often a second story was added to the atrium, and, in this case, the bedrooms were moved to the upper story and the atrium itself then became more luxurious and formal. Many houses had more than one atrium. The garden in the rear later became a colonnaded court, like a Greek peristyle, with columns and ornamentation of marble.

We have already mentioned that some of the more extensive houses had their own private baths. Even those houses that did not have such luxuries did have conveniences—running water and heat —equal, and in many instances superior, to those found in modern homes. Few modern rooms can boast of hot-air heat flowing under the floors and between the walls. The furnishings, utensils, and other necessary items were of fine workmanship and were elaborately decorated. Bronze, copper, and marble were commonly used in making these household articles.

Pompeian Art Everywhere in Pompeian houses we find evidence of the high artistic achievements of the city's artists and craftsmen and of its citizens' cultured taste. Fortunately, many of these works of art have come down to us in an excellent state of preservation. Bronze and marble statues, decorative fountains, exquisite mosaics and paintings of all types, magnificent mural frescoes—all give us further insight into the inhabitants' lives in ancient Pompeii. There is a wide range of both subject matter and color in the Pompeian wall paintings. Mythological and religious subjects were, of course, common. Landscapes and architectural paintings were popular for interior decorations to give space and depth to the rooms where they appeared. The Pompeian cupids and their activities are well known, and a large number of portrait paintings were found. A broad range of strong and delicate colors appears in all the painting brought to light in Pompeii. The reds, blacks, and yellows were especially characteristic and have defied attempts at duplication.

The past and the present merge, and the nineteen centuries intervening since its destruction disappear in the vivid scenes unearthed at Pompeii. Plaster casts have been taken by pouring wet plaster of Paris into the hollows where the bodies of humans and animals lay when they met sudden death, and letting it harden. A dog with his collar, a mother and child, a young woman who fell face downward are all vivid reminders of the instantaneous effect of the deadly pumice stones, ashes, and suffocating waves of sulfur fumes. The shops, too, present the lifelike appearance they had at the moment they were hastily abandoned. Some eggs, a partially finished vase, a loaf of bread, and numerous other tokens of the past help us to cross the centuries. In the houses undisturbed furniture, a pile of coins, some gold jewelry, a perfect statuette, a group of cooking utensils, or a drinking glass transported the excavators who discovered them speedily across almost nineteen hundred years, just as they do everyone who sees them in the museums at Pompeii and Naples.

HERCULANEUM

Location The ancient city of Herculaneum lay a little farther to the north and closer to the edge of the sea than did Pompeii. Herculaneum was named for Hercules, its legendary founder, and was situated near the Gulf of Naples on a hill at the foot of Mt. Vesuvius.

Pompeii and Herculaneum The two cities had much in common, but also differed in many respects. The early inhabitants, as demonstrated by archaeological evidence, were of similar origin—that is, Oscan and Samnite. Later, Herculaneum was colonized by the Romans, as Pompeii was. Herculaneum, however, was more strictly a residential city than its neighbor. The excavations have revealed a greater number of houses and many more residences of a large size than at Pompeii. Although Herculaneum was smaller than Pompeii, its residents appear to have had more wealth, on the whole, and their homes have perhaps more to tell us.

Destruction of Herculaneum Herculaneum suffered the same fate as Pompeii did. The city felt the effects of the earthquake of A.D. 62, but apparently it was restored and rebuilt more quickly because the majority of buildings were private houses and small shops and were therefore essential. When the disaster of A.D. 79 came, however, it took on different characteristics. Herculaneum received an even heavier shower of volcanic stones and ash than Pompeii, and in some places was buried under sixty feet of volcanic debris by the time the eruption at last subsided. At the same time the falling stones and ashes were mixed with moisture from the vapors, and quite likely from a localized rainstorm as well, which caused the deposit to become thick and wet. As a result, an even greater amount was preserved intact for posterity than at Pompeii, by the hardening of the heavy layer of volcanic mud that had shrouded the city and everything in it. Even fabrics and wood became carbonized and have been unearthed almost unchanged. On the other hand, the inhabitants of Herculaneum were more fortunate in saving their lives. Proportionately fewer skeletons have been found there, which indicates that most of the citizens escaped. This may have been because the greater weight and size of the pumice stones forced them to flee sooner and there were, therefore, fewer cases of suffocation, or because the sea's nearness supplied them with a swift avenue of escape.

Excavations at Herculaneum   In 1738 digging at the site of Herculaneum was rewarded by the unearthing of an inscription telling that a man named Rufus had built the theater. Systematic excavations were not undertaken, however, until the twentieth century, partly because interest was centered more strongly on neighboring Pompeii. Also, since Herculaneum was buried under such a deep, hard layer, it has been more difficult and expensive to carry on excavations there. To date, quite an extensive section of the city has been brought to light, and modern methods of reconstruction and preservation have made it an extremely impressive and instructive record of the past.

Houses of Herculaneum   While stucco was more prevalent at Pompeii, many of the houses of Herculaneum were ornamented with marble facing. The thick protective layer of volcanic mud destroyed far less than it preserved. A large number of splendid houses still stand, with two or even three stories in place. Columns support balconies—many made partially or entirely of wood—which overhang the sidewalks below and which once provided shady protection for pedestrians who walked beneath them or paused before a shop. The extensive use of wood in construction is noteworthy. Wood was used for support and ornamentation, and wooden panels and partitions were common. Many wooden frames and entire pieces of furniture made of wood have come down to us almost intact and in a fine state of preservation.

One of the most unusual discoveries made at Herculaneum was

the unearthing of a house that has been given the name Villa of the Papyri. Close to two thousand papyrus rolls were found in the library. Most of the writings contained in them deal with philosophy, especially the teachings of Epicurus.

The ancient city of Herculaneum, as it stands today, gives one little feeling of change. The sleeping past has been reawakened by the excavations of the present.

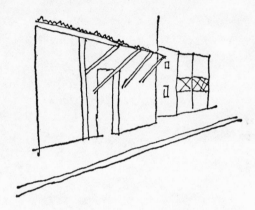

A house in Herculaneum. Notice the over-hanging balcony.

the inhabitants of a house that has been given the name Villa of the Papyri (Ghost), in two thousand papyrus rolls were found in the library work of the writing coordinated them deal with philosophy, especially the teachings of epicurus.

The ancient city of Herculaneum, as it strikes today, gives one little feeling of ennui. The sleeping dust has been reawakened by the excavations of the present.

A house in Herculaneum. Notice the overhanging balcony.

CHAPTER THIRTEEN

Archaeology in Britain

IMPORTANT DATES IN ANCIENT BRITAIN

c. 2000 B.C.	Iron Age habitations
c. 250 B.C.	Britain known to the Romans
55–54 B.C.	Caesar's invasions of Britain
A.D. 43	Claudius' conquest of southern Britain
A.D. 78	Agricola Governor of Province of Britain
c. A.D. 120	Hadrian in Britain
c. A.D. 400	Angles, Saxons, and Jutes enter Britain
c. A.D. 450	End of Roman control in Britain

ANCIENT BRITAIN

Aided by an expanding interest in archaeology and new scientific methods, including aerial photography, a great deal more is known about ancient Britain than seemed possible even a few decades ago. In the light of recent discoveries and research, many points have been clarified regarding the two large categories into which the story of early Britain can be divided—Pre-Roman Britain and Post-Roman Britain.

Barrows There are remains, chiefly in southern Britain, of settlements that archaeologists date, on the evidence of potsherds and implements that have been found, as early as the second millennium B.C. These habitations were on ridges and hills large enough to accommodate the population of a village and their needs. The security of high ground was supplemented by concentric rings of earthworks and ditches surrounding the entire mound to create a fortified plateau. These ancient defended villages and towns of prehistoric Britain have been given the name **barrows.**

Map of Ancient Britain

MAIDEN CASTLE

The best known of the numerous barrows that survive from ancient Britain and have been excavated is called Maiden Castle. It is in Dorset, not far from Dorchester. Maiden Castle is an excellent example of the fortified citadel town of the Neolithic Age. It was a huge fortress and its oblong-shaped embankments stretched almost three fifths of a mile in length. Its three rows of encircling trenches, with mounds one within another rising as high as one hundred feet in some places, were a very formidable defense against attackers, who were forced to advance along the level plain below. When we consider that Maiden Castle, with its extensive ramparts, was entirely constructed with Stone Age implements, we get some idea of the vastness of the undertaking.

Maiden Castle was attacked by the Romans when they advanced across Britain during the conquests of the first century A.D. After it

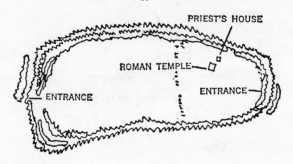

Maiden Castle

was conquered, Maiden Castle declined in importance. The inhabitants never recovered from their defeat by the Romans, and the site was gradually abandoned as the people spread through the area in the plains below and rebuilt closer to Dorchester. Three centuries later, Germanic invaders erected a temple on top of the hill. Foundations of this temple—probably built by the Celts—and of an adjacent priest's house of two rooms, all of native flint stone, are still standing and have been excavated.

STONEHENGE

Location   Stonehenge stands, majestic and alone, on the great Salisbury Plain of Wiltshire in southern England, where it was erected about four thousand years ago by early Britons for a purpose unknown to us. As one comes across the plain and approaches this stark circle of monoliths, one wonders whether the ancient Britons and Romans, seeing these massive stones outlined against the sky, experienced the same awe as we feel.

Erection of Stonehenge   Recent excavation and research have revealed that Stonehenge was probably constructed over a period of about four hundred years, the earliest stage being dated at approximately 1800 B.C. and the third and final stage around 1400 B.C. This means that the work was carried on mainly during the latter part of the Neolithic Age in Britain and therefore by Stone Age men using Stone Age implements and methods, although the Bronze Age had begun just prior to the last building phase.

Map of Stonehenge area

Construction of Stonehenge   Stonehenge is circled by a ditch and a built-up bank of earth. The circle measures over three hundred feet in diameter. About seventy-five feet outside of the ditch and earthwork and a little to the northeast, the Heel Stone was erected. The name Heel Stone stems from the fact that this stone is shaped somewhat like a heel at its base. Just within the earthen circle, fifty-six evenly spaced pits were dug. John Aubrey discovered these pits in the seventeenth century—hence the name Aubrey holes. Their function is not known. Although excavations have revealed the bones of cremated humans in a number of them, there is not enough evidence to substantiate the assumption that the pits served as a necropolis. Considering Stonehenge as a whole, it is more likely that these holes had some religious or mystical significance. All of this construction took place in the first building period, about 1800 B.C.

Those who worked on Stonehenge during the second phase, which began around 1650 B.C. and lasted over a century and a half, undertook the task of transporting a large number of bluestones from southern Wales. These were then erected in a circle in the center of Stonehenge. Whether this was done by people who migrated from Wales to Wiltshire or by the natives of the Stonehenge region, the fact remains that there was communication between these two sections of Britain. Moreover, the people had the determination and the capacity to move the heavy bluestone rocks from the Prescelly Mountains of Pembrokeshire in southwestern Wales, where they originated, to their final destination at Stonehenge. There is no way of determining the exact route which this tremendous moving task followed, but it is quite certain that the stones were carried down the Avon River for the last part of their journey. Stonehenge, however, lies about two miles from the Avon. The bluestones, therefore, had to be dragged from the river to the site. As a result, or perhaps only by coincidence, an avenue was formed at that time, leading from the Avon at West Amesbury to Stonehenge, passing the Heel Stone, and serving as an entranceway to the great circle. The Heel Stone itself was then set apart by a small ditch surrounding it.

During the next hundred years or so the rest of the construction work at Stonehenge was completed. Today, after a certain amount of restoration by the British Government, there is enough of Stonehenge standing to reconstruct it, on paper or in the imagination, as it might have looked in ancient times.

The main body consisted of the so-called Sarsen Circle of thirty huge sandstones, set upright a few feet apart to form a circle almost

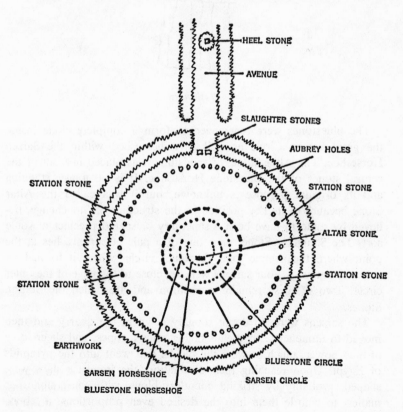

Plan of Stonehenge

one hundred feet in diameter, and rising thirteen or fourteen feet into the air, topped by great lintels, which touched each other to form one unbroken circle. Of these thirty supporting stones, seventeen are still in position as they have stood over the centuries, and five of the lintels remain in their original places. The sarsen stones came from the Marlborough Downs, a district about twenty miles away. They are of a gray sandstone and have been given the name sarsen from the word Saracen, indicating something foreign. Within the Sarsen Circle a horseshoe of sarsen **trilithons** was erected. The word trilithon means "three stones," composed in this case of two stones standing upright with a lintel topping each pair.

Trilithon

The bluestones were rearranged to form a complete circle inside the great Sarsen Circle as well as a horseshoe within the Sarsen Horseshoe. The Altar Stone, of sandstone, was placed in front of the central stones of the Bluestone Horseshoe. It is no longer standing and its original purpose is unknown, but it was called the Altar Stone because of its key position in the structure of Stonehenge, believed by some to have been a sanctuary or sacred precinct of some sort. The Slaughter Stone, once one of a pair of sarsens, lies at the point where the avenue joins the outer circle, where it formed an entrance gateway. Four sarsens were set close to the edge of the outer circle. Two of these remain in position and are called the Station Stones.

The sarsens were no doubt roughly hewn at the quarry and then moved to Stonehenge by means of log rollers, ropes, and sheer force of man power, much as were the blocks that went into the pyramids of Egypt. Upon reaching their destination, the immense slabs were shaped, probably by striking countless blows with small stones or mallets to whittle them into the desired even proportions, a laborious and tedious task requiring untold hours of exacting work. When each of the sandstone sarsens at length took its final form, it was moved, end first, into a pit prepared for it in the great circle and then was raised slowly and deliberately into position.

This Herculean labor was, of necessity, performed by physical strength, aided only by the primitive tools available, namely crude stone and wooden implements. For crowbars these neolithic men of ancient Britain must have used timber braced against timber to gain leverage, and log piled carefully upon log to build a wedge adequate enough to push, pull, and prod the gray sandstone giants into place. As to their method of raising the lintels to complete the Sarsen Circle, we can only guess. Again strong backs, and many of them, were needed, but they could not have done the job alone. It may be that ramps of earth or wood were constructed to serve as approaches along which the lintel stones might be guided and hoisted by ropes. Such ramps could have been built and later removed readily. Another method that could have been used is that of building up a crib under each stone, similar to a boat crib. The method by

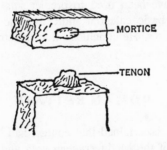

Mortice and tenon

which the lintels were secured and held in position is apparent from the evidence of the stones themselves. Each upright stone had a tenon, over which the mortice of the lintel above fitted.

There have been numerous conjectures about the function of Stonehenge. To date, this is an unsolved mystery. It may have served a religious purpose or have been erected by the ancient Britons as a monument or meeting place. The discovery in recent years of the double-ax sign on some of the stones might suggest some knowledge of, or link with, Minoan civilization, or might be pure coincidence. On the other hand, the regularity of the shape of Stonehenge and its alignment with the rising sun of the summer solstice in such a way as to preclude mere coincidence suggest a definite plan for observing the position of the sun and the changes of the calendar. If Stonehenge utilized the knowledge of the June twenty-first solstice for any other purpose, or with another meaning, we can only guess what it was.

Dr. Gerald S. Hawkins, an astronomer, undertook, in the mid-1960s, to find the solution to the purpose and use of Stonehenge with the aid of an electronic computer. Making use of clues furnished by the arrangement of the stones, he developed his theory by observations and calculations carried out at the site itself and at the Smithsonian Astrophysical Observatory. Dr. Hawkins determined the solar, lunar, stellar, and planetary positions at midsummer and midwinter by computer. He took the measurements of the Aubrey holes and the stones and calculated the positions of the missing stones on the basis of those remaining. His results showed a marked degree of accuracy in the correlation between the solar and lunar positions and those of the stones and the plan of Stonehenge. Stonehenge could, therefore, have been used to predict solar and lunar eclipses and to serve as a basic calendar indicating the calculations of the solstices and equinoxes. He concluded that the structure was planned and erected as an observatory.

ROMAN BRITAIN

Archaeologists have ascertained that contact had been established between the peoples of the Mediterranean area and Britain as early as the third or fourth century B.C., and possibly earlier. As soon as the use of tin and lead became widespread, further sources of supply were sought by Phoenician traders and others, who ventured as far as Spain and then out into the Atlantic and to the south coast of Britain to obtain the desired metals. It is quite doubtful that anything more than an exchange of goods took place during this early period, however.

Caesar's Invasions of Britain. Caesar did, in fact, invade Britain, as we know in some detail from evidence in his own writings. He tried in two successive years, 55 and 54 B.C., to conquer the island by attacking it from the nearby Roman province of Gaul, over which he was governor, but he was not successful at that time. Caesar's legions failed to get a permanent foothold on Britain and the Britons continued to live quite unmolested and unchanged, as though Caesar had never appeared on their horizon.

Conquest of Britain Almost a century was to pass before an invasion force sent by the Emperor Claudius began the actual conquest of Britain in A.D. 43. Even so, progress was slow, both in respect to the amount of territory under Roman domination and the impact of Roman civilization upon the natives of the island. The Romans were never certain of more than the southern and eastern parts of Britain, and Romanization penetrated slowly and incompletely in other sections.

Roman Occupation of Britain During the second half of the first century A.D., Rome's position in the province of Britain was strengthened by Agricola, who became governor in A.D. 78. In the next two centuries several of the Roman emperors, notably Domitian, Hadrian, and Septimius Severus, took a special interest in Britain and visited the island to reconquer and fortify various parts of the island. When the barbarians began to invade the Roman Empire in the fourth century A.D., it became increasingly difficult for the emperors to maintain the remote province of Britain, and Roman protection was gradually withdrawn. As the strength of the Romans weakened, that of the German tribes in Britain increased. Thus the Angles, Saxons, and Jutes ultimately gained control of Britain.

ROMAN CAMPS

Plan of a Roman Camp After the Roman conquest of Britain, military camps were built at various strategic points throughout the island. Some of the Roman camps were permanent and others only temporary, but they were all constructed on the same general plan. A wall, rounded at the corners, surrounded the camp on all sides. There were four gates in the wall, one on each side, with great wooden doors on pivots set in stone. Paved streets crossed the camp from one gate to the opposite gate, making four big rectangular

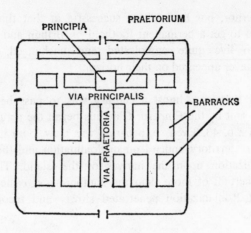

Plan of a Roman camp

divisions in the camp layout. These in turn were divided further by a number of smaller streets, crossing at right angles.

Buildings of a Roman Camp At the spot where the two principal streets met, there was a large headquarters building. This was called the **principia**, and it was built with a large courtyard, which was surrounded by a colonnade. Near the principia was the **praetorium**, the house of the commanding officer. There was also a chapel, where the standards of the military units that were stationed in each camp were kept, and a treasury, where the money and other valuables were protected by a strong room which was built into or below the ground and was reached by a flight of steps. Many traces of these strong rooms, which had heavy wooden doors and vaulted roofs, can be seen today in England. Other essential parts of a Roman camp were the arsenal, stables, granaries, workshops, and the barracks, which were set out along the streets in blocks or rows. The larger permanent camps generally had baths and an amphitheater outside the walls, and houses nearby where the soldiers' families lived.

Growth of Cities in Britain Whether or not they developed from a Roman camp site, most of the towns of ancient Britain were laid out in much the same manner, with walls, gates, and streets intersecting at right angles in a regular pattern. A good many of the towns have been occupied continuously up to modern times. When this is the case, excavation work is difficult or impossible, but there are usually some traces of the ancient city that can be seen above-ground. In a number of walled cities the later and medieval walls have been built directly on the Roman foundations. This can be seen at Chester and Canterbury. In Winchester remnants of the Roman amphitheater are visible, but the modern city has erased all but a few of the ancient remains. The two principal streets of Chichester cross in the center of the city, just as they did in Roman times. One of the Roman gates is still being used in Lincoln. In Leicester the ruins of a basilica and of the shops that once stood in the forum of the Roman town are still visible.

Place Names When two groups of people are thrown together and mingle, they must find a common meeting ground. Even the divergencies of their languages must, in time, merge to facilitate communication. This process usually occurs first with common everyday words. A glance at the map of England will show some results of this merging of words. Many of the place names of the native Britons were affected by Roman pronunciation and vocabulary and, therefore, underwent the changes that brought about their present form. The Latin word for "fort" or "camp" was *castra*. This word was used by the Britons as part of the names of many towns and cities that grew up on the sites of Roman camps and thus came to mean any city or town. It has evolved into modern English usage as -*cester* or -*chester*. The city of Chester is a good example of a place that was established as a Roman camp and is still called simply by that name. In general, however, the word for camp takes the suffix form in modern English, for example: Wor*cester,* Col*chester,* Dor*chester,* Ciren*cester,* Win*chester,* Lei*cester.*

Excavations in Britain On those sites where the towns disappeared or declined to mere villages or settlements after the Roman occupation, excavators have been able not only to unearth the remains of the ancient town but also to leave it open to view. In these cases the archaeologists have uncovered mosaic pavements, foundations and sections of walls, gates, houses, and other buildings—including amphitheaters and baths—all evidences of Roman habitation in Britain. In addition, countless objects of everyday usage have been brought to light. These include the more common articles: pottery, jewelry, and tools and implements of all kinds, as well as surgical instruments, toys, locks and keys, and various games—the most common being dice. Each find of an item of everyday or uncommon use aids the archaeologist in the vast problem of general and more particular dating. He is guided toward more definite dates by inscriptions, pottery stamps, and coins. Besides its value as a real or potential means of arriving at a date, each object brought to light plays a part in re-creating the life and history of Roman Britain for the archaeologist and historian.

ROMAN ROADS

The Romans built roads between the main towns and fortresses in Britain. These roads were necessary for both military and peaceful purposes. They were well constructed and served to make transportation, communication, and travel easier and quicker by joining all the more important centers by the most direct route. The cost of building the roads was paid for mainly from the taxes levied in Britain, as was true in all the Roman provinces. The network of roads laid down under the Romans was instrumental in binding the various parts of Britain more closely and in hastening the process of Romanization.

HADRIAN'S WALL

When the Emperor Hadrian visited Britain around A.D. 120, he had the Roman soldiers build an earthen wall across the narrow northern part of the island, from the Solway Firth to the River Tyne, as a defense against the tribes to the north who were a constant threat to the Roman province of Britain. The wall, commonly known as Hadrian's Wall, was later constructed of regularly shaped stone blocks. It extended the entire distance across the island, approximately seventy-five miles, running along the high points of the hills, and was about eight feet thick and over fifteen feet high. There was a wide ditch on both the north and south sides of the wall, and a road which ran the whole length on the south side, making all points along the course of the wall easily accessible to the Romans. The wall was protected by a number of large forts spaced at intervals, and by smaller forts, or **mile castles,** at each mile along its extent. The larger forts were garrisons where the soldiers lived and worked. In them were the soldiers' barracks, the houses of the officers, a chapel, offices, storehouses, and workshops.

Hadrian's Wall served its purpose and kept out those who attempted to invade Britain from the north for as long as the Romans were in control of the province, and it remained, through the centuries, as one of the monuments and landmarks of England.

BATH

In the modern city of Bath, healing hot springs pour forth their waters at a temperature of 120 degrees, as they apparently always have. In Roman times the medicinal properties of the mineral waters were known and utilized for curative purposes. Because of the healing powers of the springs, a small walled town sprang up to accommodate those who went there to seek health cures. An extensive and typical bathing establishment was built in the Roman style. The Roman town was given the name **Aquae Sulis,** meaning "Waters of Sul," the Celtic goddess of springs. Parts and fragments of a Corinthian temple dedicated to the Roman goddess Minerva or the Celtic deity Sul, sometimes called Sul-Minerva, were unearthed at the site.

The Baths The baths were heated by the usual system of furnace, hypocausts, and hot-air flues. The Great Bath appears today much as it did centuries ago, when Aquae Sulis was at its height. It is a large stone rectangular pool with a lead-lined bottom. In one corner a diving stone still extends out over the water, which reaches a depth of six feet and makes a real swimming pool. A tiled roof was supported on the interior by tall columns, and a fountain ornamented one side. There were smaller pools at each end of the Great Bath and the one toward the west was circular and shallow.

Excavations at Bath Although they were discovered in the eighteenth century, no excavating was done at the site of the Roman baths until the nineteenth century. Since they are situated in the center of modern Bath and are a good many feet below the present street level, the work of excavation has been difficult and limited, but a remarkably extensive area has been brought to light and has supplied archaeologists with a fine example of this type of Roman building.

The Romans brought an extended period of peace to Britain. During that time the province became Romanized in the same fashion and along the same lines as all the other places the Romans conquered. Although many Romans went to Britain in a military and civil capacity, most of the population of the island was composed of Britons. The Britons were strongly influenced in countless ways by their conquerors and patterned their towns and lives after the Romans. By the time the Roman occupation of Britain came to an end, the impact of Roman culture and civilization had been felt for a period of four hundred years and had become deeply enough rooted to be carried over the intervening centuries and emerge as a part of modern Western civilization.

CHAPTER FOURTEEN

Archaeology in the Americas

IMPORTANT DATES IN MAYAN HISTORY

c. A.D. 150 to 600	First or Old Empire
c. A.D. 600 to 1000	Migration to Yucatán
c. A.D. 1000 to 1450	Second or New Empire

IMPORTANT DATES IN TOLTEC HISTORY

c. A.D. 500	Appearance in Valley of Mexico
c. A.D. 1000	Height of Toltec Empire
c. A.D. 1000 to 1100	Migration to Yucatán

IMPORTANT DATES IN AZTEC EMPIRE

c. A.D. 1300	Appearance in Valley of Mexico
A.D. 1519	Cortes

IMPORTANT DATES IN THE HISTORY OF INCAS

c. A.D. 1000	Founding of Cuzco
c. A.D. 1400	Height of Inca Empire
A.D. 1533	Pizarro

THE AMERICAS

The archaeological study of the American continents was, of natural necessity, late in getting started. The fact that colonization was limited for a long time to the eastern seacoasts confined to those

Location of some important Indian remains: a–Central America. b–Peru. c–Southwestern United States

sections what little research was carried on by a few interested persons. Even when settlements were made in the interior and western sections of the Americas, the pressures of environment and building a life in the wilderness left little time or inclination for other activities. In addition, the great expanse of territory to be covered made any organized study difficult, so that whatever excavation and research was accomplished was focused mainly on the more obvious sites of rather widespread interest, such as the pyramids of Mexico. It has only been in the twentieth century that archaeological research has been undertaken on a larger scale in the Americas. The areas of investigation coincide roughly with the broad geographical sections, since North, Central, and South American remains show differing characteristics that developed because of, and along with, the dissimilar and varying tribes of Indians in each region.

Though still incomplete, the collection of objects and other finds unearthed so far gives archaeologists a general picture of the early inhabitants of the North American continent and the kind of life they led. Pointed stone artifacts indicate a hunting and fishing, and somewhat nomadic, type of existence in the early part of the Christian Era, but further evidence and a wider scope for comparisons could push that date back even farther. With the discovery of burial places archaeologists can determine that those who buried their dead were leading a more settled kind of existence and had evidently added farming to their other means of food gathering. With the practice of living in settled tribal communities and with the appearance of set customs in connection with burial, there came an advance to more and better artifacts and the habit of burying objects with the dead. From these pieces of pottery, implements, and weapons, the archaeologist can re-create the stage of culture reached at the time the stone, bone, clay, or metal articles were made.

By the time European discoverers and colonists began to intrude upon the scene of Indian culture and civilization, the natives of the Americas had, in many places, advanced beyond the stage of living in one settled spot to the point where their settlements had increased to considerable size. This brought about a more complex political organization and greater architectural skill, so that larger and more permanent dwellings and buildings, such as pyramids and temples, might be built. We have abundant evidence of this trend, both in the written records and accounts of Europeans of that period and in the discoveries and observations of archaeologists. As the work of digging, charting, and studying the relics of the past continues, the archaeological picture in the Americas becomes ever more complete.

NORTH AMERICA

Remnants of prehistoric habitations and traces of numerous Indian tribes have been found in many localities in the United States. Remains of pottery and artifacts of all kinds help archaeologists to record the prehistory of North America in increasing detail. Due to later building and continued habitation in many other areas, the interior of the continent, and especially the Southwest, yields the greatest amount of material and the most interesting vestiges of the past.

Early Habitations Traces of Indian cultures have been found in the Southwest that can be dated by archaeologists as belonging to the first millennium A.D. Most remains, however, are from a period of about four hundred years, from A.D. 1000 to 1400. Very little is known about some prehistoric tribes, but others left behind enough evidence to be of definite archaeological significance. The earliest houses appear to have been of a pit type and to have been built partly into the earth, with grass, bark, and wood used in their construction. The pit houses were sometimes scattered or isolated, and at other times they formed small villages. In a few places, chiefly in the region of southern Utah and Colorado and northern Arizona and New Mexico, the villages grew to some size. Later, sun-dried, or **adobe,** bricks were employed to build houses. Some of these were extensive buildings, similar to apartment houses.

Cliff Dwellings Many parts of the Southwest are filled with table-land, or mesas, and canyons which formed as a result of erosion. Some tribes of the Southwest lived in the natural rock ledges and hollows formed by nature in the walls of cliffs high above the canyons and valleys. This was undoubtedly done for protection. Those who had their homes within these long recesses in the faces of the Southwestern rocky cliffs are called **cliff dwellers.** In some instances the habitation was little more than the natural rock floor and ceiling of the cliff. In others it was a large structure built of adobe, with a number of rooms and two or even more stories, employing timber and masonry in the construction. The cliff dwelling was reached by means of rope or wood ladders, and whatever farming or grazing was carried on had to be done above on the mesa top, or in the more accessible and fertile valley below.

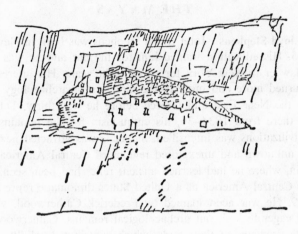

A cliff dwelling

Among the best-known of the prehistoric cliff-dwelling regions that have been excavated to date are Mesa Verde in southwestern Colorado, and Montezuma's Castle and Canyon de Chelly in northern Arizona. Here we can speculate how the timbers and adobe bricks were shaped, raised as much as one hundred feet up the cliffside and put in place to build great communal dwellings that were several stories high and had over one hundred rooms to house several hundred persons. In addition, in the many relics brought to light by archaeologists we can trace elements that appear in the cultures of modern Indian tribes, notably the Pueblo and Hopi Indians, back to their ancestors, who lived in the Southwest six centuries ago.

The people who lived throughout the Southwest practiced both cremation and interment, depending mainly on the local tribal customs. Their painted pottery, much of it on a light background, shows a wide range of color and design and a mastery of ceramic techniques. Many implements, pieces of jewelry, and articles of everyday use that were found in the course of excavation supplement the mounting knowledge of American Indians of the period before the white man's appearance.

CENTRAL AMERICA
THE MAYAS

John Lloyd Stephens   John Lloyd Stephens was born in New Jersey
in 1805. His education trained him for the bar and he was a prac-
ticing lawyer in New York for about eight years. His interest, however, turned more and more in the direction of archaeology and led
him to the Near East and Greece before he was thirty. During his
travels there from 1834–36, his enthusiasm for the remains of ancient civilizations was intensified. Stephens was attracted next to the
almost unknown and unexplored regions of Central America and to
Yucatán, where he had learned ancient relics had been seen. He set
out for Central America as a United States diplomatic representative
in 1839. He was accompanied by Frederick Catherwood, who was
equally eager to seek out archaeological remains. Catherwood made
accurate drawings of their finds, which contributed solidly not only
to their work but also to later studies of that section of the world.
Stephens and Catherwood made their way with great difficulty and
determination through thickly overgrown swamplands and jungle
maze in search of ruins left by the early Indian inhabitants of
Central America. Finally, in Copán, situated along the south bank of
the Copán River, Stephens discovered a number of **stelae,** which
stood twice the height of a man. These were stones covered with
hieroglyphics and figures sculptured in relief. He then came upon
walls close by, and a pyramid with a flight of steps leading to a
terrace almost one hundred feet in height. Stephens knew he had
discovered an ancient city of some size and importance. He continued to explore and study and in 1841 *Incidents of Travel in
Central America, Chiapas, and Yucatán* was published, setting forth
the results of his work. John Lloyd Stephens continued his interest
in the ancient cultures of Central America until his death in New
York in 1852.

Edward Herbert Thompson   Edward Herbert Thompson was born
in 1860 and went to Yucatán as United States Consul in 1885. The
young Thompson was fascinated by all he saw there and penetrated
deeply into the mysteries of Mayan civilization. He was able to

gather together a great amount of material and made a substantial contribution to archaeology. When Thompson saw the Sacred Well at Chichén Itzá, he began to think seriously about the tales he had heard concerning it. The story popular among the natives was that in ancient times maidens had been sacrificed in the well and priests had cast into it treasures for the gods. Thompson believed he could prove that the old legends about the Sacred Well were true. Although the well was about seventy to eighty feet deep, Thompson persisted and finally found skeletons and valuable objects at the bottom of it.

Thompson died in 1935 and his accomplishments, starting from faith in a legend, led to the exploration of many **cenotes** in Central America in later years. Cenote is the name given to the natural limestone sinks that are found by the score in Yucatán and in some other sections of Central America. They result from the rock formation of that area and are of varying depths, some being up to 150 feet deep.

Mayan Civilization   During the first millennium B.C. a civilization arose that has left its traces in temples, cities, and palaces constructed for the most part of stone and concrete. This civilization, one of the oldest and most advanced in the Americas, was developed by the Mayas, who lived and flourished on the plateaus of Central America and later in the area of the Yucatán Peninsula. Because of the solid, massive construction of their buildings and the durable quality of the materials they used, the remains and monuments of the Mayas were among the first in the New World to be studied and have supplied archaeologists with a fertile field for research which is still yielding useful, interesting information. The Mayas left behind a great quantity of archaeological evidence, from which it has been determined that they maintained a high cultural level until just before the time of Columbus, when wars between rival cities weakened the Mayas politically and economically, and their civilization gradually declined as a result.

Archaeological Remains   Excavations, research, and the results of modern methods of skin diving, backed by carbon-14 dating, have brought proof that the Mayas were among the most highly civilized of the ancient inhabitants of the Americas. The sections of Central America where they lived are rich in archaeological remains. The ancient Mayas were a neolithic people and built with stone on such a large scale that their structures have lasted through the centuries. Like the sites of the classical world, however, the remnants of the Mayan civilization were plundered, and much of their building material was, unfortunately, carried off to be used for constructing buildings and roads.

Mayan Art The Mayas settled originally in the southern and eastern parts of Mexico, and turned to agriculture. As a result, they lived in permanent communities, which led to the development of large villages. From the artifacts unearthed and brought out of the numerous cenotes into which they were either dropped or thrown, it is apparent that the Mayan craftsmen attained a high degree of skill. Potsherds show well-wrought and beautifully decorated pottery. Many fine statuettes and other terra-cotta objects have been found. Their cups, dishes, and storage jars, as well as their weapons and implements, were equally handsome. Metals and precious and semiprecious stones were utilized extensively in ornaments and jewelry of all kinds. Gold and jade were favored in making this type of article.

Migration to Yucatán We know now, from long and detailed study of Mayan remains, that the Mayas were forced from their homes in Mexico and deserted their cities there before A.D. 1000. Whether they were overcome by an epidemic, or by a sudden invasion, or another natural or outside force has not been determined. The Mayas did, nevertheless, enter the Yucatán Peninsula at this period in their history. There they built again with stone and achieved another high point in their culture.

Stelae One of the most characteristic of all the Mayan remains is the stele. These stelae are huge blocks of stone, generally standing from five to ten feet high, but many of them are considerably higher. They are covered with relief sculpture in the form of human and animal shapes, geometric patterns, and hieroglyphics. These do not seem to have been intended primarily as grave stelae, as was the case in ancient Greece and Italy, but rather as highly decorated stones, whose sculptured details told a historical or religious story. It will be seen that the same was true of all the carved stones of

the Mayas and other Central American tribes, who used their building materials and even their architecture as a medium on which
to record information concerning astronomy and current events with
their dates. Thus the stelae served a highly practical and useful
purpose, and were at the same time aesthetically decorative.

Mayan Building   Although the houses in Mayan villages and towns
were generally of mud brick and thatch, the public buildings were
on a grand scale and built to last. The Mayas made wide use of
the most permanent kind of building material available to them—
stone. With the primitive methods of the Neolithic Age, great blocks
of stone weighing up to forty tons and sometimes more were transported overland from the quarries and raised into place in pyramids,
temples, palaces, and other structures. In many instances, in order
to make walls wide and strong, the inner and outer facings of a wall

A Mayan stele

were built of stone masonry and then filled in with rubble. Very thick
walls were essential to support the heavy weight they had to carry,
and they could be built more easily in this way. The facing of cut

stone gave the effect of a solid stone-block wall and was pleasing to the eye, while at the same time it provided the required architectural support. The number of lime kilns that have been found bear witness to the method by which the Mayas made cement as well as their widespread practice of burning limestone to make plaster, used to coat the limestone facings of their buildings.

When the Mayas built sizable structures, they were usually ones concerned with religion or government. The city of Chichén Itzá in the jungles of Yucatán had been quite sizable when it was at its height, and excavations there have provided us with a good example of a Mayan city. The Mayas were very fond of a ball game similar to soccer and built great courts on which the game could be played. These courts also supplied a large open space, about 100 to 150 yards in length, around which big buildings could be grouped to advantage.

Mayan Temples The temples of the Mayas were usually in the form of pyramid temples. The pyramids were constructed in a series of steps or terraces, and were not true pyramids but had large flat tops, or platforms, instead of points. Staircases enabled people to make the ascent of this steep step-type pyramid more easily and slowly. The platform top of the pyramid served as a base for the temple or altar that was erected upon it and reached by steps. The temple was generally dedicated to Kukulcan, the chief deity of the Mayas. The deity was in the shape of a serpent covered with feathers or plumes. He appears throughout the remains of Mayan pyramid temples, carved in stone as part of the over-all relief sculpture which the Mayas used on their buildings to record time and events in a decorative manner.

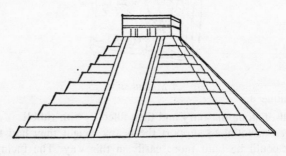

A Mayan pyramid

Mayan Writing The writing of the Mayas never advanced beyond the comparatively elementary stage of hieroglyphics. It nevertheless appears to have been adequate to serve the chief purpose for which it was intended, that of recording the months and days and other information related to the calendar and important events. The hieroglyphics of the Mayas are called **glyphs.** These glyphs were carved on stone for the most part, but were also carved on bone and painted on ceramics. The Mayan writing has not yet been deciphered, but archaeologists and palaeographers have, through careful research, reached the point at which the date and number glyphs, and a few others, are readable. A sufficient number of inscriptions have been found up to the present time, however, to indicate the possibility that complete decipherment could come soon.

Mayan glyphs

The Mayan Calendar The achievement in developing a calendar has astonished archaeologists perhaps more than any other single accomplishment of the Mayas. Related to this was their surprisingly accurate knowledge of astronomy, based on exact observations of the sun, moon, and stars. Round observatories were constructed to measure and record astronomical data. Calculations of the movements of planets and stars enabled them to predict eclipses. Coupled with their knowledge of astronomy was an equal achievement in the field of mathematics. Not only did the Mayas develop one of the most unique and exact of all known calendars, but they were able to reckon and correct the margin of error, when this became necessary, without upsetting the smooth precision of the date sequence of their calendar.

Archaeological research has worked out the Mayan system of

reckoning time. Their calendar was a solar one, composed of eighteen months of twenty days each and one month of five days, to total 365 days in the year. Each of the eighteen months and the one extra month was given a name, which was written in its own hieroglyph or glyph. The twenty days of the month were numbered, starting with zero and running through nineteen, and each had its individual glyph. In addition to its number, zero to nineteen, each day had a name and a corresponding written glyph. A further division of the solar year was made by twenty-eight groups of thirteen days, with one day extra at the end. Mathematically, a complete calendar cycle was reached every fifty-two years. Other intricate details made the Mayan calendar extremely complex, but also precise. Since all dates had a mystical as well as a practical significance, accuracy was most important, and the use of both numerals and names in all phases of the calendar helped to achieve this end.

All the Mayan buildings and sculpture, such as the stelae, had hieroglyphics on them. These hieroglyphic reliefs were related to the calendar, recording and interweaving both secular and religious chronology. Heads, both animal and human, and other parts of the body, symbols, figures, and designs appeared in the omnipresent hieroglyphic sculpture on palaces and pyramid temples. The Mayas counted by twenties and, as we have seen, mathematical numbers represented equivalent numbers of days, months, and years. Their building construction and ornamentation were all intertwined with their calendar, the whole showing a skilled knowledge of mathematics, astronomy, and architecture. The sum total indicates that the Mayas recorded time in stone and sculpture. Unfortunately, although we now understand from all the evidence at hand that it was an exact method of reckoning time, the calendar of the Mayas stands only in a broad relative position to our own. No common starting point has been found as yet to calculate in terms of our calendar. Archaeologists have, however, worked out a satisfactory comparative chronology of correlated dates for the two calendars.

THE TOLTECS

Another group of people that attained a high degree of civilization and achievement quite similar to that of the Mayas was the Toltec tribe. The Toltecs flourished in central Mexico from about A.D. 500 to 1200 and were at their height around A.D. 1000. Although traces of their remains were discovered earlier, no extensive excavation work was carried on prior to the twentieth century.

Toltec Cities Among the ancient cities of the Toltecs that have been unearthed and studied quite thoroughly by archaeologists are Teotihuacán, Tollan (the modern Tula), and Cholula. The remains of Teotihuacán, located not far north of Mexico City, are among the best preserved of all the remnants of the Toltecs, who built up a large city there more than a thousand years ago. Because the ancient city covered such a vast area, a large portion of it is still unexcavated. From the part that has been brought to light, however, we can see that the Toltecs built solidly and aristically and that their arts, especially that of pottery making, reached a high level of development and variety.

Toltec Pyramids The pyramids and temples that were erected at Teotihuacán stretch over an extensive region of several miles and are an impressive reminder of the expert handiwork and building skills of the Toltecs. Two great pyramids, one erected to the sun and the other to the moon, stand in an excellent state of preservation, giving archaeologists fine examples of the engineering skill and artistic stone sculpture work of those who erected them. For a long time these pyramids were attributed to the Aztecs, but more recent archaeological study points to the fact that they antedate the Aztecs and must, therefore, be ascribed to either the Toltecs or another tribe contemporary with them. A number of pyramid-temples were built by the Toltecs to their serpent god, corresponding closely to that of the Mayas, whom they called Quetzalcoatl. One such pyramid is really eight pyramids, each built, according to the calculations of archaeologists, fifty-two years apart and superimposed one on another.

There is still much excavation work to be done, but the Toltec ruins unearthed thus far not only show a strong resemblance to the civilization of the Mayas but pose questions as to the origin and background of groups of peoples such as these, who could achieve so much in art and architecture in the apparently brief time during which their cultures flourished.

THE AZTECS

William Hickling Prescott   William Hickling Prescott was born in Salem, Massachusetts, in 1796. Like Stephens, he became a lawyer, but he had lost the sight of one eye in an accident while he was a law student at Harvard and his other eye was so weakened that he was almost blind. Prescott was consequently obliged to give up the practice of law, to preserve what sight was left to him. He then turned to writing. He was read to, made notes while he listened, and memorized great quantities of material. In this manner he was able to pursue his interest in history, a demanding subject. Prescott mastered his subject by hard, steady work and in 1843 his great book, *The Conquest of Mexico,* a history of the Aztecs and of Cortes' conquests in that land, was published. Four years later *The Conquest of Peru* was completed and published.

William Hickling Prescott died in 1859. An armchair traveler himself, he contributed both pleasure and solid information to others in the same situation. More than that, he spurred on those who could do so to journey to the almost unpenetrated regions of Mexico and Peru, to seek out the remains of the ancient civilizations buried there.

The Aztec Empire   When the Aztecs came into Mexico from the north, around A.D. 1300, they built on the islands of a lake and, as their city increased in size, they created man-made islands. They named their city Tenochtitlán. Later they spread out into surrounding districts and began a course of conquest. Tenochtitlán, where the modern Mexico City is, became the capital of the Aztec Empire. The Aztecs gained in both power and wealth. They were skilled engineers and built dikes and bridges as well as great pyramids. When Cortes and the Spanish conquistadors reached Mexico in 1519, the Aztec Empire was cut short. The invaders plundered and carried off great quantities of treasure. Only a small portion of the many fine and beautiful articles made of gold, silver, turquoise, and other jewels was left behind to be found by present-day archaeologists.

Aztec Religion and Temples   The Aztecs adopted the feathered serpent god and called him, as did the Toltecs, Quetzalcoatl. Human sacrifice was widely practiced to appease all the gods, especially those who had to do with crops. On the whole, however, the Aztecs developed an advanced type of religion. They built, as did those they imitated, with concrete and stone, and erected temples and lasting monuments to their gods. Even though they followed the custom of sacrifice, the religion of the Aztecs and the temple they built were in most respects much like those of the neighboring Indian tribes.

Aztec Calendar Stone That the Aztecs, too, had a good knowledge of astronomy and mathematics is indicated by their Calendar Stone. This is a large circular stone about twelve feet in diameter and almost three feet thick, on which the Aztec calendar was cut. Like the calendar developed by the Mayas, the Aztec calendar was an accurate one.

Excavations carried on in the territory where the Aztecs lived have disclosed the fact that the Aztecs gradually absorbed and borrowed from the civilizations of the Toltecs and Mayas, until they themselves had attained a comparatively high level of culture. The Aztecs apparently had little originality, judging from their archaeological remains, but they knew how to utilize to the best advantage what they copied from the other tribes of Mexico. They were able, also, to develop a well-organized empire.

The Aztec Empire was a great one, but short-lived. The slaughter of the Aztecs by the Spanish under Cortes was both unnecessary and merciless. The conquistadors destroyed not only hundreds of

Aztec Calendar Stone

lives but also a splendid civilization. Archaeologists can re-create only a small part of the grandeur of Mexico as it existed before the sixteenth century.

SOUTH AMERICA
THE INCAS

The Incas entered the territory where Peru is now located from the south at some time after A.D. 1000. The word **Inca** apparently meant "ruler" and was the title given to the emperor or king. In time the term came to be applied to the whole group of people under the rule of the Inca. The Inca ruler was not only a king and emperor but also came to have the qualities of a god. The Incas made Cuzco their capital.

The Inca Empire The Incas had a well-developed system of political, land, and religious organization, and the Inca Empire was actually a socialistic type of government. The Incas' officials were placed all over the empire and selected those men who should serve in the army or work in the mines. Those who were farmers had to pay a portion of whatever they produced to the priests of the temples and a part to the Inca, or government.

By A.D. 1400 the Inca Empire had expanded over a large area in all directions, and a great quantity of building was carried on. Roads with stone paving connected the more important towns. Adobe was sometimes used in construction along the coast, but stone was the main building material in the mountainous interior. The Incas were master builders who used blocks of stone that were cut quite perfectly and shaped to fit closely together without mortar. Archaeological evidence shows that wooden beams supported the roofs, which were quite probably made of thatch.

Inca Temples Unlike the peoples of Central America, the Incas built their temples in a rectangular shape and not as pyramids. They made use, also, of rounded and circular construction in their buildings. Extensive stone walls created countless terraces on the mountainsides. The Incas erected great stone temples, some over three hundred feet long, to their deities. The Temple of the Sun at Cuzco had gold decorations and the outside walls as well as the inside were covered with gold, since gold represented the brightness of the sun.

Art of the Incas The Incas also excelled in crafts. Their pottery was well made and the colors were good. Their originality in the art of ceramics showed in the variety of their vases and in their employment of portraiture. Many pieces of pottery are in the form of human heads, some of them humorous, and animal or bird shapes. These shapes and the paintings on the pottery tell us much about the lives and interests of the Incas. The Incas' weaving and metalwork also show fine quality.

When Pizarro arrived in Peru in 1533, he and his band of followers conquered the Incas and plundered them—as the Spaniards did wherever they went in the Americas—with a complete disregard both for their victims and the civilization they were destroying. After the Spanish conquest, the culture of the Incas declined and ultimately disappeared, as had that of the Mayas, Toltecs, and Aztecs.

In the early part of the twentieth century, Senator Hiram Bingham explored the ruins of the Inca civilization and found the settlement of Machu Picchu, high in the Andes near Cuzco. Bingham maintained a lifelong interest in Peru and *The Lost City of the Incas,* published in 1948, the result of his long study, re-created much of Peru's past which had been buried for more than four centuries. Most of what we know of the Incas must come from archaeological investigation, because they left behind no records, writing, or calendar—only architectural ruins and examples of their craftsmanship.

Many questions remain unanswered and numerous problems are still unsolved, but archaeology looks ahead to new factual knowledge and further progress. As future years and the widening skills of archaeologists contribute to the picture, the history of the events, cultures, and civilizations of centuries past will appear in ever clearer and more meaningful detail.

Index